Free-to-Play

Free-to-Play

Mobile Video Games, Bias, and Norms

Christopher A. Paul

The MIT Press
Cambridge, Massachusetts
London, England

This book was set in Stone Serif and Stone Sans by Jen Jackowitz. Printed and bound in the United States of America.

Library of Congress Cataloging-in-Publication Data

Names: Paul, Christopher A., author.
Title: Free-to-play : mobile video games, bias, and norms / Christopher A. Paul.
Other titles: Free-to-play
Description: Cambridge, Massachusetts : The MIT Press, 2020. | Includes bibliographical references and index.
Identifiers: LCCN 2020002677 | ISBN 9780262539418 (paperback)
Subjects: LCSH: Video games--Economic aspects. | Video games industry.
Classification: LCC GV1469.3 .P38 2020 | DDC 794.8--dc23
LC record available at https://lccn.loc.gov/2020002677

10   9   8   7   6   5   4   3   2   1

For Erin, Piper, Ingrid . . . and Mom and Dad

Contents

Introduction: Biased Against Free-to-Play

I really like to play games. I was fortunate enough to grow up with an Atari, then a Commodore 64, a Nintendo Entertainment System, and a Game Boy. Consoles and PCs, as well as board and card games, litter my childhood with memories of playing with family and friends. Games build memories and are touchstones that allow conversation about other topics. I have turned my lifelong appreciation for games into part of my job, for which I think, write, and speak about video games and how they work, what they mean, and why they matter. It is awesome.

It is striking to me how the games I play have changed over time, as my interests and resources have shifted. There was a time where I would wake up early to get unfettered access to the television to binge on *Final Fantasy*. For a couple of years, my life was punctuated by rushing home from work, warming up some food and spending the night raiding with my partner in *World of Warcraft*. I now field weekend requests from an eldest daughter who wakes up early to play games on the Nintendo Switch with me and says things like, "I love that my Daddy likes video games. If he didn't like video games, it wouldn't be so much fun." We cruise through *Marvel Ultimate Alliance 3* as my youngest grabs "her" controller, one she will soon be old enough to realize isn't connected to anything. Now I slot my game time around work, child care, and meetings, which leaves me primarily playing games on mobile devices. And it is in this last space where I find some of the most interesting things happening in video games.

As I have moved from buying the newest console or PC game at launch into a world where I only buy a premium title or three each year, my spending and playtime have shifted to free-to-play mobile games. I am now the kind of player who will pay to save time. I know that early money beats late and starting out with a medium-sized stake can put me in a position to reap the rewards of a higher place on the leaderboards. I dabble in new games, often buying starter packs just to see if I like what I find. I have gone so far as to buy premium currency in shady deals outside of the bounds of a game's primary marketplace. For me, my time is more precious, and I use money to compensate for the time I don't have, continuing to play games, but different ones that better suit the life I have now. As my play and spending change, I continue to read and keep up on console and PC games, as well as coverage and discussion of the games I play now. I am unlikely to find the time to finish *Red Dead Redemption* even though I played through the first couple of missions, but I still find joy in reading about what is going on in video games and watching videos about flagship titles.

Using my perspective as someone with a deep history with video games, but with a positionality that has changed in recent years, offers space to analyze what is happening with free-to-play and mobile games. All too often certain kinds of games are dismissed and mocked, precisely when they are an increasingly prominent and important part of the video game industry. There are problems with the monetization structures of free-to-play games. There is also room to critique and address their game design and structure. However, until they are understood for what they are and are not, criticism of them is weak and far too often goes down a rabbit hole of red herrings.

Productive criticism is predicated on taking the object of analysis seriously. One should start with the premise that something interesting is happening and work from there. Although the mainstream game press has done an excellent job of reporting on the structural sexism at *League of Legend* developer Riot Games and the harsh working conditions at Rockstar Games in the lead-up to the launch of *Red Dead Redemption,* coverage of free-to-play and mobile games far too often devolves into deeply flawed analysis.[1] To get to the same quality of analysis and reporting on free-to-play and mobile games, the structural biases against those games needs to be addressed and owned. This project is designed to help illustrate how those biases are enacted in an effort to start a credulous, nuanced criticism of free-to-play and mobile games. Articulating what is okay in mobile and free-to-play games and where the line is requires understanding these games on their own merits and why they are designed in a manner to do things like obscure the price of in-game goods or use advertising as a secondary, or occasionally primary, income stream. The first step in getting there is developing the background and context for mobile and free-to-play games within the broader scene of contemporary video games.

Mobile gaming has taken over the video game industry, as 2016 marked the year where the mobile sector overtook both consoles and PC games to be the largest segment of the video game market.[2] Mobile gaming revenue has been growing faster than other sectors of the gaming market for years, with estimates of the market doubling in size between 2016 and 2021.[3] Mobile gaming fundamentally shifted how games work, with developers asking existential questions about whether premium pricing is a viable business model and opting to make free-to-play games because they lead to additional revenue and ongoing sales.[4] The different payment structure of mobile gaming and general promotion of a free-to-play model seeped into other video games, prompting great consternation as journalists, developers, and players wonder what happened to the recreational activity they grew up with. These fears are underlined by the trends in mobile and free-to-play gaming that emphasize a different sort of player. Although the average mobile game player who spends money tends to invest about as much as a "traditional gamer," the kinds of people making those purchases and their impact on games are different than the young men who inhabited the arcades and became the dominant image of who played video games on consoles and PCs.[5] Mobile and free-to-play titles are far more likely to be played by women, many of whom do not see themselves as gamers. Shira Chess does an excellent job of cataloguing how many game developers have changed their approach to address how their target player may be a Mom in middle America.[6] Amanda Cote uses old copies of *Nintendo Power* to argue that video games have been targeted at men and conducted interviews to assess how women cope with harassment in the games they play.[7] In a follow-up project, she found that women players have a complicated relationship with mobile, free-to-play, or casual games and argues that many women resist being associated with anything "casual" because of the implications that has within the larger culture surrounding video games.[8]

A key distinction in this different community of players is also that a substantial percentage of the mobile game industry is based on the Chinese market, which is the single most profitable one for mobile games.[9] Mobile is less dependent on the acquisition of separate gaming devices, like consoles and gaming PCs, and can be played on devices that are becoming increasingly commonplace in contemporary society. New platforms for play decenter the role of traditional gaming hubs like the United States, Europe, and Japan, which changes the audience of and focus for video games. In large part on the back of its portfolio of free-to-play video games, in 2017 Chinese company Tencent became the fifth largest publicly traded company in the world.[10] By almost any measure, Tencent is the biggest gaming company in the world, as it owns a stake of companies like Activision, Ubisoft, Riot Games, Epic Games, and Supercell, while also publishing massively successful first-party titles like *Honor of Kings*.[11] Tencent's growth has been fueled by the ability to offer access to China for Western publishers, in combination with their dominance on Chinese social media through WeChat and QQ. This shift is often made more palatable by Tencent's tendency to be quite hands-off with the companies they invest in, but the vital importance of the Chinese market is a key reason why mobile and free-to-play games signal new trends in video games.

Free-to-play and mobile games are changing what video games are because they are funded by a small percentage of players. Unlike traditional console or PC games, where the most typical case is for everyone to pay roughly the same amount for a game, excepting savings found on a deal or spending on a collector's edition, the vast majority of free-to-play spending comes from a small percentage of the player base.[12] Specifics vary based on the individual game assessed, but one aggregate analysis of over 1,000 apps and 100 million users found that only about 3.5 percent of players pay, and the small fraction of people paying typically spend 30 times more than the average player.[13] Spending is concentrated, which can change how games work and how they are played. Instead of seeking a level playing field for all, free-to-play games typically give paying players advantages over non-payers.[14] What players pay for can come in the form of additional energy to play more often, more powerful resources or characters, or items that are cosmetic rather than game-influencing. Games like *League of Legends* focus largely on spending to unlock new characters and cosmetic items, while *FIFA Ultimate Team* sells card packs to generate revenue. Card packs, chests, or loot boxes use gacha, or capsule-toy, mechanics to withhold information from the player about exactly what they are buying.[15] These mechanics, first found in Japanese toy machines, then spreading westward, can lead to massive amounts of spending as players chase low odds propositions and hope to get lucky.[16] The importance of key players and their spending decisions can also twist development of a game, as developers may seek to cater to particular, valuable players rather than the whole player base.[17] The flow of revenue is different in these games, which anchors into concerns about gambling, problem spending, and players paying to win rather than relying on their skill at play.

A final difference is that women are more valuable players than men, and women typically prefer to play different genres of games. In an analysis of the market, data analytics firm deltaDNA found that women were more likely to own a premium mobile handset, which makes them more invested in mobile as a platform. They also found a strong difference in the gender preference for the four categories of games they track, with men composing about three-quarters of the player base for action and strategy games, women accounting for about the same proportion of puzzle game players, and casino games being almost evenly split, with a slight preference shown by women. There is a long history of women playing and designing different genres of games, and excellent work has been done by Shira Chess and Anastasia Salter, among others, at demonstrating why that history matters.[18] Beyond their genre preferences, women spend more money on mobile games, with deltaDNA's estimate being that women players are worth 44 percent more than men.[19] While women are more valuable in the mobile market, they are also more quickly acquiring gaming consoles, with the gender disparity in console ownership eroding.[20] As deltaDNA's write up of the data notes, these trends have

> powerful implications for mobile game publishers—a female-focused game has a much greater chance of being profitable than a male-focused one. Given that women tend to like puzzle and casino games that are also much less expensive to produce and maintain, the economics of making male-focused action and strategy games are hard to justify.[21]

Seeking a broad appeal across audiences likely explains the growth in genre-blending games, like RPG-inspired match-three games *Empires & Puzzles: RPG Quest* or *Legend of Solgard*, as they attempt to capture traditional gamers while using mechanics that appeal to women already invested in mobile gaming.[22] The incentive structure to develop games for women can also fuel resentment from traditional gamers, as they may see the lack of games targeted at their preferences as a reason to reject the mobile platform and protest what games are made.[23] These dynamics are compounded by the fact that mobile and free-to-play games radically lower the barrier to entry to playing games, opening the door for novice and new players. From a business standpoint, this may be a compelling proposition, but it also prompts established players to defend their hobby against perceived threats. For nostalgic or conservative male gamers, the rising prominence of women can be seen as a threat to their leisure activity. Throughout the course of this project, many of the games discussed will be those aimed at the core, presumed male audience for games, as it is in those places where the biases around games are often shown in the starkest relief.

My increasing personal turn toward mobile and free-to-play games, combined with the different context for play seen in the focus on China, varying levels of investment for players, and relevance of women players gave me space to reflect on three key sets of questions about how games work and how they are received. First, how are the norms around games established? What gets valued in games and what does not? Second, how are particular modes of play normalized? And, third, how do notions of labor and skill intersect with notions of play in video games? Answering these questions helps chart the terrain of discussion about video games and how they are received. These questions are designed, within the context of analyzing microtransaction-based and often mobile free-to-play games, to help illustrate the biases held by the community surrounding games in order to show what gets placed in the center, what gets pushed to the margins, and the stakes of the discourse about what gets made and celebrated and what does not. Doing this requires beginning with a brief definition of some key terms and a discussion of the background and design for my project.

The Set-Up

Although a much more complete history of payment models in video games can be found in chapter 1, in its current form, free-to-play is a relatively newer payment structure for games that often gets linked to casual and mobile games. Free-to-play is a mode of monetizing games that hinges on using the lack of initial costs to encourage more people to try the game and then attempt to convert them into paying players.[24] The way these mechanics work in practice can vary widely. Some games choose to use advertisements as a key mode of revenue generation, with, for example, *Hungry Shark World* running ads between games and giving players an additional life if they watch an ad. In many games, ads can be disabled as a specific item to purchase or in combination with payment for other in-game goods. Along similar lines, many games exploit social connections or aggregate data, particularly those found on social networks like Facebook.

Beyond the ad support that is largely borrowed from other forms of media, monetization in free-to-play games often hinges on the use of multiple currencies. Most mobile games have several currencies, which, for game developers, can have the added benefit of obscuring the cost of in-game items. Games that use currency often introduce a soft and a hard option, with one being more readily earned in-game and another obtained through spending dollars or other outside-of-game-world money. These options take all kinds of forms, like credits (soft) and crystals (hard) in *Star Wars: Galaxy of Heroes* to coins (soft) and diamonds (hard) in *Hay Day* to coins (soft) and crystals (hard) in *Harry Potter: Hogwarts Mystery*. Dual currencies have the benefit of allowing progress and sales in the soft currency, while encouraging players to spend for greater deals and impact on the game with hard currency. Multiple currencies also let developers throttle player progress by restricting resources and challenging players with scarcity in order to frustrate them in an attempt to make a sale. Multiple currency models also lets players pursue a path through the game without paying, although they will likely progress far more slowly than those who use their wallet to move ahead. Multi-currency structures obscure the cost of goods, limiting a player's ability to readily understand how much a certain item costs. They also have a similar effect as gift cards or Disney dollars, where currency is turned from a readily exchangeable resource into something that can only be spent in a certain store or within a specific game.

Games also monetize through the addition of cosmetic elements. This style of monetization typically adds different outfits for characters, often known as skins, or other items that only have aesthetic value within the game. Developers could add items that do not have a particular game play value or seasonal additions to the game timed with major holidays or key events. *League of Legends* typifies this approach, as the developer, Riot Games, offers vast quantities of cosmetic options for players to spend money on to customize their appearance and show their devotion to the game. This style of charging players also fits seamlessly into games based on fashion or appearance, like *Design Home* or *Covet Fashion*, where items come with a cost and the most sought-after can charge a substantial premium. A cosmetic approach can also take the form of emotes and dances (*Fortnite*) and/or voice lines and celebrations for characters (*Overwatch*). This form of monetization is one that is often best received by traditional gamers, as cosmetic elements typically have no impact on gameplay and merely let players customize their own approach and display their commitment to the game and their favorite character.[25]

In many games, including puzzle and strategy games, players are faced with energy as a scarce resource. A game may charge players hearts for a failed attempt at solving a puzzle (*Candy Crush Saga, Gardenscapes*), energy for completing tasks (*Kim Kardashian:*

Hollywood, Harry Potter: Hogwarts Mystery), or any of a variety of energies for completing various levels and challenges (*Star Wars: Galaxy of Heroes, Marvel Strike Force*). The value of energy for developers is that it effectively gates play, requiring players to come back on a regular basis and limiting the length of any particular game session. It also gives a lever to sell players additional energy to complete a task or to keep moving through a game. In the case of *Harry Potter: Hogwarts Battle*, this kind of mechanic is used early in the game to limit how far players can go in completing an effort to save their character from danger (see chapter 8), which was highly controversial for those who like Harry Potter but are not accustomed to free-to-play game design.[26]

Developers of certain games can also limit access to characters. In the case of *League of Legends* and similar games, avatars typically cost resources to unlock, with the newest typically costing more than those that are part of introductory gameplay. This approach is also typical in sports games, where new players are unlocked and added to a team, and in games based around substantial, character-driven universes, like those of comic books or other fantasy worlds, like *Star Wars* or *Fire Emblem*. These characters can be sold through clear purchases, where a player knows exactly what they are getting, or in obscured ways, where players open a package or chest and are typically awarded varying amounts of characters drawn from a number of options. Games with a wide universe of characters to include in the game, or those creating their own mythology, have seemingly endless revenue streams as new characters can be added to the game over time.

Although it has largely fallen out of favor as of this writing, some games opt for a free-to-try approach that models the shareware ethos found in personal computing, which fueled the rise of games like the original *Doom*. *Super Mario Run*, released by Nintendo for iOS in December 2016 and on Android in March 2017, gave players the chance to play a handful of levels and try all of the various game modes before asking them to pay $9.99 in order to unlock the full game. Although the appeal of Nintendo's plumber led to millions of dollars in sales and eventually passed the $60 million mark in total revenue, it fell far behind the revenue generated by other Nintendo offerings that followed a more traditional free-to-play approach to monetization, like *Fire Emblem Heroes*.[27] *Super Mario Run* was plagued by complaints about the payment model, which ran in the face of what had become industry norms about how mobile games should be priced.[28] There was also pushback from business analysts, who fretted about the conversion rate of downloads to purchases, which was about 3 percent, and the lack of an ongoing revenue stream in comparison with other free-to-play entries, as players would only need to buy the game once, rather than continuing to invest in the game.[29] However, free-to-try is a model pursued by some independent game developers, like Zach Gage and his game *Pocket Run Pool*, who are not necessarily seeking a billion-dollar game, yet face resistance to any initial fee as part of the price of beginning the game.

An additional way video games generate revenue is through a subscription or similar charge assessed in exchange for a benefit in the game. Subscriptions often grant regular infusions of premium currency to draw players back to their game or, as popularized by *Fortnite*, a battle pass offering players the chance to earn rewards based on their play in the game. Subscriptions can incentivize players into regular play through daily rewards and generate a steady stream of revenue, although awarding too much premium currency via a subscription can decrease regular (and more expensive) sales of the resource. In the case of battle passes, *Fortnite* gets a regular boost of revenue for each of its seasons, which typically run for about two to three months. Players can also buy their way forward on the pass, substituting cash for playtime. At the beginning of the new season, the developer gets another injection of revenue, as players chase new goals and items on their next battle pass. A significant impact of this approach is the ongoing need for more cosmetic content to sell passes and the impact of that labor on employees. In the case of *Fortnite* developer Epic Games, this has led to reports of months of ongoing crunch development because the game is never finished.[30]

A prominent cost for free-to-play games is in player acquisition. Getting new players to choose your game amidst a sea of other options is a substantial challenge, which is part of what fuels the market for in-game advertising. Games typically have to run the balance between adding players and doing so at a price that makes sense for the game given how much it profits off the average player. This dynamic means that developing a reputation as a strong developer or being published as part of the portfolio of a large company that can cross-promote the game, like in the case of offerings from *Candy Crush Saga* developer King, enables some games to break through the clutter within the free-to-play market. Player acquisition leads to an introductory understanding of how free is not really free. There are clearly costs involved, from the developer's time to the cost of publishing a game, maintaining servers, and any additional elements of the game that need to be produced. Although players may experience the game without paying money, they are likely paying through their time, either through their role as a free-to-play player present to be beaten by higher-spending players or as a player willing to watch advertisements in exchange for some in-game currency. Just as network, commercial television is generally different than premium cable and an IMAX movie charges extra for watching a film on a bigger screen, media experiences are not the same for all people. However, there is generally less moralizing and judgment about the cost of other forms of entertainment based solely on the terms of its pricing model.

Although microtransactions and free-to-play is a monetization approach for games and stands in opposition to games that charge a price up front, mobile is a platform that is both related to and different from the core of this book. Although mobile gaming has roots that date back to Game Boys, *Mattel Football*, or *Mattel Auto Race*, and various tiny arcade cabinet games like *Galaga* and *Pac-Man*, contemporary mobile gaming is typically linked to a phone or tablet device. As markets like the Apple App Store and Google Play developed, players have increasingly embraced free-to-play mechanics, making it quite difficult for a paid game app to be successful. Free-to-play games are found on other platforms, like PCs, but there is an overlap in the discourse about free-to-play and mobile. I will separate and clarify my argument based on the focus in various case studies, but this book is generally about free-to-play and is mostly about mobile games. To complement my core focus, I use non-mobile games and games that have both an upfront cost and microtransactions as comparison points to talk about issues of norms, values, and bias in discussions and analysis of video games.

Analysis and the Industry

To analyze the questions about norms and values in contemporary video games, I primarily draw from elements of rhetorical analysis. At its most basic, rhetorical criticism is about under-standing that everything is rhetorical and that the language we choose to use matters.[31] The way we describe things shapes how we approach the world and reveals things about us and what we value as a group. The primary job of a rhetorical critic is to ask a pair of questions: what's going on, and so what?[32] Taking a rhetorical approach means understanding that the language we use is epistemic: words build our world and shape how we see things.[33] In the case of this project, taking a rhetorical approach means that assessing the way games are talked about can pro-vide perspective on the beliefs and premises held by those in the video game community. The way journalists, players, and developers talk about video games matters, and the point of this project is to give a chance for reflection in order to reveal what is generally hidden.[34] As C. L. R. James argues in his analysis of cricket, the context for play matters, and it is important to study games and who plays them, how they play, and what that play signifies about larger cultural themes.[35] Bias is a tricky thing, and studying words and norms offers an opportunity to see where assumptions and values lie.

In order to make this case, I draw from a variety of differ-ent texts. In quoted material, minor spelling or typographical errors have been corrected, but original language is retained and marked with "[*sic*]" for larger errors to avoid confusion. Pulling from reviews of games and industry analysis, I lean heavily on sites like TouchArcade, GamesIndustry.biz, and Kotaku. Touch-Arcade bills itself as a leading site in reviews of iOS gaming and typically displays a perspective of traditional gamers who have moved to mobile devices. This gives perspective on how video games have changed, as the writers are covering mobile games that are increasingly free-to-play, but from the perspective of

players who grew up on core gaming devices. GamesIndustry.
biz covers all aspects of the video game industry, with a particular focus on industry trends and how the financial side of game
development and publishing is changing. Kotaku presents itself
as a key voice for gamers and tends to focus far more on console and PC titles than mobile games, yet will occasionally cover
mobile games with a particularly high profile or level of interest.
These resources are supplemented with reviews of specific games,
sourced from industry publications and various game reviews.
However, the initial context for this project requires examining and reflecting on a general industry and gamer perspective,
which is that both free-to-play and mobile games are somehow
"lesser" than traditional games. One place to see tensions in the
game industry is in an essay penned by game-development veteran Ben Cousins.

Writing about his experience, Cousins begins by situating the
growth and change happening in the industry and announces
his qualifications for commentary, as he spent seven years in
the "traditional" games industry followed by eight years on
free-to-play projects. He announces that attacks on free-to-play
games are "often unfair and selective, and leave questionable but
traditional business practices alone. This is snobbery; evidence
that the old guard is scared of where the industry is headed."[36]
Cousins approaches and contextualizes concerns about free-to-
play, arguing that free-to-play is not a bait and switch, as most
players do not pay anything for the games. He contends that
pursuing heavy spenders, or "whale hunting," is ethical because
of surveys indicating that most players who spend heavily do so
deliberately and are satisfied with their purchases. This perspective clearly links to other hobbies, where people can spend thousands of dollars on shoes, cars, Magic: The Gathering cards, or

other items because it brings them some sort of satisfaction. He counters concerns about children's spending with the size of the overall market for games, acknowledging that there are issues but viewing them as a tiny fraction of the spending that occurs in free-to-play. Ultimately, Cousins builds to the argument that free-to-play is shocking to people because the "games are often played by children, the middle-ages, women and people in distant countries like Russia and Korea. There is a bit of snobbery and gate-keeping at play here, as the old guard is defensive about sharing their hobby with games they don't understand and gamers they don't recognize."[37] He contends that traditional developers do not know many people in the free-to-play development community, particularly as they often come from different places and backgrounds. He presents part of the fear of free-to-play as the growth of it, since data now show it is the biggest video game business model in both participation and revenue. These changes have had a substantial impact on the industry, and he reflects:

> For someone looking to preserve the industry as it was pre-2007, these are scary times. The once untouchable giants of the old industry are either going to be diminished by the bigger relative size of free-to-play or be diminished in absolute terms as consumers transfer spending to the new model and sales drop. Studios are closing, staff is laid off and traditional developers are tightening their collective belts.[38]

He likens the changes happening in the industry to the ban on pinball by those who associated it with gambling and concerns about jazz music corrupting youth, eventually asking, "why don't we come together, admit our common failings, research and learn from each other, share common ground and create something amazing for the future?"[39]

I find Cousins's position a quite interesting one, as he does a lovely job of responding to some of the major concerns about free-to-play. His argument is notable because it comes from a developer with time spent on various kinds of video games. And, I think, he does a solid job of capturing the fear and recalcitrance of those who grew used to a pay-once game model and how the growth of free-to-play as a business model impacts them. However, I also think there is a lot more going on than he discusses in his essay. He does a wonderful job of naming how the increasing inclusion of women and the locus of game development moving out of the United States and central Europe are issues for the reception of free-to-play, but he fails to address how certain free-to-play games, like *League of Legends* or *World of Tanks*, are received in a fundamentally different way than *Candy Crush Saga*. These spaces, where mobile and free-to-play collide, are where investigating how video games are talked about gives leverage to understanding how certain communities of players think about video games and what they should be. Cousins is right that there is snobbery at play, but that snobbery is intimately linked to often-unspoken values of game players. These values, which are occasionally represented as simple facts about how games are supposed to work, help articulate why some games are treasured and others are pushed to the side. Working through a variety of games, combined with a historical walk through different ways that video games have worked, enables reflection on this moment in video games, opening up room for changing what exists and building the amazing future Cousins asks us to pursue. This process starts with moving away from industry trends to focus on the values and norms that comprise play in contemporary video games.

Norms and Values at Play

Understanding how free-to-play games are received begins by looking broadly about how the norms around games and payment structures are established. What gets valued and what does not? What is legitimized and what is ridiculed? Beyond payment structure, how are particular modes of play normalized, and how are they linked to mode of payment? Is the rejection of certain free-to-play games at least in part because they contain a different style of play, a style that undermines the norms that are well established for core gamers? Finally, how do issues like labor, skill, and work intersect with notions of play in games, particularly when free-to-play games openly invite those with out-of-game-world success (and the deeper pockets that come with it) to buy their way forward? These questions are central to this project and are contextualized and answered throughout the entire book, but it makes sense to give a brief discussion of them now to show why they matter and how they get to the heart of the biases surrounding free-to-play and mobile gaming.

The central question of norms around free-to-play is an interesting one, as quotes abound about how a certain game does free-to-play right—or wrong. Statements about right and wrong are fundamentally value judgements about how things should work, even if they are regularly presented as immutable facts. An interesting set of cases involving the broad question of how norms and values are established in the payment structure of games can be seen in looking at a handful of titles published by Nintendo, starting with a 2014 release for the 3DS system called *Rusty's Real Deal Baseball*. The game is based around Rusty Slugger, a former professional baseball-playing dog whose wife just left him and is faced with raising 10 puppies on his own. Those kids are a source of Rusty's regret, as they just do not like baseball like kids used to, which leaves his massive investment in baseball games for the Nontendo 4DS in jeopardy.[40] Beyond the compelling story of learning more about Rusty and his life, *Rusty's Real Deal Baseball* is a series of baseball themed mini-games that range from batting practice to fielding, umpiring, or making your own bat. The game is a free download, which gives players a chance to try the first mini-game, *Bat & Switch*. After playing a couple of games, Rusty then asks players to pay to unlock the full version of *Bat & Switch*, which costs $4.00. However, one of his kids comes in and helps you negotiate Rusty down using a combination of chosen dialogue lines and in-game items, like doughnuts and nose-hair clippers. The game presses players toward the lowest possible price through the intervention of Rusty's kids and other prompts that typically leave players paying about $16 for the full package of mini-games for what Rusty promotes as $40 worth of content.

This novel pricing structure warranted attention, particularly coming from Nintendo, which had resisted free-to-play pricing, with one journalist using the questionable phrase "free-curious" to describe Nintendo's efforts.[41] The subject of pricing in the game was included in almost every discussion of the game, often in a similar, positive way. One article argued that this model "was the right way to do in-game purchases," since you were actually getting something for your money, whereas in many other games you can wait to get more energy; the critic continues, "why would I buy something I can get for free if I'm patient? It's garbage like this that gives in-game purchases a bad name."[42] This defense of the business model ends up contending that the game "is a wonderfully enjoyable and addicting

collection of baseball games. **It's probably not worth $40. It
is *certainly* worth $16, and that's how much you can pay to
get every single game if you haggle your buns off**" (emphasis in original).[43] In an overarching review of the game, the
same author states that, although they are not a fan of microtransactions as a whole, "the way *Real Deal* handles it is much
more welcome than any game I've seen before."[44] Ultimately,
substantial coverage of the game ended up focusing on pricing, typically explaining how this free-to-play model was different, and better, than the grubby microtransactions found in
other games. Writing for *Wired*, Chris Kohler clarified: "Now,
this is not the sort of free-to-play that you hear so much about.
There's no way for any big-spending 'whales' to pump tons of
money into this game, since the lifetime maximum that anyone could spend is $40 and that would only be if you were so
impatient that you wouldn't even bother to try the haggling
mechanic."[45] For Kohler, *Rusty's* is a home run because, in addition to good mini-games, "by delaying the part where they ask
you for money until you're already emotionally invested into
the world of the game, Nintendo's hoping that you'll be more
willing to shell out at that perfect moment. Thankfully, in the
case of *Real Deal Baseball*, what you get for your money is more
than worth it."[46] Similar sentiments are expressed in *The New
York Times* by Stephen Totilo in a review titled "Where Winners
Play, and Losers Pay," which concludes: "You're not winning
Rusty's Real Deal Baseball by paying nothing. You're winning by
wanting something more, seeing the sticker price and winning
a discount. It's not clear whether the player or Nintendo has
the upper economic hand in the transaction, but it sure feels
good to get a bargain. It doesn't feel wrong to pay for this 'free'
game. It feels, somehow, like victory."[47] Naming the game to his

list of 2014 games that should not be missed, Brandon Boyer writes that "it's a game about Nintendo's reluctance to enter the age of 'free to play' games, the kind that cajole you out of money by blocking your progress through gates of inconvenience."[48] Totilo names it his favorite game of the year, writing that Rusty sells you the mini-games "for real money, but you can haggle with the virtual dog to lower their prices. The better you play, the cheaper the entire game is. So great Nintendo gameplay mixes with unexpected meta-commentary about the many psychological tricks used to sell many modern 'free to play' games."[49] In combination, these quotes reveal a whole lot about the values many journalists and players hold about how video game should be designed and priced.

Rusty's Real Deal Baseball likely gets some of its praise because it is an elegant collection of mini-games that is quite accessible and has a strong "just one more" element to it. But coverage of the game always took a bit of time out to mention the pricing and how it was different, better, than typical free-to-play gaming. In this case, being able to get haggle for a bargain made the game more worthwhile than entries that just sought to take your cash. However, I think there is more there. Plenty of free-to-play games run sales or other discounts for players. I find it hard to believe that the positive reaction to the game was simply about getting a deal. Instead, it hinged on purchases where you get something you cannot just wait for and get in another way. It was about designing a game that was not about frustrating you into paying to get through a gate, but instead about getting players into a state where they willingly choose to buy a game. It is about designing a game where skill and consistent play can help players get a better deal on the next game. And, although it can feel like the game has a revolutionary new business model, it is more of a situation where Nintendo chose to break up the mini-games into individual packages, rather selling a group of small games in one larger one, like in the case of the *WarioWare* games or *1–2-Switch*. The game is likely praised for its approach to pricing because it appears to break from free-to-play norms, when it really is about slightly repackaging the traditional sales model for console games. This is less about Nintendo being "free-curious" than Nintendo trying to find new ways to keep the same business model moving forward, adapting it to micropayments rather than to a single, upfront fee. It is also notable that the praise for the game came from men who were largely writing for well-established outlets. Men liking a game about baseball that is priced in a manner that feels like buying things on sale makes the gendered dynamics surrounding games visible and salient. Bias around pricing and games is not just about what is happening in the game: cultural dynamics and a presumed audience of boys and men structures how games are played and received.

The norms for pricing in games and the desire for games that are based on skill and hard work have been established over years of development in the game industry. Meanwhile, the reception for *Rusty's Real Deal Baseball* makes the most sense in the context of Ben Cousins's arguments about snobbery against free-to-play. *Rusty's* is well received because it fits the norms, since it is from an established, even beloved, game developer that tried out a new pricing model, giving hope for a route around the monetization approach that upends the game industry. *Rusty's Real Deal Baseball* is fun and clever, but it is notable how it is held up as a grand exception, as the outsized praise illustrates the norms and preferences built into the preconceptions of those who write about video games for a living and the culture of Nintendo as a game developer and publisher. The game is delightfully weird and is the kind of sports game that appeals to both sports fans and those who do not watch sports, but, at its core, it is a video game that is designed to appeal to the norms and expectations of traditional video game players.[50]

After *Rusty's Real Deal Baseball* failed to revolutionize game pricing, Nintendo sought to expand its portfolio by releasing mobile phone games. Nintendo debuted beloved character Mario on mobile devices with *Super Mario Run*, which was discussed earlier in this chapter but bears revisiting in light of establishing the praise for *Rusty's Real Deal Baseball* and the almost three years between their launch dates. *Super Mario Run* got panned for a similar try-and-then-buy structure and, although critics liked the game, users and business analysts hammered it, resulting in a 15 percent drop in Nintendo's share price.[51] Between the two games, the context for play shifted. *Rusty's Real Deal Baseball* was released onto a proprietary mobile console system and targeted at the people who already had that console, many of whom likely had negative conceptions about free-to-play. *Super Mario Run* entered into a phone and tablet ecosphere that had long moved past paying premiums for titles and followed in the wake of free-to-play *Pokémon Go*. The massively successful free-to-play game led to a more than 30 percent increase in Nintendo share price and a $7.5 billion increase in market value that quickly followed after its launch, even though only part of the revenue for *Pokémon Go* goes to Nintendo. The norms and expectations for the audience were different and changing, leading Nintendo to surprise and delight on their handheld console and disappoint mightily in the broader mobile market.

Similar kinds of dilemmas will be explored throughout this book, including issues with loot boxes lifted from free-to-play games and dropped into premium titles like *Star Wars Battlefront II*. The norms and biases surrounding video games are complex, and there is plenty to unpack in statements like this one from journalist Mike Fahey:

> It's just a reality that while smartphone games may do some egregious things with their monetisation, they're now so familiar, and the games on them are so widely played, that the sting is taken out of any media attack on them. Console and gaming PCs, on the other hand, remain enthusiast devices, and are often subject to a generational barrier and degree of intrinsic suspicion from parents and other non-engaged demographics.[52]

Writing about the difference in media attention to *Fortnite*, which was being roasted in the mainstream media for its impact on children, and *Harry Potter: Hogwarts Mystery*, which was torched in the specialist press for its monetization model, Fahey's argument betrays some of the norms and expectations about games among those who write and make them. Fahey holds up *Fortnite* as a game that "is very light-touch, focuses on cosmetic items, and really does deserve to be called free, without scare quotes," while the Harry Potter game is a "sledgehammer-to-the face implementation of free-to-play monetisation."[53] These two games are subject to greater exploration later in the book, but Fahey is fundamentally making the claim that *Fortnite* fits his norms and expectations for what a game is, but *Harry Potter: Hogwarts Mystery* is abusive, while presenting his arguments about both as facts, rather than value statements. These beliefs and this general approach to discussing games underlie the core of the biases about free-to-play and mobile markets. Presenting opinions as facts is especially worthy of notice, as the approach makes it far harder to critique certain games on their own terms or see how they fit within the changing context of video games.

The difference between these two games also points toward the way particular modes of play get normalized by certain audiences. Fahey mentions the difference between the mainstream device of the smartphone versus the enthusiast device of the console or gaming PC. What is normal and acceptable on each is different, as *Fortnite*, a first-person battle royale game that is predicated on killing opposing players and building structures in an effort to survive longer than everyone else, fits neatly into traditional gamer expectations of how games should work. *Harry Potter: Hogwarts Mystery*, on the other hand, borrows heavily from mobile gaming tropes and is largely a reskinned version of games like *Kim Kardashian: Hollywood* and Glu Mobile's line of *Stardom* games. Fahey recognizes one of these games, knows the development history and genre fit of one of these games, and likely appreciates that game more because it fits within a traditional male gamer's expectation of how a game should work. *Fortnite* is a game you can play as much as you want that makes its revenue largely off cosmetics; it lets players show off their skills and is based on battle and building. *Harry Potter: Hogwarts Mystery* is a game where you tap the screen and wait for your energy to build back up before you do anything else. It is gated, there are limited ways in which to show off your skill, and the game is story, rather than battle, driven. It is also a great way to teach a child about waiting, rather than playing one more very, very last game, because once you are out of energy you have to pay to keep playing. Each of these approaches can be done well or poorly, and player preference and context certainly play a role in a game's reception. However, developing a complex critique of any game requires engaging it on its own terms. Free-to-play and mobile games violate norms based on their monetization model, but also in their particular modes of play and overarching design.

A final key normative element of games is how issues of labor, skill, and work intersect with notions of play. Certain values are held up as laudable, while others are deemed less necessary. Time spent in game tends to be praised, while the money spent to get through *Harry Potter: Hogwarts Mystery* more quickly is seen as wasted, rather than an investment in buying a new chapter of the game. In a different time, the debate surrounding pinball and whether it should be banned is one example of how our expectations about games work. Pinball was frequently banned in the United States because it was associated with gambling and seen as a game of chance. The bans were lifted at the point where courts accepted that pinball was a game of skill. Video games are often expected to work in a certain way—they are supposed to be a showcase for skill, like your ability to get a chicken dinner in *Fortnite* by being the last survivor. Jason Rohrer's *Cordial Minuet* is an example of the celebration of skill, as it is a gambling game where players put real money into the game and wager it against other players. The game involves a set of tiles in rows and asks players to pick from a variety of options, and then the opponent makes a decision about what to take. Quickly, skilled players found that the best approach to the game was to hunt lesser skilled players to win money off of them. One player's story, featured in *Kotaku*, explained how he won $6,000 on the game, largely playing against one other player. The writer also tracked down the person who lost the wagers and told their side of the story, one marked by the fact that the loser had so much money that $6,000 was not particularly important to him.[54] What I find notable about this is that there was little moralizing about a player putting $6,000 into this game, certainly not as much as generally accompanies commentaries about whales in free-to-play games. I would argue that this is likely because *Cordial Minuet* is seen as a game of skill, more like poker than a typical free-to-play game. We get both players' sides of the story, because the game is seen as normal, acceptable, and praisewor-thy. Explicit links are made to work, with the winning player's initial winnings contextualized as "less than minimum wage" until he found his whale. The losing player's out-of-game labor, as a "dot com millionaire," excuses his poor play in the game, and he makes explicit note of the fact that his losing was an experiment and there were matches where he was trying to lose. It is also notable that the game is made by a celebrated indepen-dent game developer and all the players in the story are men. Games are shaped by norms and expectations, and core video game players, journalists, developers, and scholars all hold biases about how games should be made; we use our words, design, and play to enforce and normalize those systems time and again.

An Overview

My focus throughout this project is on giving context to the norms and values that underlie perceptions of core gamers, journalists, developers, and game scholars about video games in order to map our collective blind spots. Although people will see particular examples in slightly different ways, I am trying to chart the center of the discourse and response, which I believe can illustrate biases about what games are made and how they are received. Unpacking those issues offers the opportunity to better understand how games are likely to be received and how norms and practices can be bent to move toward a more inclu-sive understanding of how games work and what they can be.

The focus of chapter 1 is to lay out the history of payment models in games. Although free-to-play on mobile is relatively new, video games have undergone massive changes to their pay-ment structures over time, some of which bear striking parallels to the current monetization structure of mobile games. The chapter traces the roots of free-to-play and how it came to be established into video games. In chapter 2, I use the history to analyze various monetization strategies and types of players to establish how norms and expectations have changed over time and how the stakes of how these changes impact game design, ending with an extended discussion of the monetization strategies typically found in free-to-play games. Chapter 3 addresses how players rationalize their spending on games and engage in strategies to resist spending. Given an understanding of payment structures, I pivot to analyzing the discussion surrounding free-to-play and mobile games to begin to illustrate how these games are discussed and the biases present in the dominant coverage of these games.

The fourth chapter specifically addresses sports games, which were a gateway for free-to-play to enter Western markets for many players. First with games like *FIFA* and then *Madden Ultimate Team*, Electronic Arts quickly found that gacha mechanics offered an additional revenue stream and a reason to purchase yearly upgrades to the game. Borrowing from Japanese vending machines and trading cards, gacha-style games use the digital equivalent of toy capsules or card packs to obscure what players are buying and entice "just one more" purchase. In addition to Electronic Arts games, I use my experience with *Tap Sports Baseball*, a leading baseball game on mobile devices, to give context to how monetization can work on consoles and mobile devices.

Chapter 5 focuses on so-called hardcore free-to-play and clicker games. Although these genres may seem to have little in common, the commentary about them is striking in how they are disproportionately likely to be considered to have legitimate monetization structures. They are frequently talked about as good, proper games, and analyzing them aids in sketching out what makes certain free-to-play games appear as normal, while others are considered abusive abominations.

One of the genres that free-to-play video games often borrow liberally from is collectible-card games. These games are increasingly being ported into digital forms, which allow players to play online and enable collections to be assembled dynamically. However, the card packs that they rely on are a traditional form of free-to-play, where players make blind purchases and then receive goods of varying quality. Analysis of card games on mobile devices opens up a reflection space in chapter 6 to talk about games predicated on loot-box style mechanics, like *Star Wars: Galaxy of Heroes*.

One of the most prominent licenses in mobile, free-to-play gaming is the Marvel Universe. Exceptionally popular, based on comic books and movies, and with a wide universe of heroes, villains, and stories from which to draw, Marvel games of all kinds of forms and mechanics abound. Chapter 7 focuses on comparing them to similar, non-Marvel games with different licenses and the relative reception of each.

Finally, the conclusion gets back to *Fortnite* and *Harry Potter: Hogwarts Battle* in order to try to bring together the threads of what leads to bias against free-to-play and mobile games. The two games give a chance to reflect on how games work, how they are talked about, and how that discussion structures who is likely to play and what games are likely to be developed. Most importantly, pairing them offers a chance to assess free-to-play and mobile games on their own terms to facilitate a critique of what is happening with these games for designers, players, and the industry at large.

1 We Can Be Really Bad at History

One of the most striking things for me in researching bias and payment models in games is how little is remembered about the history of how games have worked, particularly given that the history of video games is not particularly long. Although video games link to the much longer history of board, card, dice, and folk games, video games themselves are an invention that dates roughly to the mid-20th century. There are a number of excellent explorations of the history of video games. Some of these focus on recounting key moments and focusing on trying to recount the facts of moving from one moment in history to the next.[1] Typically, these books bill themselves as an ultimate history of video games and focus on telling a general, broad story. These books also tend to be relatively old, which means that key recent developments, like smartphone-based mobile and free-to-play gaming, are simply left out of the narrative. Focused efforts, like Carly Kocurek's critical retelling of arcade history and Shira Chess's analysis of women players and the games that they play, center on critical elements of history.[2] In spite of these histories, discussion about video games is often strikingly ahistorical. The first step in understanding mobile and free-to-play games is to look at a breakdown of different forms of games and payment models over time.

My approach here borrows from the work of these broad histories to retell elements with a critical approach focused on payment structures, norms, and how those elements have changed over time. This means the history I am telling is necessarily partial, focused on specific moments, and there are certainly parts that are left out. There are also different histories for different parts of the world; mine draws more heavily on the United States and Europe than on Asia and other locations. The point of retelling this history is to help us understand just how artificial norms are and open space for critical reflection. We have created expectations over time, and the current moment only seems natural and normal because we collectively forget how we are rooted in a history of video games that did not always look like it does now. Much like the work by Carly Kocurek and Shira Chess, retelling this history is one step toward using what has happened to inform where we are now.

And in the Beginning . . .

It is generally understood that the earliest video games were designed and developed in computer labs by those who had access to computers and a general facility with programming. Video games were a thing created in down time, something to show off what a computer could do and highlight skills at putting something interesting together. Early games, like William Higinbotham's 1958 oscilloscope game *Tennis for Two* or Steve Russell and crew's 1962 game *Spacewar!*, were designed at places that had computers in the 1950s and 1960s, which meant schools, private research labs, and government facilities.

The games were a lark, something done for fun and enjoyment and without any clear need or way to monetize them. These two titles are key examples of other elements of games as well. *Tennis for Two* was designed for a display for an annual exhibition fair at Brookhaven National Laboratory and, although it proved popular with the public, was largely lost to history until it became evidence in a lawsuit (discussed below) about the invention of video games. The game disappeared from the historical record because there was no way to play it other than to go to the lab that had the oscilloscope and custom controllers. There was no intent to make it a commercial product; it was an exhibition device to show what could be done with technology.

This early moment in video games, designing something because one could, typified an ethos of early game development. Games were made to push boundaries and show off something new, not to market a commercial product or service. These one-off games established norms about exploration, attempting new things, and showing off the limits of technology. The first video games were almost exclusively free-to play, as the commercial model for video games was yet to debut. *Tennis for Two* was also the kind of game one was likely to play rarely, maybe only once or twice. At this early point, video games were a showcase, and game development was a fun thing to try in your spare time, rather than a job.

Spacewar! marked a transition toward some hallmarks of modern game development. The game, although credited largely to Steve Russell, was a larger collaboration with students at MIT and other people in the regional computing community. Instead of being developed as a wholly novel one-off game, *Spacewar!* was designed to be played on a PDP-1 computer, which meant that the game had the ability to be played on all 55 PDP-1s that were sold. Although that was still a quite limited number of devices, it was broader than previous games, which helped establish the developer community around the game. Instead of a single game at a single site, *Spacewar!* became a game played by multiple people, most of whom had the technical capability to improve, modify, or change the game to suit their interests. The dynamic spread of the game also meant that it was ported to other systems and influenced the development of future video games. This led to new norms of collaboration, iteration, and change, as developers tweaked the game and worked together to create something new. The game had limited commercial application, as the market for PDP-1s was so small, although Steve Russell reported that *Spacewar!* was used in the testing and advertising of PDP-1s, as it exercised every aspect of the computer hardware.

There is also a greater legacy to *Spacewar!*, as it directly inspired the development of the first commercial video game. Nolan Bushnell and Ted Dabney's 1971 arcade cabinet game *Computer Space* was designed as a coin-operated version of *Spacewar!* Although the game was moderately successful, the idea of a coin-operated video game was far from a smash hit. Game distributors were concerned about possible theft of the television screens the game used for monitors, it featured extensive rules that are not intuitive for new players, and the game concept of an arcade was new and different. *Computer Space* was trying to break into a commercial space dominated by pinball machines and jukeboxes. Coin-operated entertainment existed, but a video game required convincing people that it was worth buying, distributing, and playing. Departing from a free-to-play model for video games was far from intuitive, which led to the first game that would come from the company Bushnell and Dabney created in the wake of *Computer Space*, 1972's Allan Alcorn–designed *Pong*.

Pong is a vital moment in the history of norms surrounding video games for many reasons. First, it was a breakout success. The game was the starting point of the commercial video game industry in the United States, the early point in transitioning video games from interesting explorations of what computers could do into a new industry. *Pong* was a much more straightforward game that was summed up in a line of instruction: "avoid missing ball for high score." Borrowing from the basics of traditional sports, like tennis, *Pong* is readily recognizable: it tapped into existing norms and expectations about how games worked. The business intrigue behind *Pong*, with Bushnell playing game manufacturers Bally and Midway against each other in an effort to retain the rights to the game for his new company, Atari, is a fascinating footnote of what makes *Pong* special. *Pong* is the moment where games became a business, a burgeoning industry, and a commodity to be rented by any player who happened to have a quarter. The debut of the arcade cabinet led to people going places to seek it out just to play the game. And, although the *Magnavox Odyssey* was the first home console, the home version of the *Pong* game, *Home Pong*, released in 1975, effectively led to the creation of the home console industry.

The *Magnavox Odyssey* was released in 1972, the same year as the *Pong* arcade cabinet, and featured a handful of very basic games, all based around a group of dots that would behave differently based on the game selected. The *Odyssey* was packaged with color overlays to change the color of a black-and-white television and lead to some basic attempts at immersion. It also came with traditional board game components, like chips, play money, and cards, in an effort to make the product more comprehensible in a market that had never seen a home video game console before. The system sold a few hundred thousand copies,

but it is most well known in the history of video games as the
pivotal piece of evidence in a lawsuit between Magnavox and
Atari over *Pong*. Magnavox established that Bushnell saw their
console prior to directing Alcorn to develop *Pong* and sued over
a patent Magnavox held for video games played on a television
screen. The suit established Magnavox, and employee Ralph
Baer, as the patent holders for video games played on television
screens, a case that held up in the legal system against both
Atari and Nintendo and brought Magnavox over $100 million
in patent lawsuits and hundreds of licensees. Baer's patent was
another new moment for video games; they were not just the
commercial product shown in the success of the *Pong* arcade cabinet, they were also a key piece of business, an intellectual property worth millions of dollars and subject to contention outside
of the game itself. The stakes of play changed, as money flowed
into the commercialization of what was once a hobby and way
to explore computers.

Atari continued to lead to the establishment of new norms in
gaming with their *Home Pong* system, which was sold through
the Sears catalog in 1975. Both the *Magnavox Odyssey* and *Home
Pong* were sold through the Sears sporting goods department.
Toy and electronic retailers of the time shied away from the new
home consoles, as they were thought to be too expensive to fit
with other toys, and there was no established market for them.
On the other hand, the Sears sporting goods department had a
hard time at the biggest retail time of year, Christmas, as summer sports equipment did not have much of a market in the
winter. Home video game consoles gave them a viable product
line, as they were designed to play indoors, and many of the
early games resembled traditional sports. *Home Pong* became a
massive success, one of the most successful goods in the catalog

for Sears, issuing in an era of home console video games that would soon see Coleco, Nintendo, and Mattel enter the market for video games. Atari eventually released the *Atari Video Computer System*, known as the *Atari 2600*, two years later, and these innovations created the foundations for the modern computer game industry. These systems launched a new form of payment for games, one where players needed to purchase the console first and eventually extra cartridges to play new games. Monetization moved from the rental games of the arcade to ownership in the home.

Parallel to the developments happening in arcade and console gaming, Roy Trubshaw and Richard Bartle developed a computer game alternately called *MUD*, *MUD1*, and *British Legends*. Trubshaw and Bartle built on a growing community of computer games, like *Zork* and *Colossal Cave Adventure*, where players moved through a text-based adventure, exploring, solving puzzles, and taking copious notes in an effort to figure out how to best proceed through the game. Computer games had grown along with the industry, but Trubshaw and Bartle innovated by taking the game online. Their game went through years of development as the two went through school at Essex University, and, when the school connected its network to ARPANET in 1980, *MUD1* became the first online multiplayer role-playing game. The game was licensed to internet service providers in the United Kingdom and United States, transforming a game that was once free for those who could access it into an attraction and retention tool for internet access companies. The evolution of the business applications for *MUD*, from free-to-play into a consumer-retention tool, is one more example of how the pay-once-and-own approach is only one of many pricing models for video games. *MUD* introduced its own norms, ones that persist through contemporary online gaming, demonstrating the stickiness of online communities, the attraction of games that players will sink massive numbers of hours into, and the fantasy and magic roots of many contemporary games.

This brief look through the history of games is designed to begin an illustration of how we got to where we are. Current norms about paying for and commercializing games come out of roots in a communal activity where there was no viable business market for years. Commercial interests changed games, making them far more available to people, but also altering the way they were made, consumed, and handled under the law. Perhaps most importantly, the commercial transition for games began to shape what games were made, how they were distributed, and how players started to think about how games should work. Understanding why the economic structure matters requires focusing less on the chronology of games and more on some key game platforms and examples of how they were commercialized.

Arcades, Consoles, and PCs: Oh, My!

In the United States, arcades peaked in the 1980s and diminished mightily after the widespread adoption of video game consoles. Japan has had a longer-lasting arcade culture, with arcades retaining relevance into contemporary times. Other countries, like South Korea, established other forms of communal play, with internet cafes serving as places to play games outside of the home. Strikingly, many of these developments can be tied to the commercial model of video games prevalent in each region and the norms surrounding them.

A revolutionary moment in Japanese video game development was the 1978 release of *Space Invaders*. *Space Invaders* was a billion-dollar success, a worldwide smash that dramatically expanded the mainstream cultural attention paid to video games. *Space Invaders* built on typical space tropes, with the player defending against waves of alien invaders. One of the earliest shooting games, *Space Invaders* was copied, borrowed from, and inspired generations of video game players and developers. The design of *Space Invaders* is also quite interesting, in retrospect. The game is effectively unwinnable, as the aliens keep coming faster and faster, until the player breaks and loses. This kind of design typifies many arcade games, as one of the needs of a commercialized arcade game is to ensure that the quarters keep dropping. Should players be able to defer losing for too long, an arcade game simply will not make enough money to warrant its space on the show floor. Other, later arcade games, like *Gauntlet* and *Smash TV*, expanded on and twisted these norms, developing health systems that depleted over time, requiring players to spend additional money in order to keep the game going and avoid losing all the player's progress. The design of *Gauntlet* is ingenious for an arcade game, as it expanded the notion of paying, functionally requiring players to keep putting money in the machine, as their health is inevitably exhausted and putting in a single coin would not lead to sufficient advancement to see much of the game at all. Each quarter leads to the next, as players must choose whether to keep investing or walk away from all the progress they made, a design that shares a lot in common with energy systems and the sunk costs players experience in contemporary free-to-play games.

These norms are notable in reflecting on the current state of video games. Arcade games are typically designed around ensuring regular instances of coin drop. Skilled players are able to play longer than unskilled players, but most games are situated in a way that ensures everyone's game will end after enough time to feel worthwhile, challenge them to play more, or get enough of a taste to want to come back. In this way, games like *Gauntlet* can be seen as antecedents to highly monetized free-to-play games. One can try an arcade game at a very low price, but continuing on requires regular, virtually unlimited injections of money to keep playing. Although one might feel like they are buying something, like those critics who preferred *Rusty's Real Deal Baseball* to other forms of free-to-play monetization, players are really just briefly renting the right to play for a bit longer, and each game is likely to end sooner than desired.

It is also worth noting that one reason the Japanese arcades may have lasted longer than arcades in the United States is that the dominant coin used in Japan was 100 yen, while the quarter that dominated US arcade cabinets was typically worth about a third as much. This fundamental difference in pricing, only solved by shifting to proprietary coins for each arcade chain, meant that US arcade gamers got a discount, so much so that it may have undercut the viability of the market. The death of the US arcade and the lack of success in moving away from the quarter as a primary means of payment is an ominous harbinger for a console industry stuck on a price point of $60. The stickiness of the initial purchase price also helps explain why game publishers are working hard to find new routes toward additional revenue.

Norms in arcade games were specific to the genre and formed by the commercial and design choices made by game companies. The way the games were designed was shaped by a combination of consumer taste, corporate interests, and the developers who sought to introduce new modes of play. The dominance of the quarter in US arcades stemmed from norms existing in the coin-operated business world and the limited number of coins available in the dollar-based currency system. Games were designed to beat players, to give them enough to want to play again, while putting them in a losing state that forced them to pay again. Fighting games were an exemplar of this kind of design, as a busy machine could be held for hours by one highly skilled player, but each of their matches would require a new opponent to step up and pay for a chance to take on the winning player from the last match.

Consoles, like the *Atari 2600*, *Nintendo Entertainment System*, and *Sony PlayStation* worked differently. These enterprises typically worked on selling cartridges or discs that contained a game to players for a premium price. Historically, console games are something players pay for once and then are able to enjoy at their leisure. This makes the design of a console game different than an arcade game. There is no need to ensure regular coin drop, so story-driven titles with lengthy playtimes are more desirable than games that quickly move players into a lose state. Although console ports of games like *Space Invaders* and *Gauntlet* have been extremely successful, the trends of the industry have pushed aside certain kinds of games on consoles, like dungeon crawlers, in favor of open-world experiences, leading at least some players to wonder, "where did the console dungeon crawlers go?"[3] Players can now consult websites like HowLongToBeat. com, where games are judged based on how long players can play them for, equating enjoyment and worthiness with time spent playing.[4] This fascination with length of playtime is notable, interesting, and fairly distinctive to video games. *Gauntlet* loses some of its appeal when keeping the game going is merely a matter of pushing the buttons to play again; the dramatic tension of needing to insert more money is lost. However, games like *Grand Theft Auto*, *Persona 4 Golden*, or *The Witcher 3: Wild Hunt* offer hours and hours of playtime in their vast worlds. As the business model for games shifted, the development and norms for games changed, as the point of sale transformed from coin drop into an upfront purchase price. Console manufacturing has also become a gendered occupation, as Nina Huntemann argues that women's work is vital to the production and promotion of video game consoles.[5]

The purchase price has also had knock-on effects on game design, as the initial prices of games have proven sticky, despite the costs of inflation. Full retail price for most console games as of this writing is about $60. However, in the 1980s *Nintendo Entertainment System* games cost $50, which would translate into around $100 if one considers the cost of inflation.[6] *Nintendo 64* games priced at $70 in 1998 would be the equivalent of $150 games in 2018. The *PlayStation 2* games that cost $50 would translate into about $65 in 2018, slightly more than the $60 base price of major *PlayStation 4* releases. *Atari 2600* games had a much wider price range, with some bargain games around $20, while premium games, like *Pac-Man*, sold for as much as $60 at launch, and many games slotted in the $30–$50 range. That 1982 launch copy of *Pac-Man*, if bought for $60, would be the equivalent of almost $160 35 years later, and a basic $30 game at launch in 1977 would be the equivalent of about $125 in 2018. The inflation and stickiness of prices in video games means that console video games are cheaper now than they have ever been, with one video game journalist doing the math to argue that inflation driving real costs down is "especially true when it comes to video game consoles and handhelds (or electronics generally), which have become more affordable over time, even when something *seems* to be more expensive."[7] Video game companies have tried to work around this to some extent with collector's editions and other special editions that come at a premium price, but the base price of most console games has not budged since it jumped from $50 to $60.

Paralleling the change in game design from arcades to consoles, the eroding effect of inflation means that additional revenue streams for games are an important part of making a console game work from a financial standpoint. This has led to an increase in online elements and a general approach from the industry that games are a service, rather than a product. Although arcade games tried to kill players and early to mid-era console games tried to give them more to play, the contemporary console game tries to keep a player playing and paying on an ongoing basis. This means that ongoing support for multiplayer campaigns and reasons to spend online for years after launch drive a revenue stream for games like *Grand Theft Auto V*, which at more than $6 billion in revenue is likely the highest grossing entertainment product of all time, at least until *GTA VI*.[8]

There are elements of PC gaming that follow a similar arc to consoles, as the dominant mode of sale is a single, up-front purchase price. However, PC sales for both video games and other computing products have used another model of sales that is relevant to discuss: a shareware, or try-before-you-buy, model. One of the most influential video games of all-time, *Doom*, was released under a shareware model, where players could download the game and play through a handful of levels for free, while playing more levels necessitated paying for the game. This approach can dramatically increase the number of people trying the game, much like a sample given out at a store. This also led to changes in the mode of development, as designers need to create a compelling hook in the early stages of the game, but also promise sufficient additional content to make a purchase worthwhile. This is a different approach to design, one based on blending the arcade's low initial cost with the single, larger purchase price for a whole game. It often led to games created in stages or levels, where some could be given away and others could be locked behind a paywall. It also is a model of payment that tried to make the leap to mobile gaming, as developers pursued a free-to-try model, such as in *Super Mario Run*, as described in the introduction. This payment structure establishes a slightly different set of norms, as players are trusted and given the opportunity to try something with the hope that the taste of the game will translate into a purchase later. Shareware shifts the norms of play, as players get accustomed to being able to try something, yet still retains the overall price of the product. And, given this backdrop, it is appropriate to focus on the model of payment at the heart of this project: free-to-play games.

Free-to-Play and Mobile

Free-to-play is linked to deep roots in pre-commercial gaming, as games like *Tennis for Two* and *Spacewar!* were assiduously free-to-play as long as one had access to the computing equipment needed for the game. For those who seek historical purity in debates about the pricing model of games, they must grapple with the historical payment structures for games, which were free for years before an industry started to emerge. However, contemporary free-to-play means something different, blending elements of the free-to-try shareware with the unlimited potential cost of arcade games. Free-to-play enables people to spend nothing on the cost of a game, or almost unlimited amounts, generally conferring some sort of benefit on those who spend money. As video games became a full-fledged commercial industry, free-to-play began to connote something different— occasionally the shareware that was popular in PC gaming, but more often a business model that encouraged some players to spend far more on a video game than they ever would under the pay-once model dominant in console gaming.

Free-to-play games largely emerged out of Asia, as the lack of an upfront price made the games accessible to far more players, while revenue could be made off a relatively small percentage of the player base, who could effectively subsidize the games as a whole through their spending. The dominance of the Chinese market was especially important, as it became the most valuable mobile gaming market in the world in 2016 and does not have as much of a history with console or PC gaming. There are certainly more games than just mobile in China, but by 2019 the mobile market exceeded spending on all other games in China.[9] Video games have become dominant in mobile markets, with 75 percent of App Store spending coming from video games, and Asia-Pacific countries contributing almost two-thirds of the total revenue.[10] Asian markets form an outsized portion of mobile game spending, which means their norms are more likely to shape the mobile market as a whole. Western markets were slower to come along, particularly as the dominant platforms for core gamer spending are consoles and PCs, which have different expectations with regard to design and pricing. Looking a bit more deeply at the Chinese mobile market helps unravel some of the notable differences in the reception of free-to-play games in Asia.

In an analysis of the difference between China and the West on mobile games, analytics group GameRefinery outlines many of the differences between Chinese and Western mobile games. Most notably, Chinese players had far more acceptance for multi-touch and free-movement controls, largely because the player base was not used to playing on game consoles. In the West there is a clear preference for single-touch controls, although the rise of *Fortnite* challenges that norm. Further, Chinese games offer far slower progression, hooking players over a period of months rather than days. However, Chinese games also pursue exceptionally deep social mechanics, with "multiple PvP/PvE [player vs. environment/player vs. player] modes, guilds/clans, co-operative tasks, chat, and spectator mode" as "just a few of the social game mechanics that are far more prevalent in top Chinese games compared to the West."[11] This enables these games to provide an additional hook for players, one that Western players are far more likely to find on consoles and PCs than on mobile. Almost 30 percent of Chinese games also use quizzes as a means of rewarding players for daily action while teaching them about a game, a mechanic that does not generally exist in Western games.[12]

These differences are notable and meaningful, as the biggest mobile game in the world as of this writing, Tencent's *Honor of Kings*, has had great difficulty latching on in the West, where it has been ported over as *Arena of Valor*. In its first six months in the West, the game made about as much as it made each day in China. It is impossible to know exactly why the game has not taken off outside of China, but Jeff Sue proposes three key reasons. First, multiplayer online-battle-arena games, the genre for *Honor of Kings* and *League of Legends*, are far more popular in China. Second, Tencent is able to reach out to players on social and mobile technologies far more effectively in China than elsewhere because of the company's social media dominance in China. And third, the game features a cast of heroes with deep ties to Chinese culture, making core heroes more relatable to Chinese players than Westerners.[13] In this case, focusing too much on any one game, even a multi-billion dollar hit like *Honor of Kings*, distracts from the core point that game markets have different norms, and those expectations shape what as seen as acceptable.

Although the mobile market is a growing segment of the commercial environment for games, there are a pair of other dynamics worth noting. First, because of the massive installed base of console and PC gamers, Western markets have more actively pursued the idea of premium games-as-a-service, rather than free-to-play gaming. As part of their fourth-quarter earnings report for 2017, major publisher Ubisoft released data showing that traditional games make about 13 percent of the revenue in their second year as they did in their first, a massive drop. However, games with live services are able to retain 52 percent of the revenue in their second year, promising an ongoing income stream that warrants continued production and helps elide consumer resistance to raising the initial price of the game by charging them for something else instead.[14] Developing an ongoing dynamic allows game companies to take advantage of a larger installed base and keep the game running for longer, likely at a lower cost than they would face if they released a new game. Additionally, the rise of digital distribution is particularly lucrative for game publishers, as they are able to retain the money that they would have had to give to a retail establishment in the case of a physical sale. Ubisoft has followed up on these industry trends by producing almost all their games as services, with ongoing content to engage players and serve as surfaces for monetization, including for their flagship title *Assassin's Creed*.[15] Although the notion of games-as-a-service is increasingly prevalent in console and PC titles, its roots are in mobile gaming.

Perhaps the best example of how games-as-a-service was popularized on mobile devices is how Electronic Arts has chosen to adapt one of its flagship titles, *Madden NFL Football*, for mobile platforms. Initially, EA bounced between either a premium option for football on mobile devices or annual releases with no up-front charge and heavy monetization. In 2012, EA released *Madden Social*, which was a card-collecting game themed around football and collecting players. 2013 saw the launch of *Madden 25*, which was widely criticized for aggressive monetization and poor gameplay. Additionally, the debut of *Madden 25* led to the closure of *Madden Social*, which meant that any spending done on the previous game was wiped out and players were forced to reinvest just to catch up to where they were previously. As one review put it,

> *Madden 25* is a poor substitute for an actual NFL game, and is instead just another social-oriented freemium title that seems to care more about monetization than gameplay. Who knows how long it will last either, as EA has shown they have no problem just shutting down their servers for these games, leaving players in the wings.[16]

Although *Madden* features annual releases on consoles, those are far from the norm in the mobile marketplace, where a few games, like *Game of War: Fire Age*, have been topping revenue charts for years.

In 2014, EA released *Madden NFL Mobile*, which once again reset the game, but, near the end of the NFL season, EA went on a press tour to announce that they were going to keep the game going, refining it instead of engaging in a pattern of annual releases. In an interview about the decision, EA Mobile's executive producer said that the company is "treating mobile as a very

different platform to others within EA. We're no longer thinking about annual mobile title releases. Instead, we're treating
our mobile games, including *Madden*, as a live service."[17] This
shift meant that the game was supported by a dedicated team
throughout the year, who focused on events and special activities
within the game to drive engagement and spending. EA released
year-branded updates to the game through 2017's *Madden Mobile
18* and then rebranded the game as *Madden NFL Overdrive* in July
2018 (figure 1.1). *Overdrive* is a mode of the game that "is as close
as the mobile version of the *Madden* franchise has ever gotten
to live PvP [player vs. player]," enabling players to play against
each other with a scoring system unique to the game.[18] Success
can be found for free players, but the game has plenty of hooks,

Figure 1.1
A newly formed team in *Madden NFL Overdrive*. Personal screenshot.

with multiple currencies and methods of upgrading a team to drive monetization. Switching to seeing the game as a service alters what the game is and how it is designed, pushing developers to try to find a large audience and then give a handful of players avenues for substantial investment in the game. As one review of the transition of *Madden* into a full-fledged game-as-service notes,

> I'd just prefer the old method of spending some cash up front for a mobilized take on the *Madden* console games, even if that means buying a new version every year. But more and more I'm realizing that people like me are in the vast minority, and there's a massive new generation of mobile gamers who embrace things like free to play, social media integration, and weekly events and bonuses. Taking all of EA Mobile's mobile sports games together, they've been downloaded more than 100 million times in just the past year [2014], which is a mind-boggling number.[19]

Madden NFL Overdrive and other games like it mark a fundamental change in games, transforming what is bought and how games are played and designed. Information about players and game design become vital in an effort to drive spending, the ultimate price of the game pushes ever upward, and those who grew up on games with a single fee lament what has come, even if there are clear historical precedents for the current era of pricing. Pushing toward deeper understanding of how to free-to-play works requires delving into a discussion of monetization in contemporary free-to-play games.

2   Requirements, Advantages, and Options

In an era where games are a product to be sold, variable pricing can be introduced in the form of collector's editions, special in-game items, or other elements designed to differentiate one copy of a game from another. However, most players of those games pay about the same price. On the other hand, free-to-play games chase players who will spend money in the game, pursuing the roughly 3.5 percent of players who will regularly spend money.[1] A tiny fraction of players spends substantially more than most, with one analysis indicating that these users spend 30 times more than the average player.[2] A small percentage of the spending players—around 5 percent, or less than .1 percent of overall players—are referred to in industry parlance as "whales": players who may spend thousands of dollars on a game.[3] The lore is that the term is borrowed from the casino gaming industry, where particularly lucrative customers are deemed whales. These are players with million-dollar-plus credit lines who could easily win or lose millions of dollars in a weekend.[4]

Video game companies chase high spenders, trying to find out as much as they can about them and their interests to better target their development resources and generate revenue. As one free-to-play game developer puts it, if you are a whale, we take Facebook stalking to a whole new level. You spend enough money, we will friend you. Not officially, but with a fake account. Maybe it's a hot girl who shows too much cleavage? That's us. We learned as much before friending you, but once you let us in, we have the keys to the kingdom. We will use everything to figure out how to sell to you. . . . We will flat out adjust a game to make it behave just like it did the last time the person bought IAP [in-app purchases]. Was a level too hard? Well, now they are all the same difficulty.[5]

Developers are chasing multiple purchases from players, as most spenders are spending $50 or less at a time, making it vital to provide surfaces for recurrent spending that eventually accumulate into massive total spend numbers. Companies are still experimenting with how to best do this, and perhaps the biggest departure from traditional video game pricing is dynamic, in-game adjustment, similar to the pricing that occurs with airline tickets and adapts to increase prices to match demand.[6] The value of proprietary information about spending and in-game player behavior is sizeable enough that one company involved the FBI in pursuit of a former employee who stole information from internal databases.[7]

In my experience, players of free-to-play games talk about games and spending differently than straightforward industry reports that sort players into whales and others. Players have a more fine-grained approach to spending, adding to the marine metaphors to include additional levels, from highest spending to lowest: kraken, whale, dolphin, minnow, and free-to-play. Kraken are the kinds of players who buy everything: they are the first to get new characters and items and seemingly spend without limit. Kraken readily spend thousands of dollars on a game and often hold a powerful place within the community. In the case of *Marvel Strike Force*, the top-spending player in the first few months after the global launch of the game, OXTS86V, parlayed his spending into a role as a frequent interview guest for leading content creators and then into a role as a producer of YouTube videos analyzing the game.[8] His voice, when he complained about pricing in the game, was quickly magnified, with players emphasizing that when even top spenders feel like the game is not giving value for spending, it is truly a mess.[9]

Below kraken on the food chain are whales, who are akin to the high rollers in a casino. Instead of having unlimited budgets, whales tend to be heavy regular spenders. This is why many free-to-play games are monetized in a manner to promote regular, moderate spending. Instead of spending the thousands of dollars on a single hand that a high roller may at a casino, whales are typically spending less than a hundred dollars at any one time. This pattern of spending also clearly ties to why Electronic Arts would pursue an ongoing model for *Madden Mobile*, since generating massive free-to-play spending hinges on keeping players invested and playing for years. A new version of the game wastes their investment, while rolling out new, more powerful players to add to teams can spur spending. This also means that games designed to attract whales inevitably engage in power creep, where the newest additions to the game are the most powerful. Dolphins are another notch down, as they may make regular purchases, but tend to do so with smaller dollar figures attached. They may be an important part of the spending ecosphere, but they also clearly define themselves against players who spend more and those who spend less. Below the dolphins are minnows, players who spend small amounts on rare occasion. Minnows often end up buying special promotions and introductory deals, which typically offer far more value to players for their money than regular options. These players may also buy an ongoing subscription or incur some sort of small cost to provide them with advantages in the game. Finally, free-to-play players spend nothing on a game. The term is highly policed by players, as contentions that "I'm free-to-play, except for this one thing I bought" are quickly shot down by others who contend that players are either free-to-play or they are not. To them, any spending is indicative of not being free-to-play. Somewhat separate from using whale or similar terms as a noun, whaling can also be used as a verb, as players may "whale out" on some new item or opportunity, spending money to gain an advantage in their game of choice.

The food-chain metaphor is an interesting one. Casinos and the communities surrounding them use terms like whale, high-roller, advantage players, typical players, and action players, but the words chosen by the community surrounding free-to-play games clearly connote a food chain, with kraken lording over all others. Casino players are rarely in competition with each other, and, in competitive games like poker, food-chain terms like "fish" are used to describe new players. A food-chain metaphor is largely tied to the fact that spending in a game where you can buy limited characters or gain other advantages means that you are more likely to beat, or eat, those who are not spending. Effectively, the whale is there to eat the minnow, and the minnow is there to be eaten. Players write narratives about their success in limited spending, and top YouTube creators often have a public account where they spend, along with an additional free-to-play account, to show the range of their skill and experience with the game. Free-to-play players may brag about their success at the game, implicitly arguing that they are more skilled than paying players because they have managed to achieve some feat without spending.

The way these terms break down and get implemented by players hinges on the design of a game. Although a term like "whale" has become so ingrained in the discourse that it is used throughout free-to-play gaming, finer distinctions hinge on a particular type of game design, one predicated on pitting players against each other and giving some sort of advantage for spending. A mobile game, like *Star Wars: Galaxy of Heroes*, has a wide variety of things players can spend on, and those who spend have an advantage over those who do not. However, *League of Legends* also has a free-to-play monetization structure, but the way the game is designed means that spending money does not inherently grant an advantage in-game. Players still occasionally use terms like whale, but they do so in a different way, one that is less descriptive of a social structure in the game and more about a player's relationship with spending and the game developers.[10] Within free-to-play games, there are three primary modes of organizing payment structures: a requirement for buying, an advantage to spending, and optional spending.

Three Free-to-Play Monetization Models

Games with a requirement for buying have a lot in common with console and PC games. They contain some hard and often impenetrable paywall that limits play in some sort of way until a player pays to unlock the game. These games take advantage of having zero upfront cost in order to get players to try the game, and then limit player progress in some way to encourage payment. Games like *Super Mario Run* and shareware fit the bill, as they give players a chance to try the game, but fully unlocking it requires payment. These games typically have a single cost, although they may charge an additional fee for content that is added later. In the mobile marketplace, independent games often borrow from this structure, with developers like Zach Gage using it to make his game fit an initial user expectation of free and then generating revenue as players pay to unlock the game. This design can also be used in a softer way, with players paying to remove ads from the game or making a one-time payment for some basic game advantage, like doubled coins or extra experience. These games tend to be designed in a manner quite similar to traditional console and PC games, offering players a clear value proposition and making the gaming experience consistent from one player to the next. An additional form of this sort of game integrates advertising into the core of the playing experience, forcing players to watch an ad to continue forward. Although this does not require players to make a direct financial contribution to the game, they are being required to pay through their attention to generate revenue for the game developer, much like commercial television. These games may arouse discontent if the price is thought to be excessive or if the game is bad, but they are not typically subject to the most strident criticism about how free-to-play games are ruining the video game industry.

The games that do generate the most consternation are free-to-play games where there is an advantage to buying things. Games with an advantage to buying often use energy timers where players can pay for additional refills in order to progress more quickly. There are likely special deals that allow a player to unlock more powerful characters or cards to increase their odds of success in their next battle or game. There is likely a steady stream of content to keep players engaged with the game for longer periods of time in order to continue to stimulate revenue and to make older purchases less relevant than newer ones. Players can pay to speed the game up or gain other advantages to make themselves more powerful. Some of these games will offer VIP packages for players, giving them bigger rewards as they hit higher spending targets. Many of these games also integrate advertising, giving players some sort of bonus if they consent to watching an ad. The top-grossing mobile games tend to follow this framework, likely because it enables virtually unlimited spending by players and consistent, ongoing revenue for game companies. This kind of payment structure enables developers to continue spinning off content for a game that will likely have a much longer run than a game where players only pay once. Games like *Candy Crush Saga*, *Clash of Clans*, *Game of War: Fire Age*, and almost all strategy or match-three games are designed around an advantage-to-buying philosophy. Games with scads of characters to unlock, like any comic book or fighting game, also fit nicely into this paradigm. Games with restrictive energy systems, like *Kim Kardashian: Hollywood* and the *Stardom* games that inspired it, fit here. And cosmetics-driven games, like *Design Home* and *Covet Fashion*, are typically structured in a way to make the most sought-after items premium content that is quickly followed by the release of even cooler, newer premium content.

Games where players can buy an advantage are subject to great debate, as they are typically designed with different kinds of hooks and strategies than contemporary console and PC games. They are often designed to limit the length of a play session, and they will frequently put content behind some sort of wall, requiring players to either spend to break through it or wait for months until they can catch up and climb it. They are likely built in a manner that gives those who pay persistent structural advantages over those who do not. This violates expectations of balance and "fairness" that permeate contemporary console and PC games.[11] Similar to what Mia Consalvo found in her excellent

work on cheating in games, boundaries for players and expectations are socially negotiated and subject to individual rules about
what counts as appropriate and what does not.[12] They may not
require much skill, often trading on luck or basic game dynamics that do not allow players to demonstrate mastery. These are
frequently the kinds of games that inspire moral panic, as the
spending can be veritably unlimited and may be targeted at children. There are news stories about them, like the librarian who
embezzled money to pay for his nearly $90,000 *Game of War:
Fire Age* habit.[13] However, games like *Hearthstone* and every other
collectible-card game fit into this category, as having more cards
confers a structural advantage to players. In fact, it is possible
to see the roots of collectible-card games in all the games that
contain card packs or unlockable characters, like *FIFA Ultimate
Team* and all of the Marvel- and DC-licensed games. These games
also have roots in the arcade, where paying more got a player
more chances to continue to get better and improve. However,
quarters in the arcade likely led to an increase in skill, a value
that is celebrated in the video game community, while spending
in a free-to-play game confers structural advantage to the player,
bringing up complicated thoughts about merit, social structure,
and how things "should" be.[14] These games are frequently at the
center of the bias about free-to-play games, as they constitute a
huge section of the market and symbolize something different
about the future of games. These are a kind of game where skills
and time are substituted for money, and they are far more common on mobile platforms than on PCs or consoles.

The final category of free-to-play games are often left undis-
cussed in considerations of the perils of the business model.
Games where there is optional buying typically enable players
to purchase cosmetic elements to customize their character and

approach to the game. These cosmetic elements let a player show off their support for the game developer and their dedication to a particular character or approach. Unlike *Design Home*, where all the purchases are cosmetic, but judging players on the aesthetic success of their home design is built into the game, games like *League of Legends* and *World of Tanks* make purchasing things almost entirely optional. Although there are requirements for certain modes of play in some of these games that are made easier by spending money, players can typically earn currency (slowly) through playing the game, providing a seemingly level playing field for each player to test their skill in the game. *Fortnite* also fits in this category, as a game that is free-to-play on all platforms, yet is monetized through cosmetic purchases. *Fortnite* began its monetization structure through purely cosmetic elements and then introduced "battle passes," which enabled players to make a payment each season in the game that would let them earn their way toward cosmetic items. Fulfilling the battle pass grants far more value than paying for each item individually, and it also grants the developer, Epic Games, a chance to offer players the opportunity to pay another fee to skip forward on their pass if they are short on time. Seasons are offered about every 12 weeks, and the second and third seasons have led to roughly $50 million in sales on just the first day of each season.[15] With a business model that can clear $200 million a year in four days, the battle pass model is a way of conforming to expectations of optional buying while grossing substantial amounts of revenue as long as the game has a large-enough player base.

Discussion of optional spending games often focuses on how non-paying players can succeed, and they face stiff resistance from their player communities if they attempt to break out of their elective buying model. When the mobile version of *World of Tanks* introduced a system that many players complained pushed the game from optional buying to advantage of buying, territory players revolted, leading the developer to drop prices and change the structure of payment in the game to come back in alignment with player expectations. One recounting of the situation stated the developer "agreed with those vocal players about the pricing of the consumables. . . . It's good to see a developer with its ear on the ground and one that isn't afraid to admit a mistake."[16] This incident illustrates the norms for game design in optional buying games. If developers push too hard on monetization, they are betraying the trust of players and breaking the game. The difference between optional buying and advantage of buying fuels much of the bias surrounding free-to-play and mobile games, and investigating elements of these debates is a core project of this book.

Mobile games face opposition because of their simplified control schemes and generally inferior hardware capabilities, but a primary accelerating element is that the most popular, highest-grossing games on mobile devices tend to pursue an advantage-buying model of monetization. This approach leads to deep questions about norms, as the strategy and design that come with an advantage-buying model is quite different than those players pay for once in an upfront payment. Closer to the arcade model for pricing and with links to collectible-card games, communities of players tied to console and PC video games often decry that the advantage payment structure is pay-to-win. Underlying criticism of advantage games is the belief that video games are a place where players should be able to show off their skills and talent so that the best player can win. The norm on consoles and PCs is for a style of play that showcases either skill or in-game effort, minimizing the role of payment beyond the original price of the game and system. Players are celebrated for work and talent, and games are cordoned off as a space apart from the "real world," a place where your pocketbook should not buy your way ahead, even if you have the money to spend. The barrier to entry for a console and all the elements it takes to play it is much higher than downloading a free app on a smartphone that many people already have. However, the community writing about and playing video games has normalized the idea that once you have paid the fee to get into the game, you should be able to play on the same terms as everyone else. Given the basics of what mobile and free-to-play games are, how free-to-play is designed, and this overview of different approaches to monetization, it is important to turn to just how nasty the discussion about free-to-play can be.

The Core Strikes Back

There are many different kinds of communities involved in video games. When one looks broadly at the notion of who plays video games, almost everyone in the United States plays. However, when it comes to a self-defined identity as a gamer, the focus is far more narrow.[17] The type of player invested enough to write about, read about, and discuss video games in-depth online is representative of a particular group within games, and those people are far more likely to appear in discussions about video games. Among these players, free-to-play, particularly in the form of advantage-buying structures, is seen as abhorrent and a violation to all that is right and good in gaming. Winding through the general perception of the center of the industry to free-to-play, and often mobile, games requires starting with a walk-through of reactions to free-to-play games from players,

developers, and journalists in an attempt to track why they are
so offensive to some.

One of the most eloquent articles I have read about why
some players reject free-to-play games is a 2013 essay by Justin
Davis for IGN titled "Why Core Gamers Hate Free-To-Play."[18] In
it, Davis begins with a thought experiment: what if *Borderlands
2* (a popular game at the time) was produced as a free-to-play
game, rather than a premium title? He imagines a version of
the game funded by "a real-money auction house, with the creators taking a 10% cut," instead of the $60 fee for the game and
an additional $60 charge for subsequent downloadable content
found in the status quo. The center of his essay explores the
rhetorical question: "Is there a way to make 'freemium' more
than a dirty word for hardcore gamers, or will we always push
back against anything more than paid cosmetic options?"[19] He
posed the scenario to his Twitter feed and they quickly rejected
the idea, even though it would be the exact same game and
give players a chance to get paid for their effort in the game
through item sales. He argues that the central issue with free-
to-play monetization is one of trust, because if you cannot buy
the premium currency in a game "you would *never* become suspicious, because there is nothing to be suspicious of. But once
it's for sale, the shop's mere existence puts the idea into your
head."[20] He imagines scenarios where players would complain
about possible manipulation, posting data of changes in the system and lamenting days gone by where games were a product
that could be purchased and played. For even the sober, trusting,
non-conspiratorial gamers, he argues that "there's still a certain
grossness associated with real-money values continually intruding into your mind," because when you get an amazing item in
the game you will be prompted to consider using it or selling it.

For Davis, "there's a purity in playing a paid game that's lost in most freemium alternatives. Video games are all about escapism. There's a certain indecency to thoughts of real-world money intruding into the experience. . . . Many of us will pay a higher up-front cost to protect the integrity of the play experience."[21] This straw version of an idealized free-to-play game is quickly shot down, as Davis contends that, more often than not, developers get free-to-play wrong. He contends, "many free-to-play multiplayer games include a cash shop with power-up items, undermining the game's balance. Many freemium games feature artificial barriers put up by the game designers, which players can pay to overcome. Practices like these are where the blanket fear and distrust originate from. Gamers' time is valuable. Pay up to not waste it grinding. Ick! Core gamers are a smart, plugged-in bunch that does its research. They're a hard group to fool."[22] Davis proceeds to enumerate how a game developer can do free-to-play right, discussing Valve and the trust they have built up with players over time and their games, like *Team Fortress 2* and *Dota 2*, that are largely monetized through cosmetic purchases. He concludes by arguing that, to him and other core gamers, the most important part of considerations about free-to-play are about perception, trust, and immersion, as they want to play a game that lets them play, rather than think about money—and "until game makers figure it out, I'll keep buying games for full price and playing to my heart's content."[23]

This essay and the sentiment within it gets at why many in the core community around games has an issue with free-to-play. Free-to-play games have different norms and structures, a different relationship between money and playtime, and an alternate mode of monetization. Much like games transformed in intent and design as they moved from arcades to consoles, it is reasonable to expect that games would need to adjust to move from console to free-to-play and mobile. The version of *Borderlands 2* he envisions, with a real-money auction house, probably would have many of the issues he enumerates. Free-to-play development results in new kinds of games, ones built with different systems in mind, instead of just picking up a console game and dropping it into a free-to-play business model. Arguably, this is a reason why a game like *Super Mario Run* struggled, while *Pokémon Go* created excitement. Charitably, Davis is writing as free-to-play models are emerging, but he cannot see outside of the norms of the games he is used to playing. Those games he pays for once and plays to his heart's content are based around the kinds of values he treasures: balance, regular effort in grinding, the delight of a rare drop, and the escapism that comes from not having to think about money and how it impacts the playing field in game. These are all norms that have been developed over time, rather than immutable truths of gaming. It is also noteworthy that the most strident protests come from men and are most frequently aimed at free-to-play games targeted to them, while games aimed at women are typically ignored or mocked. However, for Davis and the gamers whose perspective he is representing, there are firm expectations about what games are supposed to be. That reactionary response limits the space to accept some new kind of design, particularly one that challenges the essential fabric of the kinds of games they grew up on and have grown to appreciate. By failing to take a new form of design seriously and critique it on its own terms, the debate often hangs on preferences presented as facts.

Kirk Hamilton wrote a similar column for Kotaku in 2017, contending that microtransactions "poison the well" of games, leading players to a series of dark thoughts about the designer's intent.[24] Beginning with a review of several games that use microtransactions, Hamilton builds to the claim that "every game with a microtransaction system is a player revolt waiting to happen. That's more true of full-priced games than free-to-play ones, but making a game free doesn't necessarily make players feel any less taken advantage of."[25] Hamilton anchors his argument in a 2009 article by Stephen Totilo, who wrote about his experience in *Final Fantasy Crystal Chronicles*, where the multiple small packs of downloadable content that made the game easier left him wondering: "Is there a dirty trick being played here on gamers? Who knows. There is the possibility. That stinks enough."[26] Hamilton centers his argument around the contention that games are designed to make us fail, and "whenever some aspect of the game is locked behind a real-money paywall, every decision that developers make will be suspect."[27] For Hamilton and Totilo, in-game transactions erode the trust between player and developer, leading them to wonder about the way that capitalism and a corporate desire for profit interfere with what they portray as a relatively pure art of game design. Discussing their positions in 2018, they largely argue that in-game purchases and small transactions lead them to question the value proposition of the game versus the items offered within the game. For Hamilton and Totilo, if a AAA title costs $60 at retail, why are they trying to sell a single cosmetic horse for $7?[28] Both journalists back up the core claims of Davis, with repeated articles stretching almost a decade and making largely the same claims: microtransactions do not belong in games because they corrupt them, leading players to wonder if decisions about monetization are being made by game designers or business people.

These sentiments appear in many different forms and evaluations of free-to-play games, many of which have deep design issues, since good free-to-play design is still evolving. Writing about the different between *Peggle* and a free-to-play version of the game called *Peggle: Blast*, henrique antero claims

> *Peggle* believes in your potential, even when your parents don't. *Peggle* likes you. *Peggle: Blast* hates you. *Peggle: Blast* would want you dead if that meant you'd pay more. *Peggle: Blast* would kick your dog just to enjoy your desperation, and then would charge you money to not do it again. . . . It's everything you could expect from a free-to-play version of *Peggle* for mobiles made by [Electronic Arts].[29]

Peggle is a charming game, and *Peggle: Blast* is a version of it that builds largely on the free-to-play structure of limited lives to try levels and charges for additional attempts. *Peggle* is hopeful and optimistic, as it encourages players to keep trying to solve puzzles, which is a sound strategy for a pay-once-and-own game. *Peggle: Blast* put barriers in front of players, extracting time or money if they want another chance, as the monetization model twists the game and drives it to be cruel. He argues that "What is distasteful about *Peggle: Blast* are the subtle transformations that the original design has gone through to accommodate the habitual villainy of monetization."[30] Like Davis, a key part of antero's argument is that the injection of money into the game inherently corrupts it. *Peggle* is transformed from something you can play with a partner until it is completed into a *Peggle: Blast* that limits progress, stops play, and decreases his sense of wonder. In this regard, *Peggle: Blast* violates antero's norms of games, becoming all about the money and less about the play. The balance is off, as the monetization structure makes the business side of the game more present when compared to the simplicity of the original game design.

Similar vitriol is aimed at *Final Fantasy XV: A New Empire*, the mobile partner to the core game, which is summed up as "essentially everything you probably hate about free-to-play mobile games, amped up to a million. . . . It's where mobile games go to fester and die, staring at your screen as you wait twelve real-life minutes as a hammer motions back and forth, waiting for a building to upgrade for no discernable reason."[31] A story promoting *Transformers: Battle Tactics* takes the time to engage in an aside mentioning that the game's developer DeNA "is not shy about taking the 'free' out of 'free-to-play.'"[32] The criticism of free-to-play typically centers on how incremental payments change games and how that process undercuts what a video game is.

To be clear, my intent is not to defend all free-to-play games, as I do not find *Peggle: Blast* enjoyable and *Final Fantasy XV: A New Empire* was a quick uninstall for me, but the spaces in between why these games get rejected is notable and interesting. It is in these gaps that we can better understand how video games work and how certain kinds of games are challenging norms and expectations about what video games are supposed to be. One of the most direct explorations of how free-to-play has changed games was an episode of *South Park*, which Kotaku described as going "in hard on the unethical free-to-play menace that has been plaguing video games for the past few years."[33] The strength of the reaction is a form of gatekeeping, one designed to maintain the norms and expectations of the old system rather than develop something new. And rejection of free-to-play, or at least complicated feelings about it, is also prominent among developers and publishers.

NBA 2K18 was celebrated for the quality of its gameplay, but panned for its use of microtransactions. Although the game is a premium title, it integrated substantial gating restrictions to push players to spend money in the game.[34] Some of those prices and options were rolled back over time, but in advance of the launch of the next version of the game, senior producer Rob Jones explained his perspective on the issue, stating

> VC [victory coins, the premium currency in *NBA2K*] is an unfortunate reality of modern gaming. Every game, at some point, in some way has currency and they're trying to get additional revenue from each player that plays the game. You know, the question has to be when does it feel like it's a straight money grab versus when does it feel like it's value added, right?[35]

The desire for an additional revenue stream is painted as unfortunate, something developers are forced to do rather than what they believe is the best choice. Jones also presents a clear appeal to changing norms in his attempt to claim that the additional charges are tied to "modern gaming." He recognizes that the contemporary context of game publishing is different and attempts to bend the norms and expectations of players to encourage them to see that times have changed, contending that games need to change too. Game designers and publishing companies are working in a space where premium titles have sticky prices that have not budged in years, while they watch a new, more profitable approach to game design demonstrate a different way of doing business. Free is a particularly important price for apps, because the dominant norm of the app economy is predicated on a free sample. Pushing against that norm requires an immense, established reputation or reason for players to invest without knowing exactly what they are getting. Publishers have leaned into this change, as it make the friction for player acquisition lower, and a large player base is a key element of any free-to-play game. However, as the status quo evolves, some developers are seeking to rationalize their pricing models.

As Valve geared up to release their card game *Artifact*, which was developed in partnership with *Magic: The Gathering* designer

Richard Garfield, principal people involved in the game went on an interview tour stressing how the game was being designed in a manner that conformed with traditional norms. In her summary of *Artifact*, Rebekah Valentine wrote that, unlike other digital card games, *Artifact* would have an upfront cost of $20 and after that initial fee, "there is absolutely no way for players to earn more packs by playing the game. Everything more must either be bought with real money, or traded for on the game's market, where individual cards can be purchased or bartered for just like one might do at a physical card shop for something like *Magic: The Gathering*."[36] Similar to the real-money auction house hypothesized for *Borderlands 2*, but different because it is anchored within the realm of collectible-card games rather than shooters, designer Richard Garfield went out of his way to make the case that, even with this pricing structure, *Artifact* would fit traditional expectations about how games are supposed to work. Garfield argued that the cost for new cards, rather than the ability to earn them freely, adds a level of investment to the game, as "free play always comes along with suboptimal experiences, because you have to sacrifice something for free play."[37] A couple of months after the initial launch, Valve reconsidered their position, adding a leveling system and a way for players to earn some cards through regular play of the game.[38] However, Garfield believed that spending within the game will not upset traditional gaming norms about balance, since skill is still likely to win out in the end. Garfield claimed that *Artifact* is

> not pay to win. It's pay to participate. Any hobby you have, you have to invest something. If you play tennis, you buy a racket. So here, we've got a model where you can put in a very modest amount and be competitive. . . . If you give Pete Sampras a shitty racket and you buy the best tennis racket in the world, he's still going to beat you handily. I think this game is very similar. I think that's a key part of

it. The best way to win the game is to get good at the game, to learn how to play the game with the right kind of deck, and to learn how to make higher-level strategic decisions. I think that's really the best way to learn.[39]

Garfield, despite wandering through an analogy to tennis great Pete Sampras over a decade after he retired, sought to make the case that, although the money ensures the financial viability of *Artifact* as a product for Valve, it does not corrupt play by making those with a greater financial investment more powerful within the game. This is a clear appeal to traditional gaming norms about skill, which is backed up by his contention that players need to invest time and effort to get better and learn to play the game. The sentiment is only a step or so short of screaming GIT GUD, which is particularly interesting given Valve's hands-off approach to elements like chat moderation and their starry-eyed trust that people will simply be nice to each other.[40] In promoting *Artifact*, those behind it make clear appeal to traditional norms, while resisting the intimation that their game might be seen as featuring the crass monetization that, to many, typifies free-to-play games.

An interview with Graeme Struthers, one of the six employees of independent developer Devolver, makes bias about mobile and free-to-play gaming clear. Journalist Dan Pearson explains that both he and Struthers "recognise that free-to-play isn't inherently wrong, evil, or doomed to failure." Instead, he says, "what rankles us both is the idea that it's a zero-sum game between that model and the console market."[41] Of course, two paragraphs before that reasoned position, Pearson quotes Struthers's statement on the state of free-to-play in the industry: "The other thing I really like about what they've done is, thank fuck, I was so fed up of people telling us we should do free-to-fucking-play, in-app-fucking purchases, whatever the fuck that is, and that consoles were dead. So fuck all of those people and their fucking shitty stance."[42] Struthers makes clear in the interview that Devolver seeks to develop for PCs and then port their games to consoles. Featuring indie hits like *Hotline Miami*, Devolver makes premium games that charge premium prices, fitting in line with a core gaming business model. Industry analysts and business advisors are represented in this story as corrupting influences, people who do not understand games and are simply pushing for making more money. Although both people in this story ostensibly respect free-to-play, Devolver surely does not sully their hands in making games that way. Upholding the traditional norms of games, Pearson and Struthers vehemently reject how free-to-play is perceived as upending the structures of games.

The monetization mechanism of free-to-play games is at the center of critiques of games in the genre. Players that readily accept a single fee for games can often be quite comfortable with optional spending models and also with a requirement to spend. However, advantage spending upsets their understanding of what games should be. For game developers, advantage-spending models often have the highest capacity for revenue. Optional spending with character customization works for games like *League of Legends* and *Fortnite*, but they are exceptions with absolutely massive player bases. If a game does not garner nearly as many players, it is far harder to make an optional spending strategy work. Throughout any consideration of payment model, it is vital to remember that games have not always been priced in a singular way, and advantage spending does have connections to the coin drop that dominated in the arcade era. Gender also needs to remain in consideration, as the criticism above presumes a certain kind of (likely male) player. Destabilizing the status quo requires keeping an eye on what drops out and what gets centered. In many discussions of free-to-play games, considerations of gender, race, and class fall away, as a traditional upper-class, white, male gamer is presumed to be the target audience for games. Moving from game-design strategies to player responses, players who spend focus on rationalizing their money and resisting developer appeals. Fortunately for me, they often write about their angst in articles and on forums, offering clear perspective on how players feel about the money they pay for free-to-play and mobile games.

3 Rationalizing and Resisting

Core player concerns underline the statements made by developers and journalists, but they often attempt to be both introspective and change the industry. Part of the player discussion about spending is an effort to explain, justify, or rationalize their own spending. This approach offers insight into what players see as legitimate and where they object. Players often discuss payments in games in loaded terms, and broader stories about paying for free-to-play games are typically written as either a confessional or circus sideshow. There are also points of resistance, where players collaborate in efforts to avoid paying or to change the monetization schemes of a key game. Beginning with an overview of player discourse provides the perspective to shift to four key case studies about spending in free-to-play games.

Typical of the rationalizing genre is GB Burford's review of *Warframe*, in which Burford states: "The entire game is free to play, but it's so good that I spent a hundred bucks on it and don't regret a cent."[1] The confession of payment is immediately contextualized by the appeal of a core gamer, as the player writes, "for me, it's a point of pride that I don't spend money on free to play games. Spending money means giving in to systems designed to manipulate me; it feels like losing. That constant reminder on players to buy, buy, buy is like a movie theatre interrupting a movie every few seconds to remind people that they can buy popcorn and soda any time they'd like. Not giving in to the ads feels like winning against an intrusive and unpleasant experience."[2] *Warframe* is presented as a better form of free-to-play, one that is not grubby or in your face about asking for money and one that conforms to traditional norms about what a game should be. *Warframe* is the kind of game that is worth your money, even if you're investing more than you likely would for a premium title.

Another form of the confessional is an ode to Valve's *Dota 2*, where the author, Philippa Warr, begins by stating "Confession: I have spent approximately $357.38 on a free videogame. Three hundred and fifty seven dollars and thirty eight cents. Second confession: Actually it's a little more than that."[3] Warr proceeds through the article accounting for her spending. First, she contextualizes it in the terms of how much she has spent per hour played. Then she goes through what she spends on, justifying each kind of purchase in turn. She spends the most words explaining spending on cosmetic items, articulating the larger context of buying something "pricey or rare" and her more specific reason of seeking to "'reward' the heroes" she enjoys playing.[4] She argues that spending can drive her to try new things in the game and how certain items are just cool and buying them is a signal that whoever created the item "worked hard and deserves some cash."[5] She closes in line with how she opened, rationalizing her spending in terms of how much she spent on take-out lunches relative to her spending in *Dota 2*.

Paul Tassi has engaged in similar confessionals for his spending in *Hearthstone*, presenting his spending in this game with the caveat:

I *hate* microtransactions in video games. I have never once paid for so much as a single piece of horse armor in *Oblivion*, nor extra lives in *Candy Crush*. Despite several hundred hours of *Diablo 3* played, I never spent one dime of real world cash in the Auction House. I've never paid money to speed up my castle construction in *Clash of Clans*. "Three dollars!" I'd exclaim in horror when running into in-game microtransactions. "The nerve!"[6]

In the context of his first article, where he'd spent $639 on *Hearthstone*, a second entry three years later sees him at a total spend of over $1,800 and adding a confession to spending on games like *Overwatch* and *Pokémon GO*. He contends that his spending is not likely to be repeated, but the tone of both articles is to justify the choices he made to pay money in a "free" game.[7]

It is notable that game journalists writing about their spending on free-to-play games are admitting to spending on games that are close to the core of video games, like third-person shooter *Warframe*, the multiplayer online-battle-arena game *Dota 2*, and a collectible-card game made by esteemed developer Blizzard. The apologetic tone of these articles is designed to reaffirm the norms of traditional video games while twisting them somewhat to accommodate these new types of spending. Spending in these cases is rational and justified, as the authors seek to fit within the dominant, normal discourse about games while explaining their choices as an investment in fun or time-saving, or to reward game developers.

Narratives about other kinds of games, the mobile games with more aggressive forms of monetization are often coded differently. In the case of Chief Pat, a prominent YouTube creator of content about Supercell's games *Clash of Clans* and *Clash Royale*, he explains that his $30,000 of spending on the two games is a reasonable business expense because he's "gotta show off all the coolest shit" for his subscribers.[8] A story about the spending of UFC fighters on *Clash of Clans* includes a statement from one that "I can go to the movies with my girlfriend and get some popcorn or I can spend $50 on this game. It makes me just as happy," yet closes with the judgement that "everyone has to deal with mobile game microtransactions. They're the suffering that unites us all."[9] This latter sentiment, that spending is regrettable, is emphasized in narratives about problematic spending, like an article titled "5 Reasons I Lost $9,000 On An iPhone Game."[10] Detailing spending in *Game of War: Fire Age*, the article begins by stating the size of the marketing budget for the game and then lists the strategies it uses to ensure that players "lose" their money. Another story catalogs over $13,000 in spending that began in mobile games and spread to PC games in an attempt to raise awareness among developers and publishers about problematic spending practices.[11] These kinds of articles uphold the traditional norms of games, painting spending on mobile, free-to-play games as abnormal or problematic. Unlike the confessionals of core games that justify spending, these efforts typically undercut the choices made by players, focusing on edge cases of heavy spenders with problematic play patterns. Spending is cast as abnormal, out of control, and caused by developers pursuing abusive and addictive design practices.

The norms of video games are reaffirmed through stories that center certain approaches to spending and play, ones that make buying a game quite regular, yet spending when you don't have to is something that requires a confessional. Winning based on your skill or hard work is to be celebrated, while paying to stay at the top of the leaderboard is something that might require an intervention. Centering certain kinds of games and practices established what is seen as normal in and around games, pushing what is new or different to the margins. Academic studies of games are similarly limited, and a broad survey of what video games academics choose to study demonstrates that researchers tend to analyze limited genres of games, disproportionately focusing on online games and role-playing games, rather than looking at the broader corpus of what actually gets played.[12] These efforts, from developers and journalists and players and academics, all contribute to what is seen as normal for games.[13] And they tend to relegate a free-to-play model to a status that is something to be laughed at, apologized for, and warned about, rather than being considered as interesting in its own right, with studies about social, casual, and mobile games standing as the exception rather than the rule.[14]

Resistance!

The ultimate push of the narrative against free-to-play games is to return to a point in the game industry where players pay once for a game and own it forevermore. Although the comments of certain game publishers indicate we are unlikely to reach that point, particularly without raising the base price for games, it does not stop a substantial portion of the community surrounding games from hoping that they can turn back time or flash back, as one might in the television show *Lost*. Major industry forces have promoted the model, like Apple's debut of a game genre called "Pay Once and Play."[15] Reviews of mobile games, where free-to-play is dominant, often make clear statements about the payment structure of a game, promoting the ability to play a game for free or noting when a game has chosen a monetization structure largely in accord with the idea of paying once. *Flop Rocket*, a game largely unlocked via a one-time $2.99 fee, was celebrated with the concluding statement: "What I'm saying is that for the average reader of the site, as someone who probably likes the idea of a one-time full-game unlock, you should check out *Flop Rocket* on principle but also because it's a great game."[16] A typical version of the pay-once approach on mobile includes a shareware-style free trial, like for *Sid Meier's Civilization VI*, where a review promotes that "Honestly though, the best thing about this *Civ VI* port is that it's free to try. You can play the first 60 turns of the game as the Chinese empire in single player mode, without spending a dime."[17] The one-time cost comes after players get a chance to try the game, and there is no pesky monetization that requires additional payment. Although games like this are technically free-to-play, they are premium games for the most part, as their design lines up with expectations of other premium titles and the cost is generally a one-time fee. Effectively, *Civ VI* is a premium offering on mobile that is wearing a free-to-play mask to get players started on the game.

The lack of additional purchases is enough to help net a game special plaudits, like in the case of *Guardians of the Galaxy: The Universal Weapon*, which is praised as a solid game, "but the thing that really stuck out to us about the release of *Guardians of the Galaxy: The Universal Weapon* is how prominently it touts not having any IAP [in-app purchases] and not requiring an internet connection to play."[18] The review of the game goes on to theorize that perhaps this game and its rejection of free-to-play elements means that "chances are pretty good that even those newly-turned gamers [brought on by free-to-play mobile games] have had a sour experience with a free to play game. Perhaps this audience is now looking for what those traditional gamers have been clamoring for all along: a pay-once experience where the game design isn't compromised by the business model."[19] Given that the game came out in 2014 and almost all subsequent Marvel titles have been free-to-play, it is safe to surmise that *Guardians of the Galaxy: The Universal Weapon* was not the beginning of a new direction in pricing.

Developers promote alternate pricing models, saying things like, "we're not charging subscriptions. There's no monetization. There's no cash shop. No microtransactions. You buy the game, and you play as long as you want. You don't see a lot of that anymore strangely, but that's what we feel is the most fair way of delivering the game to our players."[20] Pay-once games are celebrated by those who grew up paying for games that way, as it is seen as normal and the expected way of monetizing a game. However, the industry has changed, and "mobile games shone a light on something a few industry types had been saying for years; that there was a massive, largely untapped audience for games out there, who would never climb over the barriers to entry to the traditional market but who could potentially be immensely valuable customers of games with lower barriers to entry."[21] Balancing the new potential customers, with their expectations for free, with established gamers and their expectations to pay once is at the heart of the debate for norms around payment. Future chapters will analyze case studies in depth, but illustrating the rationalization and resistance to payment and play in games can be seen in four cases, discussed below: Strange Flavour, *Sim City*, *Kim Kardashian: Hollywood*, and "pay-to-win."

Four Cases

Strange Flavour was an early developer on the App Store and were successful with quite basic models of monetization, like tips or small fees. However, as the market on the App Store matured, they looked at the same industry dynamics facing other developers and tried something they called Play Nice. The idea behind the Play Nice system was to cap the amount of money a player could spend on a game. They could either pay for a full unlock immediately or make incremental purchases, each of which would take money off the price of a full unlock. The company explained their hope that "the Play Nice system will allow players to enjoy the games they want, the way they want, without accidentally racking up huge bills while at the same time allowing the developers to still make a living."[22] However, in 2015, about two years after announcing Play Nice, Strange Flavour announced their intention to stop pursuing the model and simply move to paid games. An article about the change noted that "the Play Nice games haven't done well at all—Which again, is perplexing, as they delivered effectively *exactly* what the people who are always complaining about IAP say developers should make."[23] Strange Flavour noticed that the norms for games were changing. They could no longer pursue the premium payment models they were successful with in the early days of the App Store. However, in giving core players what they say they want, they effectively capped their revenue stream and fell into a middle ground: neither paid nor free-to-play. This meant that players could play the game for free, but Strange Flavour could not realize the revenue from players who were willing to pay more than the full price of an unlock for the game. They got more players, but they had to change their game design to do it and could not recognize the full benefits of a game with integrated in-app purchases, leading them to move toward an established pricing scheme and illustrating the importance of attracting high-spending players if some of the player base is allowed to play for free. Placing the cap on spending effectively gave Strange Flavour the worst of both worlds: they were unable to capitalize on a small payment from all players, and they were also unable to reap the massive spending of the top end of their player base. The failure of this pricing model is a clear example of the thing players want not always being the best decision for the companies making games.

In considering the norms around payment and games, a second brief case worth considering is *SimCity*. *SimCity* games have a lengthy history as paid offerings on PC and consoles, typically as games where players pay once for the content and can play for hours and hours, designing their city and playing through various scenarios. Downloadable content has become part of more recent versions, but largely in line with broad industry trends for PC and console games. However, *SimCity BuildIt* was released for mobile devices in late 2014 and features almost every hallmark of a free-to-play game. It is free to download, and there are tons of timers and items that players must either wait for or pay to complete in their efforts at city building (figure 3.1). In this case, the reception of the free-to-play version of the game is notable. As a write-up of the game notes,

> I know people around here love to moan and groan when a new free to play game hits, particularly when it comes from a popular or potentially nostalgic franchise, but **man** is the writing on the wall that's what millions upon millions of people are looking for. *SimCity BuildIt* is definitely not the straight up port of *SimCity 2000* that a lot of hardcore gamers are anxious to get on their iPads, but by nearly every metric there is to gauge the success of the game has shown [*sic*] that folks are loving it.[24] (emphasis in original)

Within months of the game's launch, there were about eight times as many people playing the free-to-play version of the game as there were playing the previous PC release.[25] About six months after release, Electronic Arts (EA) was promoting the

Figure 3.1
The sample *BuildIt* city of a computer-controlled "friend" designed to inspire envy.

game as the most-played version of *SimCity* ever.[26] EA argued that the success of the game was based around giving players what they want, which is notable since it was designed quite differently than other entries into the *SimCity* franchise. However, if one considers that the potential market for *SimCity* expands far beyond PC gamers, the mobile marketplace offers the ability to reach far more people who are interested in designing their own city. In this case, by deviating from norms and expectations for entries into the classic series, EA was able to hit on something that resonated with a much greater audience, garnering a massive number of players by going with a free-to-play, advantage-style monetization model.

Another game that broke from the norms of video gaming to great success is *Kim Kardashian: Hollywood* (*KKH*).[27] Launched in 2014, the game is a reskinned version of a pair of *Stardom* games previously released by developer Glu Mobile. Based largely on time management and showing up to click on items, the game branded itself to Kim Kardashian's fans and experienced enough success to cross over between celebrity and fashion discussions that regularly cover the Kardashian clan. Coverage of the game varied, largely based on the venue for the publication and its presumed audience. A primary focus of articles about the game were about how much money it was making, notably amortizing initial revenue estimates over a full year (figure 3.2). Early reports covered dynamics in the broader economy of games, like a 20 percent drop in the value of *Candy Crush Saga* developer King Digital Entertainment because *KKH* was cutting into their revenue.[28] The success of *KKH* was notable enough that Forbes ran a profile of her as a "mobile mogul," touting the success of her video game and the estimated $45 million it made her.[29]

Figure 3.2
The first meeting with Kim Kardashian in *KKH*.

Kardashian herself tweeted that she cashed an $80 million check from the success of the game, both numbers indicating her out-sized footprint in the free-to-play mobile gaming market.[30] The game even got a confessional-style article about how much a journalist ended up spending on the game, with a writer for Jezebel writing about her $494.04 in spending, which included a frantic call to the Apple help line when her game crashed.[31] The article ends with a takeaway that typifies the response to the game, "Conforming to the vacuity of modern American culture can actually offer a sense of relief and make you feel all nice and warm, if only for a minute. But you can achieve the same results by peeing your pants—which is way cheaper and less embarrassing than *Kim Kardashian: Hollywood*."[32] Skepticism about the game is also found in the initial comments to her article, where her spending choices are questioned, with one person writing "On a writer's wage she is going to blow $500 on a phone app? I haven't spent $500 on video games in the course of the last two years, and I buy the full on studio production stuff for Xbox and PC."[33] This critical sentiment is at the heart of the resistance to the game: it is abnormal to spend that much on any game, and it is certainly inappropriate to do it on something like *KKH*, which does not conform to expectations about how games should work.

Coverage of the game among established video game outlets often took the tone of Luke Plunkett's preview in Kotaku, which addressed how "various tabloid and entertainment sites are *buzzing* with teases and speculation about the game following a 'reveal' on Kardashian's Facebook page, oblivious to the fact that there's already a lengthy playthrough of the game online. And by lengthy I mean *over an hour*."[34] Running under the headline "Kim Kardashian's Video Game Is the Stuff of Nightmares," the general attitude of the headline matched the reaction of much of the video game press. The *Forbes* review began by posing the success of the game as a mystery to be solved, as Paul Tassi felt he should not "simply weep for our society, I figured I should actually give the game a fair shot to see how it could perform that well in just a few short months in a hugely crowded space."[35] Tassi writes that he had some positive impressions in the early part of the game and transitions into an analysis of how monetization works in *KKH*. To Tassi, the game is similar to many others in how it encourages

> cash shop purchases, but this is probably the most genius slash evil example I've seen. The game is well designed enough to make players actually *want* all these cosmetic items, but trying to play the game spending zero money is exhausting to the point where fans will give in and simply buy coin packs to save themselves weeks or months of effort. And that's how you make $200M in barely two months.[36]

In sum, Tassi concludes that *KKH* "may be a perfect storm of awfulness based on vanity culture, but it works. It makes money. It's killing all its competition. And that deserves a slow clap, at the very least."[37] Tassi presents a baseline respect for a game that is certainly attracting attention and revenue, but quickly qualifies any praise to be about strictly economic success. Tassi does not treat *KKH* in any manner similar to his confessionals about spending in *Hearthstone*, quite possibly because this game is new territory for him. In the piece he praises *KKH* for not being a clone, which only betrays his lack of knowledge about the history of Glu Mobile's *Stardom* games. Mashable added to the pile-on, running pieces titled "The 10 Most Disturbing Things About '*Kim Kardashian: Hollywood*" and "We Played '*Kim Kardashian: Hollywood*' So You Don't Have To."[38] The general tone of these pieces is to relegate *KKH* outside of what is considered normal. Playing it requires quotation marks. It is notable only for the amount of money it is grossing and is not even worth dabbling in beyond watching a video that mocks it.

There were some critics who engaged the game differently. Leigh Alexander put *KKH* on her list of top five games for 2014. Her assessment of the games is that *KKH* is a "hooky, unintrusive, digestible, memetic, funny, of-the-minute, fashion and celeb culture spoof" that "is really good, and no amount of brand power or lunar gravity could have made it so popular if it wasn't (and hey, look: racial diversity and player-led sexuality like it ain't even a thing. Was that so hard?)."[39] Alexander follows her opinion of the game with an example of one from the industry, writing that she "heard an entire male-dominated game industry wring its hands: It's trashy! It's a sign of the end times. It instills *bad values. All of our breastplate armor dragon babe power fantasies up till now were fine fiction, but this feminine Hollywood power fantasy deserves derision*" (emphasis in original).[40] Alexander astutely notes the rejection of this game is tied to who is in a position to write about the game and who is likely playing it. *KKH* breaks from norms. It is free-to-play. It is on mobile. It centers women and is about fashion. It does not have complicated gameplay mechanics. It makes a ton of money. Patrick Klepek's review for Giant Bomb gets at something similar, although less eloquently, where he writes, "ultimately, if judged as a *game game*, it really is terrible. Similar to fast food, it only feels good in the moment."[41] However, Klepek quickly moves to acknowledge that this is precisely the kind of game that "causes an existential divide between folks like myself and casuals, or whatever you want to call them."[42] In his review, Klepek includes harsh tweets he got from his core gamer followers when he posted an automated tweet from *KKH*. The rejection of this game is tied to who is playing it and who gets to judge it. This position is codified nicely in an essay about the game by Patricia Hernandez, who, in the wake of a conversation with her 15-year-old sister, realized that teen girls were playing *KKH* far before "the rest of the world found out about it"; she writes, "while the adults of the internet argue about the merits of Kim Kardashian and her game, teen girls everywhere continue to gleefully tap on their screens, unaware of our debates and our think pieces. They're too busy having fun."[43] The first comment after the story encourages us to realize that "at least, on a video game site, we can recognize that this a shitty game," largely illustrating the arguments made by critics like Hernandez and Alexander.[44] The game, in its design, execution, platform, and monetization scheme, is abnormal. It is different, even though it has a ton of humor and an all-time great video game rival in Willow Pape, the antagonist who pops up throughout the story to harass your character.[45] Glu Mobile tried to copy the formula of *KKH* with games featuring Britney Spears, Katy Perry, Taylor Swift, and Nicki Minaj, but none caught on in nearly the same way.[46] However, studying games like *KKH* and the reception to them illustrates how free-to-play games trigger the resistance of core gamers and prompt those who enjoy the games to rationalize their choices. Academics have also examined *KKH*; Shira Chess and Alison Harvey have argued about how the game presents a particular version of feminism and is an indicator of the future of digital play.[47] Additionally, *KKH* is a crucial reminder that new audiences for games are easiest to reach when the upfront cost to play is zero, opening the door for those who have not invested in a gaming rig or console.

The last case to assess in this overview is the resistance to a monetization and game-design scheme referred to as pay-to-win.

There is a general understanding among the core of people reporting on, playing, and designing games that pay-to-win is a bad thing that should be avoided at all costs. Games can be decried as pay-to-win based on a small change in payment structure, altered incentives, or general design. *Black Desert Online*, a Korean massively multiplayer online game, made changes to its economy as it expanded to Western markets that allowed players to buy certain items with "real" money and then turn around and sell those items for in-game currency, effectively enabling players with a large wallet to buy in-game currency. This change led to "literal in-game protests. Like, characters marching the streets, carrying angry placards, the works."[48] *Black Desert Online* is a game with an up-front charge for players, but the desire to have an additional income stream led to in-game purchases. Tying those to the in-game economy left players worried that a minority of people could buy their way forward; hence players began marching in the game's "streets" protesting against pay-to-win design changes.

This desire to avoid violating player expectations of proper balance and payment structures runs throughout games. In the lead-up to the release of *Dota 2*, Valve announced that the game would be free-to-play, with item sales designed to support the game. However, the developers went out of their way to stress that the game would not be pay-to-win. In one prelaunch feature, Kris Graft wrote that "being able to 'pay-to-win' is one of the biggest concerns with the free-to-play business model, particularly in competitive online games. In the *Dota* Store, players will be able to buy 'fancy gear to customize your heroes,' but Valve said all items will be purely cosmetic."[49] Valve is quoted more directly in Graft's piece, stating that "*Dota 2* will not be a pay-to-win game. All the items in the store are cosmetic, and don't affect gameplay."[50] Concerns about pay-to-win dynamics are laced through core games, as the default norm is that superior players should win battles contested on a level playing field. Advantages that can be purchased complicate that equation, as wealthier players can buy their victories. Much like the public relations campaign for *Artifact*, Valve tried to appeal to core users, letting them know that players will be able to play, and fund, the game as they choose. Concerns about players buying their way forward are presented in all kinds of games and situations. One developer pitched their attempt to develop a version of *Clash of Clans* that is not pay-to-win.[51] Fantasy football players got outraged at a version of fantasy football that is pay-to-win.[52] A prominent game designer was allegedly fired for objecting to pay-to-win.[53] And plenty of games flirting with pay-to-win systems have prompted outrage in their player communities.[54] However, one of the most vitriolic debates about pay-to-win is found in the story of *Star Wars Battlefront II*.

Star Wars Battlefront II was a major release from EA that received massive amounts of attention in the lead-up to its release. There is a lengthy single-player mode to the game, but the focus of ongoing play for many is the rich multiplayer combat that happens in a variety of different contexts, from massive ground wars reenacting parts of *Star Wars* lore to battles among notable heroes and villains to space-based battles between ships. The game is not free-to-play, it is a traditional release with a premium price, but it is worth discussing here because the additional revenue stream from the game borrowed heavily from free-to-play titles. *Battlefront II* used a system of "loot boxes" that players could earn in battle or buy; within those boxes, they would find a variety of items. These loot crates can be a key tenet of advantage-style monetization if items in the boxes grant an edge to players. In those cases, players are incentivized to keep buying items in hopes of getting lucky with an item that is particularly powerful or that suits their style of play especially well. Loot crates add randomness to the game, as the luck of the draw helps determine success, and players can increase their odds of being lucky by spending more on the game. Those two core notions, of luck and money being determinative of success, run counter to the way online play in games like *Battlefront II* are typically designed.

Most importantly, players could find Star Cards. Star Cards came in varying levels of quality, and more powerful cards were rarer. Players could equip these cards in battle to change their statistics and abilities, making them more powerful. In an essay about the microtransactions in *Battlefront II*, Heather Alexandra starts from the premise that Star Cards are "a mess that affects balance in negative ways."[55] She breaks down the process for the cards and how they can be gained and plays out a scenario where a player spends $99.99 on crystals to buy loot boxes, concluding that, "in other words, you can quite literally pay money for statistical advantages in *Star Wars Battlefront II*."[56] She holds that the game is fun, but "loot crates add an unnecessary layer of complication, upset the game's balance, and exist entirely to screw you over. To quote famed senator Padmé Amidala: 'So this is how multiplayer dies. With thunderous loot crates.'"[57] Alexandra reframes the original quote from Luke and Leia's mother about the downfall of the Galactic Republic and rise of the Empire in *Star Wars: Revenge of the Sith* ("So this is how liberty dies . . . with thunderous applause."), implicitly likening the changing monetization strategies seen in *Battlefront II* to the demise of a cherished era in video games. In a broader critique of the game written after paying $90 for premium currency, Owen S. Good writes that *Battlefront II*

> may hold a fig leaf over all its indiscreet parts so that it can't be directly accused of imposing a pay-to-win model. But it does something just as bad by tying multiplayer advancement to the random chance of opening a loot crate: It strips players of a sense of control over their long-term gameplay, and it clouds their broader understanding of how the game should be efficiently played, and what winning and success really means in it.[58]

Good feels the crates gave players a lack of control in the game. The randomness and ability to pay one's way forward complicated what it meant to do battle in the game and led to massive player outrage.

As the player community roiled, EA attempted damage control. The defense the company posted on Reddit for the game quickly became the lowest-rated comment in the history of Reddit, amassing hundreds of thousands of downvotes before the game's official release.[59] EA eventually pulled the microtransactions system back, seeking to retool it to better match player expectations, potentially under pressure by corporate owner Disney in the wake of the terrible press the game was getting.[60] Business analysts argued about how this would impact EA's earnings, with concerns raised about whether the company would have to issue downward guidance because of poor sales. One industry analyst took a contrarian view, arguing—in line with the lack of growth in the cost of premium games—that gamers "aren't overcharged, they're undercharged. . . . This saga has been a perfect storm for overreaction."[61] Eventually, EA mounted a more robust explanation for their choices. First, the company felt that cosmetic sales and an optional spending model were not a viable revenue stream for them, because "you probably don't want

Darth Vader in pink."[62] This is picking out a particularly odd example, as there are plenty of additional skins or outfits that could have been made for iconic *Star Wars* characters; however, it is likely an appeal to core fans who want to see the canon of the *Star Wars* universe preserved. EA's CEO and chief design officer would go on to admit that mistakes were made, stating that they want to do better in the future and that "fair" was the most important concept for the company to keep in mind for in-game economies.[63] For EA, this means that

> you have to look at it from the perspective of what's fair. Fair is the number one thing. When you buy a product from us, you should get full value for the money you spend. There should be a fair game economy in the game so you can't pay to win. We don't want you to be able to pay your way to be better than others. That's important to us. But we also look at trends in the market and see people are fine with paying for other things, such as how they appear in the game. That seems to be completely fine.[64]

In the six-plus months they took to reflect on what was done, EA eventually ended up back within the norms expected of current video games: pay-to-win is wrong and players should contest matches on a fair playing field, while advantage-spending models are relegated to the realm of grubby free-to-play. This presumption in core games and for core gamers inevitably places certain free-to-play games outside the realm of what is acceptable. The moment purchases go beyond cosmetic items, core gamers rage hard.

These four case studies—Strange Flavour, *SimCity*, *KKH*, and the concept of pay-to-win—were chosen in an attempt to start to show the boundaries and the norms for how video games are expected to work. They are spaces to first see the rationalization and resistance to monetization in free-to-play games. The case studies show what the community surrounding games values and what they do not. These four cases demonstrate certain norms of play and how they have not been eternal; they are patterns of behavior that have been normalized in the console- and PC-dominant era of video games. And they are examples that illustrate how players expect to perform in-game effort and labor to be successful, rather than use their out-of-game wealth to buy their way ahead. These examples give an overview of the norms of paying for video games, but a deeper dive into thematic free-to-play games can offer better perspective on certain elements of free-to-play games and how they are received. Furthering an analysis of free-to-play games begins with a history of how the model for microtransactions seeped into Western games through sports games like *FIFA* and *Madden Ultimate Team*.

4   Bringing Free-to-Play West: Building an Ultimate Team

There are a variety of entry points to look at how free-to-play and mobile games became an established part of the Western video game ecosphere. There are starts and stops, in addition to the games outlined in previous chapters. However, one of the most striking success stories for free-to-play games can be found in the portfolio of one of the largest game publishers on the planet, Electronic Arts (EA). As console and PC games were firmly entrenched in Western markets and price points for the games eroded the value of sales for game publishers, EA found a way to integrate additional sources of revenue. Expanding on a model explored in an earlier version of a soccer game, EA leveraged elements of collectible-card games with sports traditions and fantasy sports to build a multibillion dollar part of their business. The debut of games as live services and microtransactions in console games paved the way for free-to-play gaming for major publishers. Understanding how that came to be requires analyzing two of the biggest sports video games on the planet: EA's *FIFA* and *Madden NFL* franchises.

Looking at these two series is nominally an analysis of the monetization strategies of sports video games, but these franchises offer vital perspective on free-to-play trends in the industry as a whole. The mode of monetization in sports games puts particular emphasis on issues like labor, skill, and pricing, as video game players are frequently buying and selling representations of athletes while seeking any advantages they can get to aid their cause. The pricing model often puts players in tension with game publishers, leading to the creation of lively black markets where players can circumvent the rules and markets that are built into the game. These lessons offer perspective for the broader game industry, even as ham-fisted attempts to implement similar mechanisms fail in games like *Battlefront II.* Understanding the role of free-to-play in sports games requires a broad look at free-to-play games, followed by an analysis of EA's portfolio and the Ultimate Team mode, and then a brief look at another sports game, *Tap Sports Baseball*, which helps demonstrate how Ultimate Team has shaped other games.

It is somewhat generous to give EA the credit for bringing free-to-play into the mainstream, Western game-development market, as three things were happening at the same time. First, in June 2009 Zynga released *FarmVille* on Facebook.[1] The game fueled the rise of the company and was monetized through what are now typical free-to-play mechanics, advertising and in-game purchases. Based largely on *FarmVille*, Zynga went public in December of 2011 and was generating hundreds of million dollars in revenue each quarter.[2] Zynga peaked in value shortly before its IPO and had almost the same valuation as EA at its apex.[3] However, that dominance was short-lived, as a variety of factors conspired to erode Zynga's role in the market. Facebook changed its rules for games. More competitors entered the market, chasing the same players. And the venue for the kinds of games Zynga made largely shifted from Facebook and PCs to phones and App Stores, where other companies beat them to the market.[4] Zynga definitely had an impact on how games were paid for, but its impact was fleeting, and the era of Facebook games was important but short-lived.

A second contender for the role of popularizing free-to-play gaming is the App Store. Apple's marketplace for applications dedicated to iOS devices debuted on July 10, 2008.[5] A little over a year later, on October 15, 2009, Apple allowed in-app purchases within free applications.[6] The initial pitch for the rationale behind this change was to enable "developers to create a single version of an application to be sold for free with limited accessibility that can then be unlocked for full functionality via in-app purchases, eliminating the need for developers to create separate free 'lite' versions of paid apps if they wish to offer such products."[7] This change was largely designed to simplify the App Store, ridding it of duplicative applications and making life easier for consumers. For the run of the App Store, games have tended to be about a third of the total number of apps available; however, in spending, they play a much larger role.[8] In a retrospective 10 years after the launch of the App Store, App Annie reported that the top-grossing game worldwide, Supercell's *Clash of Clans*, had made over $4 billion, while the top-grossing non-game app, Netflix, brought in just under $1 billion.[9] Games are a massive industry on the App Store, where a handful take an outsized portion of the revenue. Of App Store spending on games, 76 percent goes to the top 50 apps, and between 2014 and 2017 only 142 games made an appearance on the top-10 grossing games.[10]

The App Store has a major impact on free-to-play games and how they work, but Apple's relationship with games has been complicated. Initially, Steve Jobs and Apple prohibited third-party apps from the App Store and believed they would be a small part of their business, likely dwarfed by music sales.[11] Even other executives present a complex relationship with games, as Eddy Cue noted: "When we first announced the iPhone, we didn't tout it as a gaming device. But games became a huge part of iPhone, because it turns out that a lot more people than just hardcore gamers love games. We expanded the market."[12] As John Voorhees contextualizes, those comments are representative of a "company that's content to collect the 'found money' dropped on its doorstep in the form of casual games."[13] Although game developers made the App Store work for them, what happened was largely organic, occurring in spite of Apple rather than because of it.

With Zynga a flash in the pan and Apple an unwitting participant in the rise of free-to-play gaming, EA's role is important. As one of the first-ever game companies, and in its current role as a corporate behemoth comprised of multiple game studios and dozens of major games, EA has a different role in the game industry than Zynga or Apple. EA's relevance means that its actions spread more deliberately, from game to game, and that it serves as an industry leader other companies have followed. The ties EA has to the core game industry also means that their popularization of free-to-play elements, instead of being relegated to Facebook or smartphones, were integrated into core video games. Ongoing in-game sales are a truly massive part of EA's total revenue, and their approach has been adopted by other developers and publishers in titles across the industry.

Electronic Arts and Sports

Although EA has many key franchises, EA games have always had a deep connection to sports. The company's first major

success was *One-on-One: Dr. J vs. Larry Bird*, which was released
in 1983 and offered a streetball style one-on-one basketball contest.[14] Licensing the rights to the images of the two famed basketball players and using them on the cover of the game, EA
broke new ground, and the game hit the bestseller list in its
launch year. The game inspired EA to pursue other sports franchises and licensed partnerships, such as a deal with football
coach and announcer John Madden that became 1988's *John
Madden Football* and eventually *Madden NFL*. By the 25th year
of the game, in 2013, the series had grossed over $4 billion for
EA.[15] EA's line of soccer games is somewhat more complicated,
although the primary game EA produces is now simply known
as *FIFA*, which is licensed from the governing body of international soccer. The series has seen a handful of branching titles,
such as special editions for the World Cup and three versions of
FIFA Street, which attempted a street-style presentation of soccer.
The games trace their lineage to 1993's *FIFA International Soccer*,
but the initial seed for what would become *FIFA Ultimate Team*
came from a game called *UEFA Champions League 2006–2007*.
Understanding the drive behind this new mode requires a brief
overview of what makes sports games different from many other
video games and of how those differences have likely given the
company more space to experiment with pricing.

Sports video games have firm, established annual-release
cycles. Although some other titles pursue annual releases, EA
and competitor 2K Sports attempt to replicate the offline leagues
they are inspired by. Annual launches fit nicely with the early EA
Sports motto—"If it's in the game, it's in the game"—as EA bills
its games as a chance to let players take over their favorite teams,
franchises, and players in simulation-style gaming. The annual
development cycle can be great for revenue, as publishers get to

sell a version of the game each year, but it also presents certain complications. One issue is that it is hard to develop a game, and a one-year time frame is quite short. This pressure means that EA is in continual development on their sports titles. A second complication is that they have to sell the game to players each year, which means they have to present a compelling reason for purchase. These two factors come together into a situation where EA has to convince players there is more to each version of the game than just an updated roster to match the league in question, offering innovations in gameplay and design that make the new version the best ever. EA responds to these dynamics in two primary ways. First, the integration and prominence of online play drives players from one version of the game to the next, since when the bulk of players move, holdouts are encouraged to move with them to keep playing. Servers can also be shut down to force movement if players want to keep playing the game online, effectively ensuring the obsolescence of each version of the game.[16] The push for online play in the sports franchises is ongoing, with EA promoting *NHL 19* as having richer options for online play, since online multiplayer is where they report players have the highest level of satisfaction.[17] The second approach is through Ultimate Team, which warrants far more attention and explanation as a gateway for free-to-play.

Ultimate Team

Retrospectives abounded when Ultimate Team hit its fifth anniversary in 2014, with one describing it as a mode that "offered a new, engrossing way to play the beloved soccer game, but it ended up being much more than that. *FIFA Ultimate Team* catapulted the series into new levels of global popularity, and heralded a new paradigm in game development just as the industry was shifting into a digital future."[18] The mode debuted in *UEFA Champions League 2006–2007* in March 2007, but only on the Xbox 360 edition. *UEFA Champions League* was a short-lived game for EA, with just two editions. The game is dedicated to the premier club-based soccer competition in the world, and the rights to the competition are held by UEFA, rather than FIFA, warranting a separate negotiation to be able to release the branded product. EA's two games in the series were based on the version of *FIFA* they released earlier each year, with slight adjustments and different commentators.

That first version of Ultimate Team was a premium piece of downloadable content and had many of the elements that became hallmarks of the mode:

> Users put together clubs with virtual trading cards for players, staff, stadiums and more, and attempt to maximize their team's attributes by maintaining team chemistry based on players' nationality, formation and position. They play games against the CPU or online, with "contract" cards enforcing a finite number of matches an athlete can partake in, to earn in-game currency to spend on packs of additional cards (or pay real money for those packs, if they want to accelerate the process). And they trade unwanted cards with other players online in an effort to fill their collection.[19]

Ultimate Team enables players to assemble their own team, linking players from teams around the globe in an effort to build something that represents them. Players can use the badge of their favorite team in a different stadium with a group of players they find in a formation of their choosing. Because players get to make their own team, Ultimate Team gives wide latitude for personalization.[20] One of the designers of the mode presented it as linking into his memories of trading playing cards on the playground, with the excitement of opening a new pack driving the compulsion to open more and leading to the social experience of trading with friends.[21]

When EA lost the license with UEFA, one of the designers proposed expanding Ultimate Team to the main *FIFA* title. Executive producer and future CEO Andrew Wilson saw that, although the mode was showing a loss based on its upfront fee, which limited the player pool, there was a massive potential stream of revenue through microtransactions for the card packs if the mode was transformed into a free-to-play offering with an advantage-spending structure. The mode was released on March 19, 2009, about five months after the launch of *FIFA 09* as a way to keep the game fresh. Ultimate Team first came as a $10 piece of downloadable content that could keep players playing until the fall launch of *FIFA 10*. By the time *FIFA 11* came around, the download was free, and with *FIFA 12*, the mode was integrated into the launch version of the game. Over the first five years of Ultimate Team, it grew to be the most popular mode in the game, with almost 22 million unique players playing about 11,000 matches per hour.[22]

A primary value of the new mode cited by two of the men who have popularized it was that "it changed up an online experience that had always calcified around the world's best teams. Instead of always going up against FC Barcelona, Real Madrid or Manchester United, you could take your eclectic Ultimate team online and play another person's carefully crafted club" (figure 4.1).[23] Eventually the game modified the marketplace and made it accessible via a web browser, which meant that players could build and manage their team outside of the game itself (figure 4.2). This expanded the role of Ultimate Team and made it much easier for players to buy and sell players.[24] EA would eventually add Teams of the Week, modifications for how players were

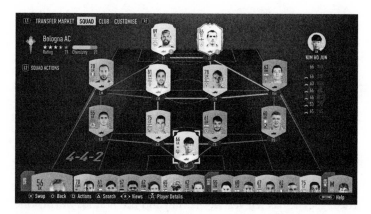

Figure 4.1
A newly formed FUT squad in *FIFA 20*.

Figure 4.2
The web app for the *FIFA 20* version of FUT.

playing on the pitch, and a variety of other options that led a producer on the game to say, "everybody knows what career mode is about, but explaining Ultimate Team in a sentence is almost impossible."[25] The complexity of the mode prompted the creation of a host of fan-made resources to explain how to best play Ultimate Team, full of advice about the players to chase and ways to play the auction house to maximize resources. The game mode is robust enough to support a massive out-of-game economy, complete with FIFA Coins that are sold alongside *World of Warcraft* gold and multi-million dollar scams that have led to FBI investigations and indictments for mining coins and stealing in-game currency.[26] Ultimate Team effectively became a whole new game bolted onto *FIFA* that was based on advantage-buying mechanics through the sales of card packs and a trading system.

Ultimate Team continues in *FIFA* stronger than ever, but the legacy it has left reaches far beyond the bounds of this one game, as the mode has been integrated into every sports game EA offers. Further, the mode is what demonstrated the potential of a microtransaction-driven live service. As the producer who brought the mode to *FIFA 09* puts it, Ultimate Team "changed the way we made games—it was the dawn of the live service. Previously, obviously, we kept the online element running, but to a large extent it was: You made the package good, you'd ship it, you'd move on. Ultimate Team completely changed that in [that] we now build the mode, put it out there and then a whole live team then supports it throughout its continuation."[27] Ultimate Team became the way that sports games could bridge from one version of the game to the next, driving interest and continuing to offer players something new to do after the sport's season was over. The financial impact reached beyond the creation of the live service, as the mode "created the whole microtransactions element. The key to that was allowing people to—the whole 'sweat versus cash equity,' as we called it and that was giving people the ability to play the game as much as they wanted and never need to have to spend a penny on it."[28] Instead of gating play through energy, the game uses contracts and card packs to drive spending, yet still conform to many norms of core gaming. Spending gets players ahead, but a savvy, skilled player can play as much as they want as long as they bought *FIFA*.

The game mode generally plays best when players stake their team with an investment up front to buy packs and establish a quality baseline, but a substantial amount of coins can be made by playing the auction house at odd hours, expanding the game in both the time spent playing and content (figure 4.3). Ultimate Team modes are not just about the sport they are representing, they are also about building a team, running it, and trying to defeat EA's systems. Finding holes and value is part of the game, and Ultimate Team dramatically changed how players can engage EA's sports games, altering the context for play and providing EA with additional revenue streams that stretch far beyond the initial purchase price of the game. Eventually, EA found that giving the mode away and monetizing through

Figure 4.3
Gold packs in *FIFA 20*. FIFA points cost about a penny, pricing the premium electrum players pack around $2.50.

microtransactions generated far more revenue than original attempts to charge for the mode.

The amount of money EA makes on Ultimate Team is truly massive. In 2016, the total was about $650 million a year across the stable of EA sports games, with most of that revenue coming from *FIFA*.[29] This was about half of the total revenue the company made from add-on content, leading one game journalist to recognize that the success of Ultimate Team in financial terms means that "it's safe to say that microtransactions are here to stay."[30] By 2017, the amount of money made by Ultimate Team had grown more than 20 percent year-over-year, to $800 million annually, leading their chief financial officer to talk about bringing the mode to other EA games: "Like *Battlefield* or *Battlefront*, our *Star Wars* game, which are very similar in the depth of play—we can possibly add a similar mechanic to that. We spend a lot of time thinking about it. Not for tomorrow, but over the next couple of years you're going to see a lot more of that in our portfolio."[31] That $800 million was 17 percent of the total revenue for EA, which is complemented by the sale of the initial game that players must have to partake in Ultimate Team.[32] Combining Ultimate Team sales with the core game, *FIFA* accounted for almost 40 percent of EA's revenue in 2017, with each unit sale earning almost $121.[33] With a list price of $60 and some copies sold at a discount, more than half of the revenue tied to *FIFA* comes from microtransactions in Ultimate Team.

An additional benefit of Ultimate Team for EA is that the revenue comes from digital content, which typically offers game publishers a higher margin than packaged games sold in stores. And, in an industry that often relegates sports games to the margins, EA's chief financial officer noted that, in 2017, "we saw a notable shift to digital in our sports titles and remarkable growth in Ultimate Team. Our sports titles have once again shown their value in delivering a stable and dependable performance. This quarter demonstrates how they can drive our business and offers a window into how our games will evolve over the months and years to come."[34] Sports games effectively created what we know as the modern EA in the form of *One on One: Dr. J vs. Larry Bird*, and they continue to push the company forward, representing an outsize share of the company's revenue and demonstrating a way to design games that has had a huge impact on microtransactions and monetization in games. By 2018, 40 percent of EA's total revenue came from live services rather than game sales, with Ultimate Team leading the way and EA refusing to give predictions for unit sales of games, arguing that ongoing revenue is a better indicator of the health of a game franchise.[35]

2018 marked a different year for EA, however, as it tried to turn the initial hints from the CFO about integrating microtransaction elements into other franchises into reality. As they did so, EA brought on the wrath of players through their choice to use loot boxes in *Star Wars Battlefront II*. As discussed at length in the previous chapter, players of this first-person shooter game revolted against the game's attempt at an Ultimate Team model. The card packs and trading that were part of the playground experience for sports fans had not previously been part of either a leading shooter game or the *Star Wars* universe. Without the additional context, players raged, because the norms of play in a game like *Battlefront* had been set over the years to include only cosmetic microtransactions, and the game-defining ones tied to Ultimate Team were beyond the pale for many players. The loot boxes were also far less fully integrated into rich play, as players were not building a squad of storm troopers or trading items in an auction house.

The controversy led to efforts to ban or regulate the kinds of transactions that typify Ultimate Team, where players purchase a card pack or loot box without knowing exactly what is in it. Politicians were concerned that the games promoted gambling. In response, EA argued that "because players always receive a specified number of items in each pack" and the company does not "provide or authorize any way to cash out or sell items or virtual currency for real money," what happens in their games is not gambling.[36] In the wake of the *Battlefront* controversy and its accompanying threat to a core business model of *FIFA*, EA argued that the games were different, since players are given choices about how they want to play *FIFA* because of all its different modes. EA Sports VP and COO Daryl Holt argued that Ultimate Team fits within a player-first model, where

> I can earn things in *FIFA Ultimate Team* just by playing the game, at whatever tier I want to play at. I can also beat you if you have a better-rated team because I'm better than you at *FIFA*. I don't worry about what my rating is as a team. . . . That aspect of choice and how we engage with EA Sports is a very different aspect with how we look at the controversy that came up around *Battlefront*.[37]

The attempt to cleave the difference between the two kinds of games is notable, because EA is clearly trying to preserve the Ultimate Team revenue that is a core part of their business. However, it is also important because of how seamlessly microtransactions were implemented into one kind of game and how quickly they were rejected in another. EA Sports games are not fully free-to-play, but a free-to-play mode ushered in a new revenue stream for a major games company that now drives their revenue and decision-making. Ultimate Team, along with innovations made by Zynga and Apple, brought a new form of game monetization westward, as publishers realized how much money they could pry from players beyond the initial cost of the game. Those innovations met with the most resistance at the points where they violated norms, changed expectations, and altered expected practice. However, tying all of this back to free-to-play gaming requires looking at another game, Glu Mobile's *Tap Sports Baseball*.

Tap Sports Baseball

Although it would be appropriate to examine one of the EA mobile sports games, they have been refined to a point where they are largely copies of Ultimate Team ported to mobile devices. They have slightly less interaction among players and simplified game modes that fit the processing power of mobile devices and the interface limitations of a touchscreen. *Tap Sports Baseball* shares some of those elements, but also adds a number of different avenues for analysis. Developed by Glu Mobile, the same developer that made *Kim Kardashian: Hollywood, Tap Sports Baseball* is an annual sports game for mobile devices. Glu pitches the game as a chance to "team up to build your roster and dominate the league in *MLB Tap Sports Baseball 2018! TSB* is now closer than ever to the real MLB, with new PICK'EM and CREATE-A-PLAY modes, and fan favorites like WALK OFF HERO are back and better than ever. Build your roster, play with friends, join clubs, and compete in daily events!"[38] Baseball is one of the more compelling sports to turn into a video game because of its focus on discrete events that can be represented by statistics and modeled in a computer program. Mobile devices give the opportunity for a lower-key style of play that can be boiled down into specific interactions, which in the case of *Tap Sports Baseball* means focusing on hitting. Prior to *Tap Sports Baseball 2017*, Glu only had a licensing deal with the players' association, which meant that players were in the game, but not the teams they represented. In 2017, Glu added a league license, which drew additional attention to the game.

In the words of one review of the game, "*Tap Sports Baseball* reduces the national pastime to its most basic confrontation, the one between the pitcher and batter. Your job is to learn to recognize different types and speeds of pitches and tap the screen to swing at the proper time. It almost literally couldn't be easier."[39] The pitching and defensive side of the game are simulated, which means that the players you have on your team are incredibly important, since your skill at play has no impact in half of the game. Teams are built through a dizzying array of options and levels and types of cards. Players can opt to buy certain listed and promoted players directly for a price. They can also open a mystery box that could contain any player, or there may be a special promotion that just provides players at a certain position, just Hall of Fame players, or just Legend players, which are somehow different than Hall-of-Famers. In addition, laying over all of this are regular promotions tied to spending. If you hit the benchmark spending amounts within a given amount of time, you are awarded items of increasing value, with the most powerful rewards requiring about $100 of spending two or three times a week. Players are graded on a five-star scale, including half-stars, and must be leveled up with experience points to maximize their power. Different types of players require different types of experience to level up, so that new Legend requires rare Legend XP. On top of all of this, there are game modes, like Home Run Derby, that require a whole additional set of players with their own currency and leveling needs. The game is a cornucopia of microtransactions.

I have played a lot of microtransaction-driven free-to-play titles, and *Tap Sports Baseball 2017* was one of the most striking. The number and level of ways it blended opportunities to spend money was simply awe-inspiring. The veneer of skill in tapping and recognizing pitches offers just enough of a cover to let me believe I had a substantial impact on the game, encouraging me to take that special offer or spend just a little bit more to get that new player to push my team to the next level. The conclusion of one negative review for Macworld contends:

> *MLB Tap Sports Baseball 2017's* supposed payoff just doesn't seem worth the massive amounts of time and/or money that you'd have to invest in it. Were this a genuinely absorbing game, then maybe the chase to build the perfect roster would be exciting and engaging, rather than a huge, likely expensive hassle. But it's entirely the latter in this case. As a simple bat-swinging diversion, *MLB Tap Sports Baseball 2017* is fine for a few quick minutes of play here and there, but the obnoxious freemium layers are thick and unavoidable.[40]

The review from Gamezebo, a website that focuses on mobile games, states, "there isn't another baseball game out for mobile devices that walks the line between arcade action and sim quite like this one, and even though it leans toward the arcade side more than a little, it's still versatile enough to be fun for a wide range of sports gamers"; the reviewer also notes that the team-building system "requires some skill but also a lot of luck, as the game's gacha-esque player drafting system has received more wrinkles in the form of mystery boxes [that add additional randomness to which player you will receive]."[41] In an advice column for the 2018 version of the game, the Gamezebo reviewer simply stated, "*MLB Tap Sports Baseball 2018* is all about the gacha thing, as the primary way to add new players to your team is by way of draft picks. Some draft picks are available to you just by spending the game's basic currency, while better ones can only be earned as rewards or purchased with gold, the premium currency."[42] When I read this kind of background information for the game and was thinking about norms in free-to-play games, *Tap Sports Baseball* became like catnip. An aggressively monetized free-to-play sports game with a veneer of skill and a whole lot of luck involved? I can have the opportunity to spend so much money that it blows the mind? Of course, I had to sign up to reflect on how this game took the basics of the *FIFA Ultimate Team* model and pressed it into a different context.

The average *FIFA* player spends about $60 on Ultimate Team, but that amount would not get much in *Tap Sports Baseball*. The 2017 version, which I played, requires spending more than that each week to stay at the top of the leaderboard. And, unlike *FIFA*, where skill at playing the game can enable a player to win with an inferior team, because so much of *Tap Sports Baseball* is simulated, the quality of the players on a team really matter. As I began to play, I spent a relatively small amount of money, buying up the one-time offers for new players that often give better-than-average value and moving through the various early moments of the game designed to get players invested. I started to play the various modes and quickly found myself outgunned by players who were scoring multiple orders of magnitude more than I was. The range of results struck me, with some absolutely crushing others, and set out to do some research on what was going on and how I could get better.

The first thing I figured out is that I needed to join a new club. Clubs function in *Tap Sports Baseball* in a manner similar to guilds or clans in other games. Players can communicate with each other, often through third-party chat applications like Line or Discord, and are grouped together in competitions, working as a team to score more points and get better rewards. Shortly after I joined the group chat, I started reading about teammates who were accruing premium currency and players far faster than seemed reasonable. I politely inquired and learned that many of the top players contracted with a group of people called loaders who would log into your account and modify it so that you got a whole lot of gold, key players, or almost anything else your heart desired. In a way, loaders link to the gold farmers of games like *World of Warcraft*; they transform a labor-heavy industry of farming for in-game materials into one predicated on knowledge and access to tools to circumvent the best efforts of game developers. The risk of the black market transaction is that your account could be banned by Glu, or, in the parlance of players, jailed. Jailed teams were still owned by the player, but they were unable to compete in multiplayer competitions, making them effectively worthless. As I learned more, including the fact that our club leader had recently had an account jailed and another member of the club had recently quit after a jailing, I saw a research opportunity.

My club leader referred me to the third party he had paid for advantages in the game. I was told about the general parameter of things that could be requested and what it might cost and was offered the opportunity to buy 100,000 gold for $40, while Glu was selling 10,000 gold for $99.99. In addition, I could request players at certain positions or even certain players to improve the quality of my team. Suddenly I understood how some players were moving through the game so quickly: they were buying $1,000 worth of premium currency for $40. In the terms of a free-to-play game, $40 is a minimal amount for those who are willing to pay, and the deal is even more attractive when placed in the context of the prices set by the developer. One purchase is enough to revolutionize a team and make it highly competitive, while offering the chance to top the leaderboards with energy refreshes and other time-sensitive investments. Loaders and those who buy from third-parties were always under a cloud of worry. If you tripped the warning of having 100,000 gold in game, would that be the thing that would get you jailed? Fortunately, loaders also sell the ability to get you out of jail. This system clearly works for those making money outside the game and those paying for it. But how does this tie back to Ultimate Team and norms in free-to-play games more generally?

In the most direct terms, games like *Tap Sports Baseball* liberally lift elements from Ultimate Team and sports-card collecting in the design of the game. The game is designed to directly appeal to sports-card collecting, and the dual license with the league and player's association is hailed as "letting you use real life major league stars and puts them on real teams as well. If you don't understand why that's a big deal, I'll just assume you never collected baseball cards as a kid."[43] Borrowing from the Ultimate Team model, and then transforming it with leveling cards and experience points that are an additional prize to be won or bought, gives *Tap Sports Baseball* all kinds of surfaces for advantage-style monetization. It takes the business scheme of one of the most profitable enterprises of EA and pushes it more aggressively—almost requiring payment if players are seeking success. Some of the latitude for the more aggressive form of monetization is tied to the fact that *Tap Sports Baseball* does not come with an upfront fee. Unlike EA's game, which generally comes with a $60 charge for the game, *Tap Sports Baseball* is a free download, which means it is received within the expectations of purely free-to-play games, rather than premium titles. The game escapes some of the tension of loot boxes because the business model is transparent from the beginning: Glu will try to find the levers to drive payment on as many levels as possible.

I suspect the loaders also serve an important part of the ecosystem of the game. Although Glu cannot let the illicit market get out of control, having some players press the limits of what is possible gives all players something to chase. Players who either do not know about the third-party market or are not willing to participate in it still see those numbers at the top of the leaderboard and are driven to catch up with them, under the promise that players who are cheating are being banned.[44] Glu jails enough players that the market has to operate in the shadows and cannot get too greedy, but players who use loaders are an implicit advertisement for what players can get by spending in the game. Developers cannot let a market like this operate unencumbered, as it is drawing purchases of premium currency out of their pockets, but for products with aggressive pricing, black markets will likely emerge. In a larger context, and for several other games I have encountered, it is rumored that loaders like these are funded through the use of stolen credit card numbers, attracting clients willing to pay at a steep discount and then buying resources in-game, but never paying the bill. Games like *Tap Sports Baseball* demonstrate some of the new norms of free-to-play games, as Glu found a way to aggressively monetize tapping on a smartphone, instead of tapping on a video game controller or keyboard.

Norms and Sports Games

Ultimate Team modes changed the norms of sports video games. They ushered in ongoing, year-round play and microtransactions that could diversify the revenue streams of what were once single-purchase console games. EA took care with their sports titles, measuring the tolerance of their player community for engaging in microtransactions and adjusting accordingly, moving from a single purchase for the download to a model based on card packs and contracts. The model is still evolving, as 2K Sports rolled back some of the microtransaction-based charges in *NBA 2K19* and made light of the changes in a cut scene within the game.[45] Over a period of years, Ultimate Team shifted the business priorities for EA as a whole, leading to a massive fiasco with their release of the monetization scheme in *Star Wars Battlefront II*. Establishing Ultimate Team took years, but adding it to a different genre and a beloved franchise license left a new group of players outraged. Moving too quickly and failing to develop norms for monetization of game-impacting elements put EA out of sync with their player base, decreasing sales and alienating players. Ultimate Team also arguably addressed an issue with online play in *FIFA* and *Madden*, while a similar system undermined expectations of fair play in *Battlefront II*.

However, Glu Mobile took advantage of the trail blazed by games like *FIFA* and, using a sports license and a purely free-to-play approach, became a fairly consistently earning game, especially during baseball season.[46] *Tap Sports Baseball* also changes norms, pushing for aggressive monetization by raising the price for items within the game and challenging players to meet it. Although this has led to a robust black market for premium currency, it creates the impression of enticing early buys and enables the developer to add many modes of play and levels of players to allow the players at the top to keep paying their way ahead. Perhaps most notably, the rise of a black market for the game shows a different kind of norm for free-to-play games. Instead of simply playing in competition with other players, players are playing against the developer, seeking edges and ways to take advantage of pricing schemes to minimize their spend and maximize their outcomes. Free-to-play gaming changes the norms of who is a player's true opposition, as players seek to do the best they can in spite of an aggressive monetization scheme set by the developer.

This tension, between players seeking to spend less and developers seeking to make more, normalizes a different kind of play in free-to-play games. Sports games may have set some initial bounds for play, but other games are picking up elements and applying them within new contexts. Players are often seeking to find ways to commit less, while the game seeks to get them to engage and pay more. Developers have to find the balance between pushing too hard and burning players out, while preventing them from churning to another game. Developers also have to find the right balance of labor and skill, seeking to avoid being presented as a dreaded pay-to-win game and enabling players to show off enough of their skill to warrant investment in the game. This is a key lesson to take from the example of Ultimate Team. Not all contexts or norms within game communities are the same, and a monetization approach that lines up with audience expectations will decrease the odds of a vocal player protest. Subtly shifting norms and finding ways to build out new avenues for play allowed space for Ultimate Team to grow into a dominant mode for EA, while trying to port something similar into *Battlefront* without context, a reason, or ramp-up time led to a revolt. It is notable that Ultimate Team took years to develop into a major part of EA's financial plan. It likely works, in part, because the moves to expand it were slow, allowing players to acclimate to the changing cost of the game over time. A finer point on notions of labor and skill can be seen in studying a pair of different game genres—games that are perceived as hardcore free-to-play and those that are all about clicking.

5 Hardcore Clicking

One of the most notable things about analyzing bias around free-to-play games is that there are places where free-to-play mechanics are accepted by the community of players, journalists, and scholars studying games. There are certain games that are seen as legitimate and not really even thought of when free-to-play gets deployed as a slur. They are the type of game that gets the credit for how the low, low price of free enables anyone to play, while not getting the vitriol for a monetization scheme that can lead to players spending many times what they would on a console title. Like the potentially unlimited spending on arcade games that is often forgotten in a discussion of monetization schemes and free-to-play, certain games are notable because they are seen as appealing to core gamers while using a payment approach that, in other circumstances, causes the core to retract. Games like *League of Legends* and *World of Tanks* present a version of free-to-play that is seen as acceptable to many of those who reject *Star Wars Battlefront II* or *Candy Crush Saga*. Assessing certain games, particularly a genre of games referred to as "clicker games," offers an additional reflection point on the norms surrounding video games, payment, labor, and skill.

Although academic research on video games skews more toward online and fantasy games, a group of academics has set out to study the perception of free-to-play games among players and game developers.[1] In the case of a study about perceptions about free-to-play games, developers largely defended their practices, while players were more skeptical.[2] The research indicated that all parties involved were skeptical of pay-to-win design, or the perception of it, while certain games got a pass on their monetization practices. Games like *Team Fortress 2*, *League of Legends*, and *World of Tanks* were seen as standards to be upheld. These are "good" games that use free-to-play in a "proper" way. Both players and designers expected games to be balanced environments where time and talent outweighed the role of spending. The authors of the study note that these games are received differently than games like *Kim Kardashian: Hollywood* or *Candy Crush Saga*, but they largely stop there, acknowledging the difference and expressly wondering why it exists.

The inability to account for the fundamental difference in reception points to blind spots and subconscious bias in the minds of those making and writing about games. We are part of a system, and getting outside of it to reflect on it is quite hard. It is clear there is a difference in the discussions surrounding these games, but accounting for it is more difficult, since doing so implicates all of us. Unraveling that relationship and getting perspective for reflection requires looking more deeply at the kinds of free-to-play games that tend to be accepted and critically reading the discussion about them to better understand what these dynamics indicate about video games and their norms.

Hardcore Free-to-Play

The term free-to-play is exceptionally broad and is even used flexibly in the course of this book. It stands in for a set of monetization practices that encourage ongoing spending by players, typically with no upfront cost, but there are also games that charge a fee for the initial game and use additional monetization approaches that parallel free-to-play games, like the various modes of Ultimate Team in Electronic Arts sports games. *League of Legends*, *Team Fortress 2*, and *Overwatch* enable players to spend massive amounts of money, but are seen as legitimate, core games.

League of Legends (*LoL*), which launched in late 2009, is the preeminent example of this sort of game, for years holding a status as most-played PC video game in the world as of this writing.[3] *LoL* grosses billions of dollars a year and popularized a genre of gaming known as multiplayer online battle arena, or MOBA, which now includes games like *Dota 2* and mobile titles like *Honor of Kings*,[4] *Vainglory*, and games that blend elements of the genre with other things, like the card-collecting battler *Clash Royale*.[5] Although *LoL* occasionally ends up in lists of free-to-play games, particularly in discussion about the revenue it generates, the game is exempted from the same kind of criticism leveled at *Tap Sports Baseball*. *LoL* is largely monetized through optional purchases of new heroes or distinct appearances, known as skins, of those heroes. *World of Tanks*, released in 2010, and *World of Tanks Blitz*, a mobile version of the game that launched in 2014, are two more examples of games that are treated differently. Their developer, Wargaming, presents itself as sensitive to core player concerns, yet aggressively monetizes the game through a series of skins and optional progression advantages that let those who pay move through the game more quickly. Valve's *Team Fortress 2* launched as a paid title in 2007, but it went free-to-play in 2011, with a representative of the studio promising the game would not be pay-to-win, while asserting that Valve was seeking to get as many people playing as possible. The belief at Valve is that "in multiplayer games it's generally true that the more people playing the game, the higher value the game has for each individual customer. The more players, the more available servers in your area, the wider variety of other players you'll find, the greater opportunity for new experiences, and so on."[6] Astutely pointing out that the game will get more players with no initial price, *Team Fortress 2* transitioned to a business approach based on selling items, particularly hats, to let players distinguish themselves within the game. Blizzard took a similar approach with *Overwatch*, where they charged an upfront fee at launch in 2016, but dropped the price as time passed, including the game as part of the Humble Monthly bundle in late 2018.[7] Recognizing that more could be made from charging for appearance and other in-game cosmetic items, like tags players could spray on surfaces in the game and custom voice lines, *Overwatch* is another example of a game that tends to get a pass when it comes to concerns about free-to-play style monetization schemes.

In a brief overview of what makes these games work, it is notable to point out that the MOBA and first-person shooter genres are overwhelmingly male. They are games largely designed by men, for men, and most frequently written about by men. Unlike many mobile free-to-play titles, like *Covet Fashion* or *Candy Crush Saga*, which have large numbers of women players, so-called hardcore free-to-play games have a player base that is quite similar to other games on consoles and PCs. These games are typically predicated on selling items that have little to do with in-game performance. There may be characters one must buy to unlock, but it is typical that the purchases are optional, and spending more does not confer a substantial in-game advantage. Although I personally find it quite interesting from a gender-performance perspective that the monetization of these games can largely be reduced to boys shopping for clothes, they are assiduously trying to avoid being deemed pay-to-win. Doing so means continuing to produce art and other elements that can be sold to players and exploiting their desires to demonstrate their appreciation of a given character and dedication to the game.

Analyzing these games with an eye to how certain monetization schemes are referred to as free-to-play done right and others are cast to the side opens space for reflection on why that happens. These games are different than Ultimate Team, as they target a different player base. They are seen as acceptable because they let players still show their skill and talent. However, studying the reaction and reception of them shows another angle of the bias against certain forms of free-to-play and how norms are developed in and around video games.

Assessing Hardcore Free-to-Play

Typical discussions of hardcore free-to-play games start from the foundational premise that these are valid, interesting games that are worthy of your time and effort. A sidetrack may be made into a discussion of how much players can pay, but those stories of money spent are carefully situated within a discussion of how the game works and why the spending was worthwhile and valid. These kinds of stories typify coverage about *League of Legends* (*LoL*); for example, a Kotaku article makes a case that the game is too expensive, but never questions the fundamental business structure of the game.[8] The author, Yannick LeJacq, pulls from a discussion on Reddit to argue that, because so much new content has been added to *LoL*, something needs to be done to change the structure of payments in the game. For LeJacq, the added content "creates a prohibitively high barrier to entry for new players" and limits diversity in player choice, since they can only play as characters they have unlocked. However, underlying his argument is the belief that the problem is that prices are too high, not that the game is engaged in questionable business practices. LeJacq suggests that the game pursue alternative approaches to monetization, like ads, in order to drop prices for players. In the end, he concludes with light criticism for *LoL*, while saying that games with a free-to-play business model eventually come to the "saddest realization" players will inevitably reach "when playing a free-to-play game, even a great one like *League of Legends*: the game can only afford to be free when it's relentlessly badgering you to spend money on it."[9] In this, LeJacq effectively differentiates *LoL* from other free-to-play games. *LoL* is a great game, largely because it adheres to his fundamental conceptions of what a game is. And, although there is plenty of opportunity for spending built into it, players do not have to spend that money in order to play the game.

In a summary of a player discussion about spending habits in *League of Legends*, Harrison Jacobs argues, "one of the most interesting things about the thread is that, despite spending a large amount of money on a video game, the users were mostly satisfied with having done so."[10] To an outsider audience, spending hundreds or thousands of dollars on a video game is presented as aberrational, although the article begins with an acknowledgment of the billion dollars *LoL* made in the prior year, which clearly came from somewhere. Player accounts defend their spending based on two primary lines of reasoning: that they are justified in doing so because they could choose to spend time to unlock the same things, and they have enough disposable income that they are simply electing to spend some of that on a hobby. The second line of reasoning mirrors the *Cordial Minuet* player from the introduction who wanted to press the limits of the game, but the first rationale is particularly interesting. In justifying spending in *LoL* based on the fact that everything can be earned for free if players devote enough time to the game, *LoL* players appeal to the core values of those that defend hardcore free-to-play games, while denigrating other games with largely similar monetization strategies. A fundamental premise of hardcore games is that they should not be pay-to-win—victories should be earned on an even playing field. Spending in *LoL* is justified because it is simply speeding up time: players could have gotten that new skin anyway by playing a lot, but defend their decision to pay based on a rational appeal to economics and the value of their time. Players talk about the amount of money they make at their job or the time they spend with their family; instead of grinding away, money lets them spend their time most efficiently. Payment in the game is rarely questioned, and the core of the game is accepted as valid and legitimate, with the primary concerns coming from issues with the technical execution of it, like bugs and server outages. The way players defend the game and their spending habits anchors neatly into conceptions of player labor and work within games, while preserving the role of competitive video games as proper tests of skill.

Oddly enough, the use of core video game player norms to defend *League of Legends* as a valid game may be best presented by a website that sells "smurf" accounts. To join ranked play, *LoL* players must be at level 30 and have a certain number of champions available for selection. The process of leveling to 30 takes a substantial amount of time; in their marketing material, the site contends that it takes players about 100–150 hours to achieve level 30.[11] In an opinion piece entitled "Is *League of Legends* Free to Play? You'd Be Silly to Think So," the author breaks down how *LoL* is free to start but then charges money for Riot Points, the premium currency in *LoL* that is used to unlock new characters or skins. The notable turn happens in a section addressing whether or not *LoL* is pay-to-win; the author contends that the design of the game

> made it so people can't just buy themselves to the top like you can in other games. These items [that you can buy] might make you look cooler, but they're not going to help you climb the ranked ladder any faster. In fact, for the average player, most of these items are actually a waste of money. With that said, there is one thing that every player should spend money on to make their *League of Legends* experience even better.[12]

Of course, the site offers just the service players need to "skip the boring stuff and jump straight into the action," complete with a guarantee of a new account if the one you buy from them is banned. What is notable about the piece is that the monetization model of *LoL* is presented as acceptable precisely because the spending is optional. Spending on *LoL* is even presented as a waste of money in most cases; the money is extraneous, and the game and its ranked play mode are the kinds of things that players can enjoy. Monetization in the game may be necessary to keep the game going, but it is unobtrusive and does not get in the way of play.

These points, where microtransaction-based payment models are excused and justified, are where it is possible to see the norms and values underlying contemporary beliefs about video games and how they should work. *League of Legends* is the biggest game in this category, but there is also richness and depth to be gained in studying *World of Tanks Blitz*, the 2014 mobile version of the 2010 PC game *World of Tanks*. Both games are based on tank battles, where players are placed on a battlefield and grouped into a pair of teams that square off against each other. The developer of both games, Wargaming, has gone on to release several other games, including *World of Warplanes* (2013) and *World of Warships* (2015), rounding out their stable of war simulations (figure 5.1). All the war games are free-to-play on PC, mobile devices, and consoles and are monetized by charging for things like experience boosts and new tanks, planes, or ships. Based on the profile of *World of Tanks*, the release of *World of Tanks Blitz* was highly anticipated by many players. Taking the PC experience to a mobile platform enabled players to play a quicker game while away from their computer. In the adaptation to mobile devices, the game was streamlined, with smaller maps, fewer players on each side of the battle, and a six-minute time limit for games. Notably, "teams are sorted based on the strength of the tanks each person uses, so at least as far as equipment goes, things are generally balanced between the two sides."[13] This balance is crucial to perceptions about and discussions of the game, because the way monetization in *World of Tanks Blitz* is talked about inevitably comes back to the contention that the

Figure 5.1
Gameplay in *World of Tanks Blitz*, with a freshly destroyed tank in the foreground.

free-to-play mechanics do not intrude on the balance that allows skill at tank battling to overcome payments made to purchase something within the game.

The launch reviews of *World of Tanks Blitz* are overwhelmingly similar across a number of sites. The reviewer starts with some general background on the game and clarifies that this game is "good" free-to-play, moves into a longer explanation of the game and how it works, then closes with a reminder that the free-to-play in this game is acceptable. TouchArcade's review has a pair of clarifications in the first two paragraphs. First, Shaun Musgrave notes: "It's a rare free-to-play game that manages to pull in casual players and hardcore alike, with its fair economy, approachable gameplay, and surprising depth."[14] In the next paragraph, he compares the game to the PC version, writing, "it's also still free-to-play, and like its PC papa, it somehow manages to mostly avoid the devastating imbalance that often occurs in multiplayer games that allow people to pay their way ahead."[15] In the middle, Musgrave clarifies:

> The gameplay itself has such a heavy skill component to it that even a weaker tank can make useful contributions in the right hands. If they cut all of the premium content out of the game tomorrow, you'd still be left with a game that feels well-designed and enjoyable, and that's certainly something worth applauding in the scope of the overall free-to-play scene.[16]

This is a point where the values about how games should work shine through. For Musgrave, *World of Tanks Blitz* is a good game because it is about skill, where the "right hands" can make all the difference, and where the monetization is not gauche enough to get in the way. He ends by claiming that *World of Tanks Blitz* is "a rare free-to-play game that respects both your time and your money, and it's definitely worth checking out."[17]

Owen Faraday offers a similar perspective in a review for Pocket Tactics, starting with the clarification for readers that

> If you never played *WoT* (*World of Tanks*) on PC, you're probably wondering why I'm so excited about a game that violates two of the most important dicta of the *Codex PocketTactica*: not only is *WoT Blitz* a touchscreen shooter, but it's a free-to-play game to boot. Surely we are preparing an effigy burning/pig roast here on Mount Hexmap?[18]

Making the suggestion that "there's never been a better touchscreen action game than this," Faraday asks readers to give the game a chance. He says it is a faster version of the game than its PC predecessor, but it is a far more deliberate game than many shooters and the touchscreen makes the whole experience more forgiving.[19] However, Faraday is merely building to the core of the argument—that the game features "free-to-play that isn't grubby."[20] Developing his position, Faraday first sympathizes with his imagined readers and then turns them back toward this version of free-to-play. He writes: "Free-to-play is a bad word around these parts, and that's for good reason: F2P games are total rubbish, by and large, because the way that they're monetised intrudes into the mechanics of the game. *World of Tanks* succeeds at making an F2P game where there's a nice church/ state separation between the gameplay and the money."[21] Faraday goes on to break down how players can spend in the game and how each type of spending fails to interfere with core game mechanics in a way that he finds distasteful. Although players can pay to unlock tanks, they can also use in-game currency that they earn in battle to do the same thing. Premium currency will let players choose from more tanks with which to play, but the premium tanks players can buy "aren't super-powered monsters, but rather get a bonus to how much credit [the soft currency] they generate."[22] The premium ammunition players can buy does give a slight bonus, but Faraday quickly breaks down how "gold ammo isn't a pay-to-win button. Because the skill ceiling is relatively high here, a smart player always has a chance in *World of Tanks*, no matter what kind of shells the other guy is loading."[23] Faraday then goes on to give tips about how to best play the game, since the breakdown of the payment structure in the game is presumed to be effective in convincing players to try it.

In an analysis of *World of Tanks Blitz* about a year after its launch, Michail Katkoff makes the case for how *World of Tanks Blitz* could make more money. Perhaps unsurprisingly, much of his argument is couched in the same set of values and norms about how games should work. Katkoff begins with the admission:

> I love *World of Tanks Blitz* because it's simply a great game. There are no timers. No lives. No farming. No crafting and resources caps. There's just the fun and engaging multiplayer battle where progress is made by playing instead of waiting. *World of Tanks Blitz* makes the most out of touchscreen devices offering players an experience that none of the other games are willing nor able to do.[24]

Katkoff goes on to break the game down, pointing out flaws in the tutorial and making suggestions about where the game could be improved. He praises much of the monetization strategy in the game, writing:

> The best thing about the monetization through Premium Account is that it doesn't give these players any in-game advantage. The biggest mistake is to allow players pay-to-win in a competitive PvP [player vs. player] game as it destroys the skill element and discourages the majority of players (the non-paying players) to continue playing on uneven turf.[25]

Premium accounts in *World of Tank Blitz* allow players to get greater rewards after each battle, and the option is offered to players after every battle with a visual reminder of how much more currency and experience they could have earned if they had purchased a premium account (figure 5.2). Katkoff is echoing the compliments of the initial reviewers, pointing out how *World of Tanks Blitz* is predicated on skill and is a game where players can fight against each other on largely equal terms in an effort to demonstrate their facility in battle. The game is special to Katkoff, and worth the time to analyze and suggest how it could be better, precisely because this game conforms to his expectations about what a game should be and how it should work. In the end, he writes, "I want to believe in [the] success of games like this because this is something we the players deserve after grinding through all those *Clash of Clans* and *Kingdoms of Camelot* clones. Rooting for *Hearthstone*, *Vainglory*, and *World of Tanks* is rooting for core games on touch screen devices."[26] The provenance of *World of Tanks Blitz*, as a free-to-play mobile game, is sufficient to lead to questions, but Katkoff argues that this game is special. Through a focus on skill and payment design that aligns with what he believes are the proper norms of

Figure 5.2
An end-game screen in *World of Tanks Blitz* with the notice of the additional rewards I could have gotten with a premium account.

free-to-play gaming, Katkoff is making an argument much like Musgrave and Faraday. This game is different. This game follows the right norms. This game is a good one that is worth your time and possibly your money. Games like these help illustrate the belief system of players, indicating what is normal and what is atypical and scary.

However, the ride for *World of Tanks Blitz* was not universally smooth. Update 2.8, released in 2016, was designed to make higher-level tanks worth playing in order to grow the top end of the game. Prior to the update, many players refrained from playing the top-level tanks because the repair costs for fixing damaged tanks often exceeded the amount of soft currency won in battle. As a result, players played with lower-level tanks, decreasing the variety in the game and limiting the appeal of grinding toward the highest tier in the game.[27] However, the update also introduced a consumable item called provisions. Provisions were relatively expensive soft-currency items that had a passive effect throughout the battle, enabling players to move more quickly across the battlefield and gain other advantages. Players expressed concern that provisions gave those who could afford to use them a substantive advantage in battle, making the game pay-to-win. Unlike the consumables that had previously been in the game, provisions had no cool-down time, and they impacted the whole battle when they were equipped. This dynamic led one critic to write that provisions featured "no strategy behind their use, and that's part of the issue here I think. If you add a consumable that clearly makes a player better and has no downside to its use, then all you've done is ensured that those who can afford to pay for that consumable for every single battle will have the upper hand."[28] Echoing concerns of reviewers about the appropriateness of the monetization strategy in the game, an article about provisions concludes with the statement: "What I can say is that paid advantages in F2P competitive multiplayer games are not the path to an entertaining game."[29]

Despite all of the paid advantages that come with things like sports, airline flights, and life in general, games are cordoned off as something different, a place where a certain kind of player expects a certain kind of fairness. Within about two weeks of the initial patch, the developer announced that the pricing in the game was incorrect and needed to be adjusted in line with player requests.[30] In doing so, the developer of the game, Wargaming, better aligned themselves with the expectations of the community and furthered the norm that games should be designed in a way that does not allow players who spend money to get a competitive advantage. Wargaming upheld norms about how games should work, leaning into a community of players that praised the game at release as something different than other mobile free-to-play games. Wargaming sees their offerings as games that should last for decades, arguing that it is an "easy" prediction to say their games will "remain popular 10, 20, or even 30 years into the future because of frequent updates that will keep it [Wargaming] abreast of whatever hits the market in the meantime."[31] However, maintaining that kind of longevity requires the game to be in sync with its players, steering away from pay-to-win and toward a level playing field and free-to-play monetization that is not seen as grubby or out of step with dominant norms.

World of Tanks Blitz is far from the only game treated this way. *Vainglory* is a mobile MOBA game that was hailed as the possible arrival of *League of Legends* for smartphones. Of course, reviews point out things like "it's important to note that I considered no aspect of *Vainglory's* freemium facets to be considered pay-to-win. Instead, its monetization favors the more established free-to-play MOBAs and is very fair."[32] It is essential for games like *World of Tanks Blitz, Vainglory,* and *League of Legends* to be perceived as fair and balanced contests of skill. In discussions of these kinds of games, players and reviewers frequently present beliefs along these lines as something that just is, rather than a norm and a value. Games do not have to be monetized this way, but swimming against the stream is far more difficult than going with it, especially if a game company is making an attempt to get a game to last for decades. Players see these games as contests of skill, where money is something that does not intrude, and reviews of these games must quickly and repeatedly make note of how their expectations will not be violated. Pressing harder on this idea requires looking at a kind of game that takes skill out of the equation but still maintains a high profile among the kinds of players in hardcore free-to-play games.

Just Keep Clicking

At the other side of the skill spectrum, a genre of clicker games has sprung up in which the primary goal is to accumulate more, and the only way to do that is to click, or—if one wants to be even less involved—wait. Clicker games are the antithesis of games like *League of Legends*: they ask players to sit back and interact minimally, with little precision and no real way to demonstrate mastery. One of the first games in the genre was a web-based game called *Cookie Clicker. Cookie Clicker* was largely an art project, an attempt to push the boundaries of what was considered a game, but it also introduced a number of mechanics that would soon become commonplace in the genre. Players start by clicking to generate something, but as they move forward in the game they can use currency they have made for upgrades and quickly grow to a point where they no longer need to click. In the case of *Cookie Clicker*, within about 15 clicks players can simply watch the game play itself.

A mobile version within the idle clicker genre, *Bitcoin Billionaire*, was released in late 2014 to great praise. In the game, players mine hypothetical bitcoins, starting by tapping the screen and eventually growing their operation so that it continues to accumulate bitcoins with minimal interaction (figure 5.3). Players can choose to pay to double their bitcoins earned or get an auto-miner than lets them hold the screen, rather than tap; plus, there is a requisite cat available for purchase as a cosmetic item. Negative events can occur that cause a setback to mining, and those can be skipped either by paying a small amount of premium currency, called hyperbits, or watching a video, ensuring an ad revenue stream for the game. Notably, reviews of the game often single out how the game is monetized, much like in the case of *World of Tanks Blitz*. As one review puts it,

> the game doesn't require spending anything on it, it's literally only to speed up progression, which is what this game is all about. The fun is in watching the numbers get higher and buying things to make the game progress faster. The hyperbits are pretty much the only paywall of any sort. . . . If you want faster progression without setbacks, well, Noodlecake is happy to take your money. This is truly a **free**-to-play game, though I admit I have spent a couple of dollars on this.[33] (emphasis in original)

Bitcoin Billionaire was successful, earning a five-star review from TouchArcade and landing on two of their writers' top-10 games lists for 2014.[34] The game would go on to launch a massive update the following year, tripling the amount of content in the game, demonstrating the viability of the genre and its ability to get players to pay in a game where there is no skill required.[35]

Figure 5.3
A new game mining bitcoins in *Bitcoin Billionaire*.

Idle clickers are consistently talked about as dumb but compelling games. They are games that somehow get a hook in players and keep them playing despite their inherent inanity. *Bitcoin Billionaire* is described as a game "you can't help but keep playing," one where a reviewer "know[s] it's dumb, but this game absorbed my life for weeks."[36] There are several other popular games in the genre, with *Clicker Heroes* for PC being one of the most played games on Steam at its launch, competing with titles like *Grand Theft Auto V*, *Dota 2*, and *The Witcher 3*.[37] Invariably, the review gets to the question of why anyone would play the game, then quickly pivots to how much the reviewer played it and the complicated feelings that invokes in them when they could be playing something more tightly knitted to mainstream expectations of video games. *Clicker Heroes* introduced role-playing-game-style progression, complete with boss battles and the chance to gather loot. *CivCrafter* is a mobile game that pushed the genre farther, effectively becoming a resource simulation set within a clicker game.[38] *BitCity* took the clicker genre in the direction of city simulators like *SimCity*. The game also introduced a pair of fairly novel purchase options to generate revenue: a chance to double the speed of the game, and the Pension Pig, a $2.99 purchase of a piggy bank where money accumulates over time, but once it is emptied another payment must be made the next time a player wants to crack it open.[39]

These games are designed in a manner that strips a game down to its most basic element: clicking. Almost every other game in this book, including those praised for their inclusion of skill, are fundamentally clicking games. Games like *Bitcoin Billionaire* embrace their fundamental nature as clickers; these kinds of games strip away all pretense and show what games are at their most basic. They lead to questions about what counts as skill, how players show mastery, and the dynamics of labor and the grind. They are rewarding in certain ways, but they also show a specific angle on what it means to be free-to-play, as pretty much the only things that are sold in the game are options to speed the game up, when the whole game is about taking time and grinding one's way through it. The genre is popular enough that the sequel to *Clicker Heroes* dropped the free-to-play model because of the developer's complicated feelings about certain players spending thousands of dollars on the game. *Clicker Heroes 2* was an immediate best-seller on Steam, Valve's digital distribution platform for PC games.[40] Even with a payment model in flux, what is successful is not always about skill or purity: there are more complicated issues at play, although it is far more likely to be acceptable in certain communities to say you are playing a game to show off your skill than to show your persistence at clicking or patience in waiting. That said, for many at the core of games, anything is better than buying your way forward. Just as *World of Warcraft* players were likely to hide the fact that they bought gold, gamers often believe that buying their way forward is an indication of a lack of skill or effort.

Hardcore Pay-to-Win

The point of blending comparisons of games like *World of Tanks Blitz* and *Bitcoin Billionaire* is that they show opposite sides of similar approaches. They use a roughly similar monetization approach, and both are praised, but the reasons *World of Tanks Blitz* is venerated run counter to the gameplay present in idle clicker games. It is not just about the money or paying-to-win. It is about the themes in a game. Notably, bitcoin mining and role-playing games are accepted, but a similar kind of game, *Kim*

Kardashian: Hollywood, is lampooned. It is about fitting norms and expectations and being comfortable for your players, while gently pushing them in a direction toward microtransactions and generating additional revenue. There are deep systems of norms at play, and if games step outside of expectations, they must have a compelling reason for doing so. The examples also show the importance of masculine theming when battle-driven games can sell players a new outfit, while some players will mock those who do the same in a fashion game.

Labor and skill are key tropes, as players seek to show off skill and demonstrate dedication through their labor. In these cases, examining disparate genres of games that are considered acceptable by core gamers illustrates the consequences of that praise for video games more broadly. After this focus on games that studiously avoid accusations of being pay-to-win, it is appropriate to turn toward games where paying really does matter: collectible-card games and gacha-based strategy games.

6   Hoping You Get Lucky

Luck plays a complicated role in video games, as players in many games try to limit randomness within the computer simulation. However, there are games subject to a heavy influence of luck, particularly within the free-to-play sector. One of the dominant ways in which to generate revenue is through some sort of gacha, or capsule toy, mechanic, like card packs, loot crates, or loot boxes. This kind of design puts players in a position to try their luck in an attempt to get that super rare, awesome reward. Games in this category use blind purchases to enable players to buy something without knowing exactly what they will get. In so doing, players invest money into a system, largely under the hope that they will be the lucky ones to pull the best prize. Layering on releases of new cards or characters, these games have a virtually endless stream of things players can buy, and the importance of chance means the amount that can be spent is vast.

In the free-to-play space, games predicated on selling mystery items have a tough challenge: finding a way to engage free-to-play players, and keep them playing, in order to have a large-enough community of players to sustain a lively multiplayer game. This kind of design is more like the process in the card packs of an Ultimate Team game than the purchases of cosmetic items in a multiplayer online battle arena, but there are key difference in how games with this monetization approach are talked about in terms of skill and paying-to-win. Building a game around a loot box element necessarily invites luck into the game, as one player's success might be largely based on an exceptionally lucky result they got early in the game. However, the presence of that luck has to be weighed against the more dominant norms of core video games, where skill and work are far more likely to be accepted as valid and appropriate in adjudicating success or failure. These dynamics are compounded when certain players invest more money in the game in an effort to bend the curve in their favor, a dynamic that can cause a game to get the oft-dreaded label of pay-to-win.

Gacha mechanics are a powerful advantage monetization strategy in free-to-play games that have also been integrated into many premium titles on mobile devices, PCs, and consoles. When implemented poorly, they can lead to the backlash that followed in the wake of the *Star Wars Battlefront II* launch, but this approach can also fuel the success of multi-million dollar flagship titles. Studying a pair of very different games that use this mechanic, Blizzard's *Hearthstone* and Electronic Arts and Capital Games's *Star Wars: Galaxy of Heroes*, offers perspective on how games in this genre are received and how this kind of optional spending plays out in practice.

Hearthstone

Hearthstone is a collectible-card game officially released by Blizzard for PCs on March 11, 2014. The game was expanded to tablets, and eventually phones, with a full iOS and Android launch on April 14, 2015. The game is set in the universe of the massively popular video game series *Warcraft*. In the game, players assemble decks of cards to complete battles. Some of these battles are against the computer, but the most active modes of *Hearthstone* involve combat against other players in a variety of play modes, including ranked, casual, and arena (figure 6.1). Distinctive to this card game is that players must pick a class avatar from *World of Warcraft* to represent them, such as a mage, shaman, or warrior. The class a player chooses dictates the cards they can play with and their general stylistic approach, as most cards are limited to a single class. Cards have different levels of rarity, including legendary, epic, rare, and common. Players are tasked with building a deck of 30 cards for casual and ranked play, using only neutral cards or cards that match their class. Players are also limited by a rule that they cannot have more than two copies of most cards in their deck and cannot have duplicate legendary cards. Casual and ranked mode were further divided by the introduction of wild and standard mode in

Figure 6.1
My mage battling against a computer-controlled hunter in *Hearthstone*.

early 2016. Wild mode includes all the cards that have ever been released for *Hearthstone*, while standard mode is limited to basic and standard cards that are available early in the game, plus the most recent sets of expansion cards for the game.[1] The addition of standard and wild modes enabled Blizzard to normalize their addition of expansion cards, integrating them more fully into the game and rotating old sets of cards out.

A typical game of *Hearthstone* plays out with two players doing battle with their 30-card decks, drawing cards and using abilities in order to try to defeat their opponent by exhausting their hit points. Players gain "mana" over the course of the game, starting with one and adding a point each round, to enable them to play cards from their hands or abilities tied to their class in an effort to protect their hero, do damage to their opponent, or exhaust their opponent's deck of cards. The game ends when one player runs out of health and, based on the mode played and level of the game, players are awarded rewards based on their performance. *Hearthstone* has a number of modes of play, with players using their own chosen deck of 30 cards in ranked and casual play, choosing a deck out of consecutive sets of three options in arena play, and completing what largely amount to puzzles in the adventure modes that have come with a handful of expansions to the game.

Players can get the cards for their decks in a variety of different ways. The most common way to get cards is to open packs. Packs can either be purchased by playing the game and earning gold, through in-game activities like completing quests or playing matches, or by paying money to either buy gold or package deals that are offered to players. Players can also craft their own cards, as they get "arcane dust" anytime they get cards they will not be able to add to their deck, like the third copy of a common, epic, or rare card or a second copy of a legendary card. Based on the dust they acquire, players can then choose to "craft" a card they are missing in an effort to customize their decks and compensate for the randomness of a card draw. New sets of cards are introduced into the game through a series of expansions that happen about three times every year and have solidified into releases of 135 cards that can only be obtained by opening new card packs or crafting them with arcane dust. The appeal of new cards is twofold. First, it gives Blizzard a way to keep players spending money in the game. Second, it keeps the game from getting too stale, as most players eventually coalesce around similar approaches that are considered the most powerful. Each new release is designed to mix up the game and force players out of their comfort zones.

Hearthstone follows in a long line of collectible-card games, like *Magic: The Gathering*. Collectible card games have roots in the baseball cards and other sports cards that inspired *FIFA Ultimate Team*, and their business strategy works in a very similar way. Collectible card games have a rich history and a careful line to walk when it comes to game balance. Most collectible-card games make the most powerful cards rare, which makes them valuable and hard for players to obtain.[2] That combination of rarity and power makes certain cards especially desirable, driving the price for them ever upward. One of the rarest cards from *Magic: The Gathering*, the black lotus, has become a cherished collectible, with prices for well-preserved versions of the card nearing \$100,000 at auction.[3] The card is valuable precisely because it is both rare and is considered one of the most powerful cards in the game, so powerful that it has not been reprinted in subsequent expansions and releases.[4] Collectible card games are built around spending; it is understood that players who spend more will likely have an advantage over those who have not spent. Buying more cards means having more options and, typically, means having more powerful cards as part of your deck. Luck surely matters, but in the long run, luck will even out, and money can overcome a run of bad luck. Even more importantly, in pre-digital collectible-card games, players needed to spend money in the first place to even have a chance to find good cards. In making *Hearthstone* a digital game, rather than on offline card game, Blizzard took advantage of the opportunity to let players craft their own cards, personalizing their deck and limiting the downside of bad luck. Throughout their various strategies for monetization, *Hearthstone* manages to make a substantial amount of money, with revenue estimates ranging from $20–40 million a month, as the biggest game in a digital card game market estimated to be worth as much as $1.4 billion annually.[5] One of the most striking aspects of *Hearthstone* is that it is effectively a blended player community, drawing Blizzard fans and collectible-card game fans together. In addition, the community of collectible-card game players has a different set of norms and understandings about how games should work, one in which they have accepted that spending more increases odds of winning.

There are two key areas of discourse that are important to track: the way players talk about building decks in *Hearthstone* and the general reception to the game and its design. The blended community of players offers an excellent opportunity for reflection, as players come with different norms and expectations. Collectible card game players expect spending to have an impact on performance in the game, while Blizzard fans expect a balanced competition in which skill is the most important element. Blizzard does what they can to bring players into the game, with a rich tutorial and a series of matches against the computer to practice playing and getting used to the way the game works. On the forums for the game, Blizzard hosts a set of new player guides that breakdown all kinds of aspects of the game, but they struggle in negotiating the different expectations of players.[6]

One of the most interesting types of guides is the advice to players on how to build a deck. Guides are generally written with three kinds of decks in mind: free-to-play, budget, and ultimate. True free-to-play decks are incredibly limited, as there aren't many cards that are guaranteed to be in a player's possession. Budget decks are generally built around a combination of the cards from free-to-play decks and a handful of cheap cards that can be readily crafted with dust. Taking advantage of some of the gold that can be achieved through early quests, players can build a thin bench of cards, enabling them to specialize and try to develop their first budget deck. A guide from 2013 focuses on how budget decks can be quite powerful and how playing with them can be far more fun than playing with free decks. However, this requires players to make a choice early in the process to focus on a single deck. Deviating from that plan could lead to a substantial setback, since crafting a card of your choice costs the dust from several disenchanted cards. However, the guide states, "once your budget deck is complete, you can go beat people up in play mode! Never again will you be able to complain, 'He won because I'm using a free deck.' Budget decks may not be the very best decks possible, but they are often pretty damn close. With a free deck, skill matters more than cards. With a budget deck, skill is 90% and your missing cards are only 10%."[7] This closure, with its appeal to skill, is notable, as it cycles back to the kind of concern expressed in other free-to-play games. Electronic Arts Sports executives defend Ultimate Team as acceptable because weaker teams with strong players in control can beat stronger teams with weaker players, and the same line of argument is used to justify play in *Hearthstone*. Although the cards matter, the appeal to skill is notable and important, as it is the ongoing focus of whether *Hearthstone* is portrayed as a proper, worthy game.

In a guide written about two years later, Aidan begins with a preface stating: "The concept of free-to-play becomes more and more daunting with every passing release and adventure, leading more and more players to test their skills in the Arena or give in to microtransactions. With this in mind, I've brewed 20 budget decklists, all costing less dust than a Legendary, ready for action!"[8] Writing after far more cards had been released, the pressure on players had changed. More cards meant that it became harder for new players to slot in and keep up, as they not only needed to overcome the advantages held by those players who had been playing for years, but they were also competing in a landscape with far more cards from which to choose. In the perspective of this author, players were faced with a pair of choices: try their skills in the arena mode, where players wager a set amount of gold in an effort to win prizes based on cards they draft, or "give in" to spending money on the game. In the case of arena play, particularly skilled players can actually make a "profit" in the game, winning more gold then they pay as an entry fee, while getting other rewards, like card packs and dust for crafting. Presenting microtransactions in this way, as a submission to the mechanics of the game, is interesting given that players engaging in any offline collectible-card game would need to "give in" to those microtransactions to simply sit at the table and play in the first place.

Similar themes show up in the forums of the game, with players promoting their ability to achieve what others think is impossible based on their skill. The cards are not what makes the game, some say: players just "have to play harder. And Hard-core."[9] Players post about the bias they perceive the game holds against new players, since someone joining the game does not have access to the same resources as a veteran player. Others chime in with advice and thoughts such as, "if you wanna have a chance. Expect to pay at least $100 a set. And that with the 80 free packs you can 'earn' between sets";[10] and "at this point its pay2play for newbies."[11] The cycle is ongoing, as new expansions drop new players farther behind and tilt the playing field toward those who spend on the new set to add fresh options to their decks. This provides ongoing revenue to Blizzard and supports the continued development of the game, but it does so at the cost of putting a presumed wall in front of new players—one that just keeps getting higher and higher. This bitterness fuels the community surrounding the game, as they work through their beliefs about the relative level of success they should expect and the level of money they need to invest in the game to reach their goals.

Writing for Kotaku, Joshua Calixto refers to the process of loving and then hating a game as a cycle of salt, where "any change to the game is viewed with intense scrutiny, every developer decision interpreted as either a money grab or completely out-of-touch. On this familiar seesaw between excitement and brutal criticism, hype is never just hype—it's also a precursor to eventual disappointment."[12] Calixto argues that all games with engaged communities have a cycle of bitterness, but the one for *Hearthstone* is different. First, he notes that "The amount of money it takes to build and play with the top-level decks that inspire all this discussion is much higher than it is in other online games of its stature. I read (and talk) about Control Paladins and Taunt Warriors all the time, but I still don't actually have the cards it would take to build those decks for myself."[13] Despite noting that he has spent $120 on the game on the most recent expansion alone, he is still missing most of the cards he would need to build key decks, so that when he is playing with his best deck and loses to "a rank 20 scrub with a Boulderfist Ogre and back-to-back lucky Primordial Glyph draws, I get salty."[14] For the purposes of my argument, understanding the specifics of the situation of the game in that quote is less important than the general values behind his argument. It takes players so long and so much effort and so much money to put together an ultimate deck of cards that when they lose to a lesser deck they are likely to get frustrated. For Calixto, this is

> the paradox of *Hearthstone*. You start off as a scrub, you get your ass handed to you by higher-level players with strategies you don't understand and decks full of Legendary cards, and you want to get better at the game. But when you put in the hours it takes to get to their level, all of a sudden you find that you're tired of your deck of Legendaries and you want to toss your keyboard out the window when you get beaten by a scrub.[15]

Hearthstone is different than other games, as players can readily sink hundreds of dollars into the game, yet any single match has a substantial amount of luck involved. And, eventually, players will face a game where their bad luck overcomes any advantage they may have in terms of cards and skill. Although players focus on the role of skill in the game, that is rewarded over the long run, rather than in any single game where luck can play a major role. This runs counter to the norms held by core gamers, as individual rounds of *Hearthstone* favor luck and spending over skill and hard work. Calixto notes, "as long as the game favors random hijinks and costs real-world money, the *Hearthstone* Salt Cycle will continue uninterrupted."[16] *Hearthstone* features a different kind of game design, but the hostility comes from running in the face of established norms in video games. *Hearthstone* is free-to-play with advantage spending and can be played on many different platforms, but the central issue is that the game effectively requires spending to get past a certain point of play. If players opt not to spend, they are putting themselves substantially behind those who do. However, skill is a key appeal in defending what makes *Hearthstone* different than more "tawdry" free-to-play games.

Between Blizzard's reputation as an exceptional developer of premium games and the design of *Hearthstone*, which is set up to reward a combination of both skill and spending, *Hearthstone* gets talked about in a manner quite different from other free-to-play games.[17] The microtransactions model largely parallels existing collectible-card games, like *Magic: The Gathering*, making it easier to swallow, in spite of the fact that it also parallels the loot boxes and loot crates that can evoke substantial discontent and laws banning the practice. The focus on skill is a call to traditional video games, tying the norms of *Hearthstone* more closely to PC and console games than free-to-play mobile titles. Beyond the discussion of deck-building or salt, the reaction to the game and how it is designed is notable. A post on Gamasutra hailed *Hearthstone* as a game changer for mobile devices, largely because it broke with existing conventions of mobile free-to-play games. Ed Biden argues that *Hearthstone* has no energy system that limits play, the cards players can buy are permanent items, the game is largely skill-based, and it features synchronous play against other players.[18] Biden states that because of these differences, *Hearthstone* "appeals to a lot of self-designated 'gamers' that find other mobile games somehow below them."[19] Although he notes that the ability to tap into the larger *Warcraft* brand is an advantage other games will be unable to replicate, the core parts of Biden's argument are fundamental to how some mobile or free-to-play games are judged as different and as better than other options. They conform to the expected norms of non-mobile, non-free-to-play games.

First, Biden makes the case that the lack of an energy system in the game means that players can play as much as they want. Dropping an energy system that restricts play enables players to play as much as they like, just as they would on a console or PC title, where they spent money upfront to buy the game. Players are not gated and can binge on a game they enjoy. Second, the cards are permanent items as long as the game is running, which links into existing norms about buying a game and having it, rather than the temporary boosts and advantages that are often sold in other free-to-play games. Buying cards in *Hearthstone* is more like buying a digital download; they are additions to a player's collection, which warrants a purchase since players are getting something, even if it is just bits, that feels tangible. Third, Biden contends that matches in *Hearthstone* are determined by good fortune, by meeting up with an opponent who has a set of cards you can counter, or by the superior skill of players. The focus on skill is a key piece of ensuring that *Hearthstone* is not tabbed with the dreaded pay-to-win label. Finally, the synchronous matches against other players may seem superfluous at first, but it complements the broader feeling that *Hearthstone* takes from console and PC norms, rather than what is more common in other mobile games. Synchronous play requires a massive player base to ensure that no one has to wait too long for a game, and it is an established norm in the PC and console games that

Biden's "self-designated 'gamers'" are likely to play. Competitive, synchronous play is also a chance for players to battle and prove their merit without having to trust game designers to make a fair battle against computer-controlled opponents. These four traits of *Hearthstone* are not just about breaking the norms of mobile free-to-play games—they are about disrupting the norms of mobile free-to-play games in a manner that accedes to the expectations of PC and console games that core players already accept. *Hearthstone* is praised because it fits with what feels familiar and comfortable to those who are used to getting their games on a different device and with a different monetization strategy.

This approach to developing *Hearthstone* is notable and interesting because of the impact the game had on the mobile marketplace. In 2015, as the game was rolling out and space for mobile games was still developing, collectible-card games like *Hearthstone* were the top-grossing category of games on mobile. This standing was consistently matched up against other games, with statements like

> what makes CCGs [collectible-card games] such a fascinating category, always according to the report, is the way they combine microtransactions with strategic competitive game play, a combination that will continue to inspire the gaming industry at large in the future. In other words, unlike games like *Clash of Clans*, CCGs don't give the (true or false) impression that the IAPs [in-app purchases] are there to "trick" the player into spending more money.[20]

This is a notable sentiment, given that the card packs in *Hearthstone* are effectively loot boxes—blind chances to get items with limited information about what is being purchased. Players seeking a complete set of cards consistently need to invest more into the game, especially with the release of new expansion packs of cards and given that older expansions inevitably cycle out of standard play decks. A purchase in *Clash of Clans* is durable or exchangeable: players will always have the extra builder, the chance to upgrade their buildings or troops, or that novelty decoration. But, perhaps even better, they generally know exactly what they are getting. There are real differences between the monetization strategies of the two games, but it is rather rich to contend that *Hearthstone's* is superior because players are not tricked into spending more. Like many other sentiments surrounding mobile, free-to-play gaming, analysis of the payment structures of various games often feature value-laden sentiments presented as anything but.

Notably, the demographic trends of collectible-card game players are also quite similar to core PC and console games, as one of the "most male-dominated gaming categories, with about 80% being male, and an average age of 31."[21] It makes sense that a game that draws a community of players who match up with "traditional" video games would seek to employ norms and approaches that are consistent for those players, refraining from pushing them too far out of their comfort zone. However, it is striking that, even in areas where payment and play strategies overlap with more typical mobile, free-to-play games, excuses are made for *Hearthstone*. Players consistently seek to pull it back into the realm of what is normal and acceptable to them, rather likening it to the "abhorrent" games that Ed Biden argues are beneath them. This sentiment runs through an essay about the *Un'Goro* expansion to *Hearthstone*, which marked a new approach to selling the game, with more cards being released and all of them being offered in random card packs, rather than as rewards to preset adventures where completing the adventure would guarantee all players some new cards. After explaining how this would almost assuredly make the game more expensive for players, Joshua Calixto argues that increasing the number of cards in the game "would allow for more switch-ups in strategies, meaning the 'metagame' would evolve at a more acceptable rate, and competitive play would ultimately end up feeling more merit-based."[22] He goes on to explain how this will create a hierarchy of players, as those who spend more will have more cards and be able to respond more quickly to changes in strategy, but never invokes the term pay-to-win. It is somewhat astounding that a move to effectively reward additional spending by players is presented as something that will make the game "more merit-based," rather than determined by the size of a player's wallet. Even as players are getting soaked for a greater investment, and Calixto calls out the approach as a way for Blizzard to give "whales more opportunities to spend, spend, spend on random drops," he closes by hypothesizing that "it's possible it might be the best move to keep *Hearthstone* around in the years to come."[23] *Hearthstone* may have a salt cycle, but players rarely tie the monetization of this game to others they despise.

Hearthstone is received as special, as different than other mobile free-to-play games. Part of that is likely because it taps into *Warcraft* and Blizzard's broader history as a developer.[24] *Hearthstone* also benefits from the fact that it came out on PCs before mobile devices. However, part of the reason why it is seen differently is that the players want to see it that way, as they go out of their way to rationalize changes and bring them into the accepted norms and understandings of the games they appreciate. Instead of calling the increasing expense of *Hearthstone* pay-to-win, or even just as adding pay-to-win elements, the defense of the game circles back to how the changes increase the skill level of the game and how they enable talented players to show off what they can do. Getting better perspective on these norms and how they work can be obtained by looking at *Star Wars:*

Galaxy of Heroes, a game that borrows from elements of many established game genres.

A Galaxy of Microtransactions

Developed by Electronic Arts's Capital Games, *Star Wars: Galaxy of Heroes* (*SWGoH*) was released worldwide on November 24, 2015, and borrows heavily from gacha-style mechanics, massively multiplayer online games, and collectible-card games. Initially presented as a collectible-card game, *SWGoH* hinges on players collecting characters and leveling and gearing them up to do battle with computer-controlled opponents.[25] Multiple modes have been added to the game over the years, but the primary objective of the game is to repeatedly play certain game modes in order to first unlock characters and then make them more powerful so you can defeat stronger opponents, in a cycle that repeats over and over (figure 6.2). *SWGoH* has a dizzying array of different energy and currency options, including

Figure 6.2
The central part of the cantina table in *Star Wars: Galaxy of Heroes*.

Cantina Energy, Ship Energy, Mod Energy, and just plain Energy. Those go along with currencies like Credits, Crystals, Squad Arena Tokens, Guild Tokens, Guild Event Tokens, Guild Event Tokens Mk II, Cantina Battle Tokens, Ship Building Materials, Galactic War Tokens, Fleet Arena Tokens, Championship Tokens, and Shard Store Tokens. This is, of course, in addition to special events in the game that feature limited attempts set over a time frame, rather than any of those kinds of energy, and may or may not reward one of the types of currency. As an initial breakdown of the game notes, "there's obviously a lot to keep track of in turns [*sic*] of currency and timers. While that's obviously a turn off for a lot of players, there's plenty here in terms of depth and character variety to make it worth trudging through for *Star Wars* fans."[26] Instead of the praise awarded to the glorious *Hearthstone*, *SWGoH* is a game to suffer through, requiring management and a tolerance for confusion to be able to make it in the game. To facilitate success, guides to the game generally lay out the basics and give players initial and interim goals on which to focus by providing lists of characters to obtain and benchmarks to mark their growing success in the game.[27]

Monetization in the game comes in a variety of forms. Players can spend crystals, the premium currency in the game, to refresh their energy, with the cost for energy refreshes going up over the course of multiple purchases. Players can also use crystals to buy gear or character shards from a variety of stores that are refreshed over the course of the day. More attempts for many key battles can be purchased with crystals and, in general, players can pay for a chance to speed up the rate at which they collect characters and equipment. However, the primary way that the game gets players to spend is by releasing new characters and then limiting access to them in some way. In the case of Grand

Admiral Thrawn, *SWGoH* runs a limited-time event where players need a five-member Phoenix Squad capable of defeating the event. For General Kenobi, players need to team up with their guild to defeat the Heroic Tank Takedown raid dozens of times to collect enough character shards to unlock and then maximize his potential. Legendary characters, like Commander Luke Skywalker and Rey (Jedi Training), are released through events that require assembling a specific team and, for the initial release, players are given a tight time frame for gathering what they need, often leading to "panic farming" and spending.

The developer, Capital Games, has also experimented with different ways to sell off other characters brought into the game. In conjunction with the release of *Rogue One: A Star Wars Story*, Director Krennic and Death Trooper were released in packs that cost about $20 in crystals and were estimated to require a total investment of about $1,100 in order to get them to the top level.[28] Players actively discuss the most effective ways of spending money in the game, generally agreeing that the most value is obtained by purchasing items that have defined outcomes, rather than those that offer a low-percentage chance of a big reward. One of the first pieces of advice players give each other is "avoid packs like the plague. They are just money dumps."[29] However, there is still plenty of debate about items with defined outcomes by comparing spending in *SWGoH* to other video games. In the case of a package of shards for various First Order characters, players compared the cost to premium titles, like *Final Fantasy XV* and *Civilization VI*.[30] Over the course of 2018, *SWGoH* largely settled on a release strategy for new characters and communicated it to players. They set expectations about the rarity of new characters and different modes for their release, with most new characters coming in as "marquee." Marquee characters are released in an event and accompanied by offers to pay money to get them to their full seven-star status. Doing so is subject to some randomness, but likely costs most players around $310 to max them out. If players wait six weeks, they can buy shards for the new marquee character in the store at a cost of about $140. Or, players can pay nothing, but it will take them roughly six months to get the character to seven stars while requiring them to forgo other options for their energy.[31]

The key piece of game design that lies underneath this advantage-buying and character-release process is that each new character is generally better than those that came before. Most characters have roles in the game, but the newest ones are generally best suited to beat the challenges or teams that have emerged as most powerful. This means that those who choose to spend, and spend big, have large structural advantages over those who do not. It also means that the game is generally accepted to be pay-to-win. Although there is enough randomness in the game that having a more powerful team does not always guarantee winning, it certainly makes it more likely. This also produces some interesting dynamics in the game, most notably players working together to try to minimize their spending and maximize their rewards. Although there are competitive elements of the game, for the most part players work together to progress their roster, leaving plenty of space for cooperation. This cooperation shows up in some interesting ways. In many cases, players are looking for a different result than players in other games. Instead of trying to find the most likely outcome, players attempt an event over and over in an effort to find the most favorable, luckiest outcome in order to win with the least investment possible. Players write guides and approaches for how to complete new modes with the minimum viable team, breaking down their strategy and possibly playing a battle hundreds of times to minimize their spending on the game while maximizing their rewards. For group raids, successful guilds often document their approach, breaking down how to build a guild and how to best deploy resources to win.[32] The competition among players in raids and various events often comes from trying to win with less, in order to demonstrate what is possible and aid others in their efforts to avoid spending on the game.[33] Players often work together to share bugs and loopholes to defeat modes more quickly, testing and reporting what works and occasionally figuring out things the developers just missed.[34]

The most distinctive type of this play, in my experience, is the way that top players organize themselves in the limited player-versus-player elements of the game. All players are assigned to arena and fleet shards, where they battle against a large number of other players in order to try to achieve the highest rank they can at the time of their payout. Each player is assigned a payout based on their time zone, so there are 24 possible payouts each day.[35] Rewards are far greater at the top and drop precipitously as players move down the rankings, with the top ranks paying out premium currency and other lucrative rewards and those finishing under rank 10,000 walking away with very little. Players are limited to five battles each day, each on a timer requiring players to wait between battles, although premium currency can buy players more chances or the ability to skip the wait (figure 6.3). In an effort to maximize their results, players self-organized into groups, often on third-party chat applications like Discord, in order to coordinate and share the rewards. When players at the top work together, they can save time, since they do not need to use as much effort fighting each other, and they can rotate their rewards to maximize their collective payout. They can also work

Figure 6.3
An arena mirror battle between two Darth Revan teams in *Star Wars: Galaxy of Heroes*.

together, knocking those who do not follow the rules downward, creating an incentive for players to play nicely with each other and shutting newcomers out.[36] There are substantial incentives to join the group and play together, but play is fundamentally twisted, as the arena shard collusion is largely targeted at defeating the developer and driven by player efforts to avoid putting money into the game, while extracting maximum rewards.

The initial pitch presenting *SWGoH* as a collectible-card game is an interesting comparison point for *Hearthstone*. At their core, both are about collecting a whole lot of something, over and over, whether building a deck or a team, and doing battle. *Hearthstone* is praised in reviews, as it conforms to the norms of console and PC games, but *SWGoH* is different. Although not generally reviled like *Kim Kardashian: Hollywood*, it is a grind, something that is suffered through and not really reviewed or discussed beyond its community of players. Gender and fandom likely also play into these considerations, as *SWGoH* is about a celebrated sci-fi property, while *Kim Kardashian: Hollywood* is targeted at women and about fashion and celebrity. However, the other inspiration for *SWGoH* is worth discussing, as the game carries a lineage as a massively multiplayer online game as well. Through its language use, like raids and guilds, and the way players organize, there are key notes in common with games like *World of Warcraft*. The most prominent guild in the game, Team Instinct, has an application process that is highly reminiscent of a raiding guild in a massively multiplayer online game. They lay out standards and expectations, ask players to introduce themselves, and then weed through applicants to try out those who seem like the best fit.[37] Many members of the development team, including former Senior Producer Carrie Gouskos, come from backgrounds that include working on massively multiplayer online games. The tie makes sense in some ways, as they are both games that run for years and feature players who make substantial time and resource investments in the game. However, the primary difference is that the investment in a game like *World of Warcraft* hinges on time, while *SWGoH* measures in dollars. This means that one of the key things included on the Team Instinct application is a question about applicants "estimated financial investment in *SWGoH*," with categories quickly jumping to four digits of spending on the game.[38] This spending treadmill, combined with the power creep of new characters that are necessary to stay on the front edge of the game, means that top guilds are constantly vetting their members to ensure they are keeping up with their wallet or removing them from the guild and finding a new person who will keep up.[39]

The rewards and expectations for group play distinguish *SWGoH* from *Hearthstone*. The communal pressure changes the game and encourages players to agglomerate in like groups.

When the heavy spenders get together, this can also warp their perspective, since they can directly see the need to keep up with their guildmates, rationalizing their growing spending to keep up.[40] However, the game also enables ways for players to work together to minimize their spending, through collusion and shared information, similar to the basic *Hearthstone* decks that are offered online for new players to get into the game.

Not Quite a Loot Box

It is notable that, in both player communities, there is far less concern about random rewards than in discussions surrounding *Star Wars Battlefront II*. Even though purchases are often blind and generally game-altering, collectible-card games warrant a style of monetization that can fit within player expectations while violating the norms established in other video games. As Cecilia D'Anastasio's review of *Magic: The Gathering Arena* observes, the pricing of the digital version of the card game is not likely to be a problem for "people who play a lot of *Magic*. Cards were the original loot boxes. Microtransactions come with the territory."[41] Video game norms about the investment of time and money can be flexible and inconsistent, as *Call of Duty* is in the midst of a multi-year partnership where players who buy Doritos and Mountain Dew can get in-game advantages for their out-of-game consumption.[42] However, the difference between *Hearthstone* and *SWGoH* shows how it is necessary to adhere to the central tenets of core gamers to get attention as a revolution for mobile, free-to-play gaming.

The norms surrounding games are tricky things, and violating them holds the risk of provoking backlash. Blizzard and *Hearthstone* worked around that by emphasizing the role of skill, while *SWGoH* adheres to some norms, but the movement into pay-to-win design means that the game does not get the same kind of broad praise. However, fitting norms is not just about game design, it is also about the content of the game itself. Some games get a pass, probably including *SWGoH*, because they are themed around intellectual properties and franchises that are beloved by a core gamer audience. The best way to see some of those differences is to look at a franchise full of mobile, free-to-play games: the Marvel comic book universe.

7   Marvel Does It All

Perhaps the most pervasive licensed property in mobile, free-to-play gaming, Marvel games abound with all kinds of forms and features. There are Marvel versions of match-three games (*Marvel Puzzle Quest*), aquarium-style building games (*Marvel Avengers Academy*), collectible-card-style games that mirror *Star Wars: Galaxy of Heroes* (*Marvel Strike Force*), fighting games (*Marvel Contest of Champions*), and action role-playing game hybrids (*Marvel Future Fight*), among others. Marvel licenses abound, likely in part because the games are so well suited for free-to-play design. A Marvel game guarantees a certain amount of attention for players and press, while ensuring the game can draw from an enormous universe of potential heroes and villains. In an ecosphere where releasing new characters is a key route to an advantage-style monetization of the game, a Marvel game can launch with a handful of characters and then regularly add more, likely always having another fan favorite or two that can be added to the game later to drum up attention and stimulate spending.

The majority of the book up to this point has focused on how certain norms are tied to the design mechanics and approach of the game, generally featuring comparisons between a game that is widely praised against one that is not. The point of this chapter is somewhat different, as my argument here is that the theming of a game, independent of the mechanics, is one of the norms surrounding games that frame how it is received. In the case of theming, fitting in with the dominant press, development, and discussion around games requires being about something that the core audience for games already appreciates. This is likely part of the reason why there are so many fantasy- and space-themed games, but it also fuels the nostalgic appreciation and buzz for a game like *Pokémon Go*. Marvel comics are at the core of the experience of many people, and there is a particularly large overlap between the kinds of people who play video games and the types of people who read comic books. However, investigating the role of theming in the norms of games requires thinking more deeply about the implications of how a Marvel license impacts a game and perceptions about its monetization structure. Unlike the game mechanics, which may be relatively neutral, theming choices of games are often tied up in issues about gender and expectations of preference. More directly, the popularity and centrality of a Marvel license reinscribes games as boy things. Looking at overwhelmingly similar styles of games and mechanics puts the focus on what is left—the license and theming—while coverage of games generally plays out in favor of the preferences that are more likely to be core to the experience of boys and men.

Matching-Three

One of the most dominant genres of games on early mobile devices were match-three variants. Easy to render graphically and easy to play, match-three games do not require much processing power and are not really restricted by the touch interface of a mobile phone. Following in the wake of the massively popular *Bejeweled*, PopCap's 2001 browser-based game, mobile match-three games widely adopt a free-to-play format, typically charging for the ability to get additional tries at completing a puzzle or chances to stock up on powerful items that can help solve a tricky challenge. The format is massively successful in the free-to-play mobile gaming space, with juggernaut *Candy Crush Saga*, which started as a Facebook game, at or near the top of the highest-grossing mobile app charts since its release in 2012, while it sports almost a billion dollars a year in revenue and almost three billion downloads.[1] (figure 7.1) Match-three games are typically based on moving colored symbols around a game board in order to match like symbols, and, when successful, the game explodes in colors and dynamic animation. The game is divided into stages, where each represents a new puzzle and challenge for players. Matching more than three tiles together generally results in some sort of bonus tile on the board, enabling players to clear the board of obstacles more quickly. Stages may introduce novel challenges, like blocks that cannot be removed or a board layout that requires substantial planning to clear all the required elements. Games can be played to a certain point value or a number of times, matching a certain color or any other challenge a game designer can dream up.

The match-three genre has seen innovation and change, with games like *Puzzles & Dragons*, *Empires & Puzzles: RPG Quest*, and *Legends of Solgard* taking the basic aspects of a match-three approach and adding role-playing game elements. These games generally blend in elements of base-building games, where players harvest resources, and characters that can be powered up, which makes matching a certain color more powerful than

Figure 7.1
An early board in *Candy Crush Saga*.

others. Adding in additional elements potentially draws a different player base and offers the opportunity to add depth to compel more play, while adding additional avenues for monetization, like selling packs of more powerful characters to use. However, these twists on match-three still have great difficulty in cracking the top of the games revenue charts, with traditional match-three games *Candy Crush Saga* and *Candy Crush Soda Saga* taking the top two spots on the game revenue charts in 2017, grossing almost $4 million a day between them.[2]

Marvel entered the match-three space in late 2013 by adapting an older game, *Puzzle Quest*, with Marvel characters. *Puzzle Quest: Challenge of the Warlords* was a 2007 release that took the match-three gameplay of *Bejeweled* and translated it into a fantasy role-playing game setting. Players pick character classes and go out on battles, using their ability to match tiles to defeat their enemies. *Marvel Puzzle Quest* uses a similar format, replacing the fantasy setting with the Marvel universe and changing the generic fantasy characters into Marvel heroes and villains. The game also made a key shift in monetization, as the original version of *Puzzle Quest* was a premium title that was available on all kinds of operating systems, notably PCs and gaming consoles. *Marvel Puzzle Quest* takes a free-to-play approach. The game debuted on mobile devices and was later ported to PCs and consoles.[3] The game has a handful of modes, with a central story mode surrounded by a player-versus-player arena, where you battle against computer-controlled versions of other people's teams. Events drive ongoing competition among players, and rewards are doled out based on both a player's individual efforts and those of their chosen alliance, which is the *Marvel Puzzle Quest* version of a guild or clan.

The trick that makes a *Puzzle Quest* match-three different than something like *Candy Crush Saga* is that, instead of trying to solve discrete puzzles, the primary goal of *Marvel Puzzle Quest* is more about building a strong team of characters to use to defeat opponents. Players are able to pick a group of three characters, like Iron Man, Black Widow, Spiderman, Thanos, or any of their variants (figure 7.2). Characters come in star levels with different relative power, with the most exclusive five-star characters far harder to gather than the plentiful, and much weaker, one-star characters. Collecting multiple covers of a character lets players add to a character's power, eventually with the option of gathering 13 covers to maximize their strength. Revenue comes from a variety of streams and is based on an advantage-spending model. The most direct spending comes from players buying chests to try to get covers of new characters. Players also need to gather ISO 8, which is generally hailed as a wonder material in the Marvel universe, in order to level their characters up so that they have more health and do more damage when tiles are matched. There are regular chests that are always available and special themed chests dedicated to particular events. Beyond paying for new characters or more powers for characters that have already been unlocked, players can purchase boosts, which give them a head start in their next battle. However, what may be the most ingenious pressure point in the game is that players can only have a limited number of characters at a time. If players want to hold on to more characters, they can pay some of the premium currency—hero points—to expand their number of roster slots. Eventually, roster slots cost about $5–10 to unlock, making them a prime area for revenue generation, since each time a player gets a rare character they are forced to make a decision: will I get enough covers of this character to make it worthwhile to keep

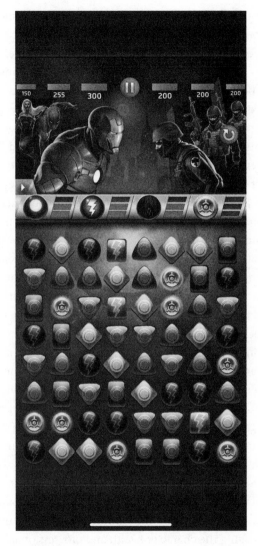

Figure 7.2

An early *Marvel Puzzle Quest* battle where I'm using Iron Man, Spider Man, and Storm.

them? Should I pay for another roster spot or sell someone off the bottom of my roster? This pressure often makes it reasonable to consider selling a newly obtained, rare cover because, without multiple covers, the character may not be worth keeping.

Gameplay typically hinges on a team of three player-controlled characters battling against a group of computer-controlled characters. Players match tiles and do damage to their opponents based on the color of the tile matched and the relative power of their character. Matching tiles also allows a player to collect them, and, when they gather enough, they can be spent on powerful abilities that can damage opponents or heal allies. Some characters also have passive abilities, enabling them to do things like steal tiles from the other team or otherwise manipulate the game board. When player-controlled characters suffer damage, players must either wait for them to heal, use a health pack to immediately heal them, or fight with them again in battle, taking the risk they will be defeated. If player characters are defeated, there is a lengthy wait time before they can be used again.

The game is notable for a variety of reasons, but one of the most interesting is how reviewers for traditional gaming publications quickly took to the game. On IGN, Rowan Kaiser wrote that the game takes "the idea of a puzzle game with a strategic/ role-playing element overlay" and turns "it into an intricately crafted, remarkably deep experience."[4] Kaiser believes the game lives up to the reputation of previous *Puzzle Quest* titles, noting that what the "interlocking mechanics add up to is a game that's compelling at each level. Fighting other players, advancing the plot, managing the character health and progression all happen at once, and all mean that there are constant challenges and goals to work toward. *Marvel Puzzle Quest* doesn't merely meet the expectations of its name, it exceeds them."[5] TouchArcade was slightly more moderated in Joseph Leray's review, but still held the game out as an exception to other, similar match-three titles. Arguing that as long as players bought into the central gameplay of *Puzzle Quest*, "perhaps surprisingly," the game is "more robust than its fan service or freemium boondoggles would suggest, packing in enough content and new ideas to keep devotees matching jewels until the inevitable heat death of the Marvel universe."[6] Brad Gallaway's review of the game for GameCritics.com goes out of its way to begin by noting how "it's been quite a while since I found an iOS title that kept my attention for more than five minutes," but builds into a full-throated defense of the game.[7] It closes with high praise:

> As of today, I've probably spent at least fifty or sixty hours on *Marvel Puzzle Quest*, and I'm still hungry for more. It's exactly the sort of game I want on my phone—deep enough to keep my attention, but small enough to shut off at a moment's notice. The use of Marvel characters is great, and the core idea of connecting special abilities to matching crystals is just as good now as it was back in the original *Puzzle Quest: Challenge of the Warlords.*[8]

PC-focused site Rock Paper Shotgun took up the mantle when the game came out for PCs, titling Ben Barrett's review "*Marvel Puzzle Quest*: No, Really, It's Good" and framing the article around a defense of the games structure. The review makes light of free-to-play, beginning

> No, don't run screaming from the jaw of free-to-play tie-ins, they're your friends! Okay, that's a lie, but *Marvel Puzzle Quest* is different. It's almost exactly what it says on the genetically-modified tin: a take on the classic match-3 formula with Marvel's endless stream of heroes, villains and miscellaneous others injected for framing and plot. By all rights, mathematics and universal laws it should be at best a cash-grab and at worst a soulless husk of un-fun. Somehow, it's neither.[9]

The review goes forward to praise the game as more than could possibly be expected of the genre, largely because of the Marvel license and role-playing elements.

The Kotaku review by Mike Fahey begins with the reviewer discussing how he had dreamt of this game for years, although the free-to-play dynamic is worrisome. He writes, "I wanted Marvel Comics characters facing off against Marvel Comics villains in match puzzle-based combat, with special gem-affecting powers for each individual character. I got that, and it's even team-based—I imagined picking a character and sticking with it. So far, better than I'd hoped."[10] Fahey talks about all the reasons why he likes the game—the depth, the playstyle, the Marvel theming—and acknowledges, "it's more than I hoped for. It's also a little less."[11] The primary drawback for Fahey is the monetization model, as he "imagined a game where players could eventually unlock an entire roster of Marvel characters simply through besting enemies in puzzle combat. I've almost got that, but there's also the ability to purchase additional resources to randomly acquire rare characters or upgrade the ones I already possess."[12] And, as player-versus-player elements are integrated into the game, Fahey worries that "the idea that players can spend money to strengthen their characters stinks a little. The shadow of pay-to-win is hovering closely."[13] He closes with a dream that he could simply pay $60 for the game, as he would rather do that than play a free-to-play version where paying money confers advantages within the game. His review is by far the most focused on the monetization structure, but it is largely framed as a lament rather than an objection to the game in the first place. He enjoys the game, it is something he has dreamed about for years, and the payment structure is the one sore spot. I suspect his longing for this game also prompts some internal conflict from the fact that he likes the game and is getting something from it, even though it is free-to-play.

Marvel Puzzle Quest is a game that provokes dissonance, as it targets the kinds of people who like games and Marvel comics, but it does so with a payment structure they are predisposed against. Free-to-play violates their norms and values about how a game should work, pushing them to defend the game with humor, as in the case of Rock, Paper, Shotgun, or talking about how the game is an exception to all those other games, or focusing on how this is one of the few true games worthy of hours of play on the App Store, or loving and loathing the game at the same time. Simply examining the initial reaction to *Marvel Puzzle Quest* points to some of the norms and expectations around games and how free-to-play sits outside of a core video game belief in how payment structures should work, but comparing it to the coverage of *Candy Crush Saga* gives additional perspective.

Candy Crush Saga is arguably the single biggest free-to-play video game in the history of mobile gaming, with the success of the game fueling a $5.9 billion acquisition of their parent company King Digital by video game industry giant Activision Blizzard.[14] *Candy Crush Saga* is a really big deal, as it is consistently at the top of the revenue charts for both Apple and Google, but the game and those that have followed it are largely uncovered in the press that praises core games and dabbles in stories about *Marvel Puzzle Quest*. On IGN, coverage of *Candy Crush Saga* focuses on news and business reporting about the game, mainly regarding how much money it makes. The site also ran a series of guides for the early levels of the game, ostensibly to pick up traffic around its release. However, even business reports about the game are framed in a particular way, largely to center core games and marginalize *Candy Crush*. One such example is a report on the wealth of Britain's 1,000 wealthiest people, which notably includes the people who started *Candy Crush Saga* studio King Digital and those who created the *Grand Theft Auto* franchise. The article breaks down the game-focused individuals on the list and closes with, "while there are naturally a range of other factors, including licensing, the nature of business and the like, it should give you some idea of the volatility of the games industry that the gentlemen responsible for the *Grand Theft Auto*, *Red Dead Redemption*, and *Max Payne* franchises can be financially surpassed by astute mobile game creators."[15] The framing to this kind of article is rather odd, but the whole piece implicitly expresses regret about what the game industry has come to when the people who create a free-to-play mobile game are worth more than those who create beloved premium worlds. *Candy Crush* is a signal of a "volatile" world, one that those who read IGN may not find all that familiar or comforting.

Kotaku takes a similar tack, as the articles about *Candy Crush* or King focus mostly on business aspects of the game or the other parts of culture involved. A short-lived television show gets a couple of articles, one of which is a preview that notes: "Trying to imagine what that [the show] will look like is likely much more amusing than the actual show will wind up being. So sticky."[16] Another article discusses the tie-ins between the show and host Mario Lopez and the games, in an effort at corporate synergy.[17] Finally, there is a lengthy preview of *Bejeweled Stars* titled "*Bejeweled* Is So Over *Candy Crush Saga's* Bullshit." The game reminisces over the dominance of *Bejeweled*, pointing out that it was simple and compelling and a big enough deal that it was integrated into *World of Warcraft* through an add-on. The new version takes lessons from *Candy Crush*, integrating levels and a general theme with the conclusion that "the whole affair [*Bejeweled Stars*] feels like a deeper, more refined version of the game the competition has been pumping out in slightly modified form over the past several years. The puzzles are more challenging and rewarding. The extraneous bits are more entertaining and worthwhile."[18] Even in a recap of an overly similar free-to-play game, Kotaku chooses to attack *Candy Crush* and praise almost anything else. Despite that praise from Kotaku, *Bejeweled Stars* never caught on, and *Candy Crush* continued its dominant run.

Rock Paper Shotgun also focuses on business news about King rather than on *Candy Crush Saga* as a game. That makes some sense, as the site is mostly focused on PC-based games rather than mobile, but the tone of the writing is notable. All but one of the articles on the site that are tagged with *Candy Crush Saga* are about legal actions by King, specifically their attempts to trademark the term "candy" or their actions against the PC game *The Banner Saga*.[19] From my perspective, the most interesting article is one that makes suggestions about games to play that are similar to *Candy Crush Saga*, but are not King Digital properties. Beginning with a quick refresher on the business sins of the company, John Walker writes:

> Bearing all this in mind, it would seem rather nice if an enormous number of people were to stop playing their games, if you ask me. But of course, a lot of *CCS* [*Candy Crush Saga*] players aren't going to be RPS [Rock Paper Shotgun] readers, but rather your mum or dad, cousin, colleague or friend, and maybe they'd be less keen to play if they knew who made it. Maybe you are too. So, with this in mind, below are my suggestions for games to play instead.[20]

Walker splices out types of players, as those folks who play *Candy Crush* are not the ones reading his article, they are something else, someone different. Those that read Rock Paper Shotgun know these people, but they are not core video gamers and simply will not know enough, without being educated, to skip

Figure 7.3
A match in *Candy Crush Soda Saga* setting off a Soda Crush.

over King's game in protest. The article breaks down a number of match-three games, with their relative strengths and weaknesses, as well as how people can find them. Throughout the essay, Walker focuses on promoting pay-once titles while relegating anything with in-app purchases downward. Representative of this sentiment is his note about *Triple Town*: "It's F2P with what were awkward IAPs [in-app purchases] to keep playing, but you can now put down $4 and play the whole game unlimited." *Candy Crush* is an affront, because the company that made it does not behave in a proper way legally, overstretching their rights and behaving like an aggressive business, not a benevolent game company. Furthermore, the payment structure of the game is offensive, particularly when there are so many other games that can be purchased and played over and over again, even though many people play *Candy Crush Saga* for free.

The one place *Candy Crush* does get some credit is on review sites that focus on mobile games. TouchArcade praises King games for their polish and clear monetization structure, concluding their highly positive review of follow-up game *Candy Crush Soda Saga* with:

> Like all things that are popular, it's inevitable that *Candy Crush Soda Saga* will have its fair share of very, very vocal detractors. It's an easy game to dismiss as "just another match three," much like the original. Hell, I even did that with *Candy Crush Saga*, as the initial out of the proverbial box experience isn't all that different from any other matching game. If this sounds like you, I seriously suggest giving *Soda Saga* a fair shake as it's an incredibly good game. Once you give it a chance to grab you, it won't let go.[21]

Pay-to-win may still be an issue for reviewers on TouchArcade, but free-to-play games are frequently discussed on the site and are well within the norms of what is considered acceptable.

Mobile games are not just normal on TouchArcade, they are central to the site, the focus of all the games that are covered. Touch-Arcade's positive review indicates how shifting the focus from PC- and console-oriented sites to mobile-oriented sites changes norms and expectations, opening space for a follow-up to *Candy Crush* to get legitimate attention and praise. However, the review on Pocket Gamer, another mobile-focused site that targets traditional gamers, shows the limits of that approach, expressing significant concerns about monetization in the game. Timers and limited lives are framed as a restriction on possible enjoyment, as players must pay, or wait. In sum, "*Candy Crush Saga's* a sweet treat in some ways then, but one with a disappointingly bitter aftertaste."[22] The game is provocative because of its size, scope, and power in the industry. It is a lighter game, aimed at a different group than those who have encyclopedic knowledge of games and love rich, deep role-playing systems like what can be found in *Marvel Puzzle Quest*. Moving away from these sites and to other places where *Candy Crush* is discussed offers additional perspective.

Gamezebo focuses on mobile gaming, typically with a tilt away from core gamers and toward a broader audience. The site actually reviewed the game when it was still only on Facebook, giving it a really strong review and only limited criticism. The review begins by praising King, then known as King.com, for producing high-quality games that would generally otherwise be premium PC titles yet letting players play for no upfront cost. *Candy Crush Saga* is hailed as a splendid rendition of a match-three game executed in a strategic, tactical gameplay where players can plot their moves and how they can accomplish their goals. The increasing challenge of the levels is emphasized, since players are forced to plan their moves out and maximize their outcomes; as the reviewer puts it, players are not just "simply looking for matches, *Candy Crush Saga* is all about looking for *the right* matches."[23] The review contends that the game is monetized in a player-friendly way, claiming that it "might be the least aggressive game I've come across on Facebook in terms of asking you for money."[24] The only real complaint is the hint system, which the reviewer finds a bit too helpful and active in a strategic game that is about picking the right move. In sum, "*Candy Crush Saga* wows us with what it accomplishes. The puzzles are challenging and plentiful, the microtransactions are unobtrusive, and the presentation is top notch. If you're a fan of a good match-3 puzzler—whether you typically play Facebook games or not—*Candy Crush Saga* should be the next game on your playlist."[25] This alternate perspective on *Candy Crush Saga* is largely about norms and what is expected. Gamezebo is comparing the game to other match-three and Facebook games, while other sites are viewing it in light of the games they tend to focus on and the communities for whom they typically write. What is considered normal hinges on what other things are being examined. And, in the case of core game websites and forums, there is precious little room for a free-to-play match-three game that is largely played by folks who would rarely touch a traditional PC or console game.

Another interesting review of the game comes from Common Sense Media, a nonprofit that bills itself as helping families make smart decisions about media. I generally find the site to lean toward a conservative perspective, and it provides an interesting touch point in thinking about games and how they are received by an audience that is well outside sites like Kotaku, IGN, or Rock Paper Shotgun. Common Sense Media has reviewed a variety of *Candy Crush* versions, from the original Facebook game, to the app, to *Candy Crush Soda Saga*, and all of the games are taken seriously on their merits.[26] Reviews of the free-to-play mobile apps have concerns about monetization and the pushiness of the free-to-play elements of the game, but the games are consistently given four out of five stars and referred to as "incredibly fun and engaging, bringing enough of a new twist to the match-three genre to stand out from the crowd."[27] The games are treated as worthy of play and discussion, with reviews framed toward parents who may be concerned about their child's media use.

The vast difference in how *Marvel Puzzle Quest* and *Candy Crush Saga* are treated by core game review sites is indicative of the norms of the video game playing community. *Marvel Puzzle Quest* is taken more seriously, in part because it has role-playing game elements, but also because it is about the kind of theming and universe that Kotaku writer Mike Fahey would spend six years dreaming about. Part of the norms around play are about payment, play structure, and design, but they are also about a game's overall theme. A similar match-three concept is taken more seriously if it is about Marvel comics superheroes and villains than if it is about candy. Or, in the case of match-three game *Gardenscapes*, being a butler at a mansion that is in desperate need of upkeep. These games are created with content outside of the experience of core gamers and for an audience that is fundamentally different than those who self-identify as gamers. The target audience for these games does not spend time reading and writing reviews of video games. The norms of that community are set by those in it, and they self-perpetuate, putting a game like *Marvel Puzzle Quest* clearly in the center of what could be acceptable and shoving *Candy Crush Saga* into a marginal space where it is deemed abnormal. *Candy Crush Saga* becomes the kind of game that is a curiosity only because it is played by so many people, people who are so strikingly different than those who are setting the norms and expectations about what games should be like. The bias about free-to-play is not just about payment structure or game design, it is also about theming and what a game is putatively about.

High Schools and Theme Parks

Another like-for-like comparison of a Marvel game is between *Marvel Avengers Academy* and *Disney Magic Kingdoms*. Both games are roughly aquarium simulators or, in the most charitable framing, city-building games. In *Marvel Avengers Academy*, players are tasked with remaking a Marvel-themed high school environment, constructing key buildings and executing events to unlock new characters. All of the events and buildings are on timers to gate play and keep players coming back. *Disney Magic Kingdoms* is an overwhelmingly similar game, released about a month later and tasking players with creating their dream theme park and overcoming curses and darkness laid out by classic Disney villain Maleficent.[28] The two games share a whole lot in common in their design, parent licensing company, and execution, but the reception and communities for the games are quite different, indicating a core difference in how certain norms of play are accepted and the role that theming plays in what is considered an appropriate game.

Marvel Avengers Academy is developed and published by TinyCo and is designed to give players the experience of setting up their own training academy for Marvel characters. The game bills itself as a chance for players to "customize your dream campus, unlock your favorite heroes and villains, navigate their social lives, and go on epic missions."[29] In practice, the game plays

154   Chapter 7

Figure 7.4
A growing campus in *Marvel Avengers Academy*.

out in a slightly different and less grandiose fashion (figure 7.4).
The game was originally predicated on a series of timers, where
heroes could use various buildings on the game's campus in order
to generate items. The primary point of the game, initially, was
to consistently keep your heroes busy, as each task would take
a certain amount of time and then turn around and use them
again. This system rewarded players with a larger stable of heroes
and buildings, as they are simply able to do more. Each task gave
a reward, which were typically used to unlock more buildings
and characters. Completing quests gave players access to more
materials, coins, and experience points, all of which help players
progress through the game. *Marvel Avengers Academy* also used
a number of limited time events primarily aimed at unlocking

new characters to put players in a position where they had a consistent reason to come back to the game and play actively. Developer TinyCo eventually added combat to the game, in which players took their characters into battle, then massively revamped the combat system on the second anniversary of the game.[30] The addition of combat pulls the game slightly out of the aquarium-game genre and pushes it a bit more toward many other Marvel games.

The attention granted to the game was substantial. Core game journalism sites covered the release, with TouchArcade writing "I've been spending a lot of time with TinyCo's *Marvel Avengers Academy* recently. What can I say? I have a documented weakness for Marvel fan-service, and this app really packs it in nicely."[31] The article then delves into a guide on how to best put together a team in the game, encouraging players to actively send their characters out on missions and focus on completing the most valuable story missions. *Paste Magazine* covered the launch party, complete with Kiernan Shipka, of *Mad Men* fame, as she voices Spider-Woman in the game. The party was full of celebrities, as it tried to portray what Marvel executives said would make the game different from other offerings—the social life and relationships.[32] The story quoted one attendee, Blake Anderson of *Workaholics*, saying "Usually anytime I get an email with something that says Marvel in it I check it out. I like superhero stuff." Anderson continued, noting that he liked the recently released *Deadpool* game because "it was cool. It was violent. I always like when Marvel takes the gloves off and gets nasty."[33] The quote is immediately followed by the observation, "there's nothing nasty about *Avengers Academy*. It's cute, amiable and meant for everybody."[34] And this is the interesting space in which the game gets credit with a certain kind of audience who will pursue anything Marvel, an audience that has a tremendous amount of overlap with those who get to decide what gets covered in game-related publications.

One way to see how this works out in practice is to simply look at the reviews of the game that followed its launch. Reviews of *Marvel Avengers Academy* follow a structure much like any other, breaking down what the game is about and how it works. However, for this game, there is an exceptional amount of attention on the integration of the Marvel license and how it plays out in the game. In a review for a site like Comics Alliance, it makes sense for there to be a deep digression on how this version of the Marvel characters fits within the broader Marvel universe, but it is striking how similar themes emerge in reviews as sites putatively focused on video games. The focus on the characters and the storyline is the first tell of how important the narrative is in this game and how its license helps it elude some of the troublesome criticism about free-to-play games.

Android Central took the time to review the game twice, first with a breakdown of the game and then with a follow-up 30 days later. The initial review begins by talking about the omnipresence of all things Marvel in pop culture, stating, "if you can't get enough Marvel into your day, or you've always dreamt of a world in which you could see all your favorite heroes as they went through high school then *Marvel: Avengers Academy* might just be the game for you."[35] The review explains how the academy is structured and how players can build it out as well as the various students you can recruit and how you can use and upgrade them, and includes a discussion of the bulletin board that drives questing in the game. It emphasizes how there is a lot of waiting in the game, in which players send characters off on activities and come back later to send them on another activity.

There is a clear explanation of how the game can be played without spending any money but that spending money will speed the game up and allow access to content that must be bought with premium currency. In sum, the review closes with advice for readers to check it out, "provided that you enjoy the type of game that *Marvel: Avengers Academy* is. It's done well, it's absolutely adorable, and really who doesn't want to guide the Avengers through school as high school students? For anyone who enjoys base building style games, or the Avengers, this game is plenty of fun."[36] This is ultimately a central conceit of the game: appreciating the Avengers and the Marvel universe is vital to enjoying the game. In integrating the license so tightly into the game, reviews and impressions become a referendum on a core comic property, rather than just a game. The 30-day follow-up to the review dishes out some additional tips and strategies, while discussing how the game has become predicated on limited-time events that drive smaller story arcs in the game and keep pressure on players to check back to unlock beloved characters. The last paragraph of the game continues in a similar line of reasoning as the first review, stating

> *Avengers Academy* has easily become one of the games that I keep playing. I've wandered away for a few days at a time, but I always find myself coming back again. The events continually add new, if temporary, ways to play the game. I'm still miles away from exploring everything the game has to offer, and I'm enjoying watching as the story unfolds. *Marvel Avengers Academy* is a fun twist on a genre of game that I've never enjoyed overmuch, the town builder game. With a story to entice you keep playing, and plenty to do, this is one game I'll be playing for quite a while.[37]

In this opinion, Jen Karner lays bare many of the notable elements that make this particular game different from many others. She feels compelled to play it, even though it is in a genre she does not normally like. There is plenty to do, which keeps drawing her back. But the crucial element in all of this is the story and how it ties the pieces together. This game, in a marginal genre with little broader appreciation, becomes important and worth playing because of its theming and license. Initial resistance to an aquarium-style game, or a town builder, or a sit-and-wait-for-things-to-happen game, or whatever else we seek to call it, is lessened because it is about the Avengers and that, in and of itself, is cool and worthy of time and attention.

The review in Polygon, a website that rarely delves into reviews of free-to-play mobile games, let alone in the aquarium genre, clarifies the special dynamics of *Marvel Avengers Academy*. The beginning of the review notes that the game is effectively a high school alternate universe for Marvel characters that "has a glacial pace and begs me for micro-transaction money at every opportunity. And yet, I've been hooked on it for two weeks."[38] The reviewer, Susana Polo, states that "every review cites the slow pace" of the game and "its insistent push toward spending real money" as the primary issues with the game and, although Polo can't disagree with either objection to the game, she still finds herself "counting the minutes until the timer on my next quest action ends."[39] She argues that the character design of the game is polished and compelling, but it is the story and the depth in characterization of beloved characters that drives her to keep going. She is playing the game to try to solve the mystery of what is going on with "a Very Bad Secret Super Science Multiverse explanation for why all the Avengers are teenagers except for Nick Fury and Hank Pym."[40] Polo breaks down her favorite character interactions and elements of the story, focusing on why she finds it so interesting, which is mostly praise of the game and its execution. She leaves the review with the acknowledgment, "so you've hooked me, *Avengers Academy*. And if you did it with story and character instead of engrossing game mechanics . . . I think I'm OK with that."[41] This closure is an acknowledgment that the interesting piece of *Marvel Avengers Academy* is not the game, it is the world and the storytelling occurring within it. However, it is still treated like a game worthy of attention, because, although it does not conform to expectations about how a game should be made compelling, its subject matter is sufficiently interesting to overcome violations of accepted norms.

Other reviews are less complementary than Karner or Polo, but they still land in much the same place. Writing for Comics Alliance, Luke Brown bashes the pace and the monetization of the game, largely holding on to traditional norms about video games. He laments that "there's no real way to experience all that *Avengers Academy* has to offer in a short-term situation without opening your wallet," which props up the central notion that games should be bought once and played to their completion.[42] He ultimately finishes with:

> It's almost a shame that this particular incarnation of the Avengers is trapped away in this mobile game, as there's certainly enough mileage here to get a comic story or animated feature out of this world. TinyCo and Marvel have done a nice job developing *Avengers Academy* for this platform though, and the continually expanding Marvel mobile games library shows that Marvel doesn't necessarily need to focus on consoles to provide interesting and worthwhile gaming experiences.[43]

The lament of mobile is a continuation of the aspersions cast on free-to-play and mobile games, but it is immediately chased by the celebration of the depth and interest in a new Marvel property, one that should be expanded and engaged more thoroughly because Avengers in high school has so much potential.

The Gamezebo review is similar, praising the narrative depth, character development, and overall polish of the game and noting: "Even if the 'play it for a few minutes and set it aside' nature of *Marvel Avengers Academy* doesn't speak to you, there's a good chance that the characters and story will."[44] The praise for the game focuses on how players should engage a game like this, one that takes a beloved franchise in an interesting new direction. Even a review for Pocket Gamer, which blasts the game for actions that "take a ridiculous length of time and cost an extortionate amount of gems to speed up," resulting "in a game that takes about 30 seconds of your time every few hours to set your heroes on a task and then turn it off because there's nothing else to do," holds out some praise for the game.[45] For Chris James, "If you seriously love Marvel, have a high tolerance for free to play, and have the patience of a saint you may just get a kick out of *Marvel Avengers Academy*."[46] He does not find as much joy in the high school setting, seeing it as irritating and annoying, rather than a fresh new twist on established characters, but even in the most hostile review of the game that I could find, he singles out the narrative and license as a reason to play the game.

Although I find the reviews of *Marvel Avengers Alliance* quite compelling when it comes to considerations of what can give a game permission to violate establish norms in gaming, looking at a similar game provides additional room for reflection. About two months after *Avengers Academy* was released by TinyCo, Gameloft released *Disney Magic Kingdoms*. The games are overwhelmingly similar, with characters and buildings to unlock, quests to complete, time to wait, and the opportunity to spend money to speed it all up. The twist on *Disney Magic Kingdoms* is that players are tasked with building their own dream theme park, complete with classic Disney rides and characters, while trying to undo the destructive curse Disney villain Maleficent put on their park (figure 7.5). Some of the discussion of the game explicitly compares the two games, as the central mechanic of both is leveling up characters so they can do more activities in the theme park (or high school) you are building. In addition, discussion of *Disney Magic Kingdoms* mirrors some of what marked discourse around *Marvel Avengers Academy*. Both games are slow but well polished, with compelling graphics and elements of nostalgia. However, they tap into different fan bases, as *Disney Magic Kingdoms* eschews comic books for Disney parks and the Disney universe. However, *Disney Magic Kingdoms* did not benefit from the same sort of broad review by traditional outlets. It never landed on Polygon, and, although several publications covered both games, they typically did so in a different way.

Eric Ford wrote a number of pieces about *Disney Magic Kingdoms* for TouchArcade, but almost all of them were brief updates to the events that were running in the game.[47] In each of his short updates, he makes note of how he is enjoying the game,

Figure 7.5
A developing theme park in *Disney Magic Kingdoms*.

but the posts are quite thin, with a couple of pictures of the new content and a scanty paragraph or two designed to provide the most basic amount of information. Posts also stop after an early December 2016 post about a new event based on the hit Disney movie *Frozen*, presumably because Ford stopped playing the game and there was no one interested in picking up the baton.[48] In his one extended piece on the game, Ford writes a classic TouchArcade piece: a guide for playing the game without spending money on it. Ford provides a basic breakdown of the game, encouraging players to emphasize development of their characters and focus their efforts to get the greatest result with limited resources.[49] However, the post never proceeds past a surface-level engagement; all of the advice is straightforward and there is no larger argument about why the game should be played. Instead of finishing with a call to download the game and start playing, Ford ends with a warning about how much of the game is "locked behind the premium currency, but there's still a significant amount of content that can be easily played without IAP [in-app purchases]."[50] Gamezebo also goes into less depth than they did for *Marvel Avengers Academy*, spending a couple of paragraphs nailing down the genre of the game and then proceeding to give a brief overview of how this particular game plays. The overall graphics and audio are singled out for praise, while the rides and attractions are criticized for their limited initial appearance. Ultimately, the game is described as claustrophobic, with limited room for play or engagement by new players. The review leaves the game for a specific group of players, as "if you're a big enough Disney geek, this [the limited space] won't bother you much, as playing *Disney Magic Kingdoms* long enough really does seem like it will open up the promise of building 'your own' Disney Park. Just know that it's going to take some effort to get to that point, and it'll be a very small world in the meantime." Again, Gamezebo stops before recommending players try the game. Unlike in the case of *Marvel Avengers Academy*, where all readers are presumed to be fans of Marvel, "Disney geeks" are a special breed, separate and distinct from those who typically play video games.

Pocket Gamer's review of *Disney Magic Kingdoms* singles it out for the same kind of harsh criticism that *Marvel Avengers Academy* got, but, like in the reviews above, the criticism of the game about Disney is treated somewhat differently. Both games are blasted for their long timers, lack of traditional gameplay, and aggressive monetization, while they are praised for their aesthetic elements. However, the specific mechanics of activities in *Disney Magic Kingdoms* and overarching design are singled out for criticism for their lack of fidelity with reality. As reviewer Ray Willmott puts it, he cannot let his criticism of the pace of *Disney Magic Kingdoms* go, because

> when the game tells me Goofy is going to take 4 hours to change a lightbulb, the boundaries of my leniency really get tested, irrespective for how true it may be. *Disney Magic Kingdoms* isn't particularly generous either. You spend most of your time collecting stars and potions to increase your overall park level, but when most of the attractions have to be paid for with rarely dispensed gems [the premium currency], that grind starts to feel a bit superfluous.[51]

The monetization process and overarching delays are the primary reasons to reject the game, since, for those who "don't want to spend," the game presents "an exploitative system that manages to ruin a sometimes very good game."[52] There is no comeback at the end to praise how the game could be interesting to Marvel or Disney fans or to try to find the common ground for those who might play this game. Much like the reviews for TouchArcade and Gamezebo, *Disney Magic Kingdoms* is treated as an oddity, a game that is getting covered, but an aberration, something different and outside of the norms of proper games.

The one place where *Disney Magic Kingdoms* was treated as more than an oddity was on sites that cater to Disney fans. Unlike Comics Alliance, whose review of *Marvel Avengers Academy* was overwhelmingly similar to those found on video game sites, the reviews of *Disney Magic Kingdoms* on Disney sites read quite differently. Writing for Disney fan site Inside the Magic, Corinne Andersson makes liberal use of Disney terminology, referencing pixie dust in the title of the review and events like D23 Expo, the Disney version of video game conferences like E3 or PAX. Andersson likens the game to theme park simulator *Roller Coaster Tycoon*, instead of parsing the genre of the game and emphasizing the lack of depth and focus on timers. The review focuses on how the game is accessible, something that is easy enough for children to play and compelling enough for adults, as she is "certain that collecting the different attractions, concessions, decorations and even characters are going to turn into an obsession for several Disney fans."[53] The one downside called out in the essay is the monetization structure, but it is described in a fundamentally different way than on video game websites. Andersson writes:

> The free app has numerous avenues built in for you to spend some money, which probably comes as no surprise to anyone. This is not something new in mobile gaming and as per usual, if you, for example, want to acquire an attraction immediately or not be obliged to wait to reach level 2, you need to spend some dollars. But "Disney Magic Kingdoms" does make it easy to avoid by just being patient.[54]

This discussion of monetization is benign, emphasizing that only the impatient would need to spend money. She is viewing this differently than the Pocket Gamer reviewer, who sees the aggressive use of timers as a block to his ability to play the game. Moved out of the context of the norms of traditional video games, Andersson sees the purpose of play in an alternate context, as *Disney Magic Kingdoms* becomes a way for her and fellow Disney fans to have another way to engage one of their passions. The game is praised as "one of the most exciting and advanced mobile games Disney Interactive has released so far" because it is being compared to other Disney games and activities, rather than the broader corpus of video games.[55] The lengthy timers are resituated and reframed, as Andersson sees it "Does waiting for your attraction to build and your characters to finish their quest occasionally become a little old? Yes it does, but it also makes the game last longer."[56] In this light, the primary objection others see to the genre is a praiseworthy element, something to let you keep playing and enjoying the game more than if you could speed through it.

Discussion of the game on the personal blog of Disney fan Jaysen Headley is quite similar, emphasizing that players should be patient and stressing how this game channels his appreciation of Disney in a new direction.[57] Headley's advice is not wildly different than Eric Ford's work for TouchArcade, with two exceptions. First, his post is all praise, singling out all kinds of richness in the game. He encourages players to "take time to appreciate the little things," since "there is some magnificent detail built into this game and a lot of fan service, if you're willing to take the time to look for it."[58] He also encourages players to participate in the community around the game to make it more social and engaging, adding to the story that he loves that his mother "has also become a fan and now posts in the Facebook group we are in even more than I do. It also helps to have a sounding board for any issues you might be having."[59] Headley takes *Disney Magic*

Kingdoms seriously from the beginning, not wondering what genre it is in or about the monetization structure, because he is interested in a Disney experience rather than a video game. His writing is less about how the game is designed in a particular kind of way to violate certain norms of video games and more about how it serves Disney fans.

Although the two games are overwhelmingly similar in design, the reception of them is quite different depending on where one looks. Furthermore, the communities surrounding the game are different, with *Marvel Avengers Academy* players engaging in theory-crafting and other conventional video game attempts at optimization on Reddit, while *Disney Magic Kingdoms* players congregate on Facebook to share advice and click on each other's social requests. After two years, *Disney Magic Kingdoms* continued on much of the same path that it started on, while *Marvel Avengers Academy* leaned in to the drifting direction of emphasizing combat and battles, transforming what was "once little more than a Marvel-themed fishbowl of sorts" into "a much more involved game."[60] In the wake of the changes, the Reddit for the game and the player base dwindled, with one player observing that "this game is a mere shadow of what it once was," and

> I do hope they improve upon this model, if I were TinyCo, I would observe *Disney Magic Kingdoms* and try to move in that direction. The game is both f2p and p2p friendly, with huge area [*sic*], characters walking around, uncomplicated and spaced events that are achievable. And they don't seem to be losing money nor slowing down.[61]

Marvel Avengers Academy tried to lean into the elements of it that are more traditionally game-like, creating a game that risks pushing away those who picked up the game for its story, while being unable to compete with more combat-laden Marvel titles like

Marvel: Contest of Champions and *Marvel Strike Force*. It became a game in between, while *Disney Magic Kingdoms* has continued to push out content to provide fan service for Disney fans looking to build their dream park. In February 2019, *Avengers Academy* shut down, yet *Disney Magic Kingdoms* was still pushing out seasonal content and seeking feedback from its player base months later.

A License Matters

The point of these two examples was to provide space to reflect on how these four overwhelmingly similar games are received differently based on what they are about. For the match-three games, the design of *Marvel Puzzle Quest* is set up to chase the strategy and combat typical of Marvel titles, while *Candy Crush Saga* is bright, colorful, and focused on quick puzzles. In the case of the two aquarium-style games, video game sites give more credence and coverage to Marvel games, regardless of how they are initially designed. The reception to these four games further illustrates the norms of what counts and what gets counted. Marvel games, and other titles and designs that are neatly integrated into video game fan communities, are covered and treated with respect from the beginning, while outliers will stay on the margins.

Free-to-play mobile games also exist in a space beyond just video games. *Candy Crush Saga* became a summer television show and *Disney Magic Kingdoms* is targeted at a Disney fan community. Although this opens up space for those games to be accepted by a broader audience, they are also a counterpoint to the insular community of video games where free-to-play mobile games are disproportionately likely to sit outside the norms of what is acceptable and encouraged.

These games also demonstrate how norms of what is acceptable and what is not reach beyond elements of design or gameplay and into the license, or skin, the game comes with. A Marvel
game, regardless of content or design, fits within the norms of
what is expected and appreciated by the traditional community of video game players. That acceptance and expectation
means that the norms around games are not just about payment
mechanics, design, or mode of play, they are also about what is
getting played. In addition, things that adhere to the community's expectation of how games should work are likely to get a
pass, even if they are heavily monetized free-to-play games.

Conclusion: Where We Dropping Dumbledore?

The central animating premise of this book is that there are biases within communities of video game players, journalists, and scholars that limit how we think about and receive free-to-play and mobile games. Appropriately assessing and critiquing these games starts by assessing them on their own merits so that we can clearly see the issues they present. However, I think that the dynamics of our biases are complicated, as issues with the reception of games are not always about the payment structures of them or about the platform on which they are played. There is far more at work, from the theming of a game to the community of players for whom it is designed, that shapes the reaction to them. One last chance to get perspective on these issues is to look at a pair of quite different free-to-play games that can be played on mobile: *Fortnite* and *Harry Potter: Hogwarts Battle*.

Fortnite became an almost all-consumptive craze in 2018. The game was everywhere, from World Cup final post-goal celebration dances to stories about parents hiring *Fortnite* coaches for their kids or final exams being refocused onto *Fortnite* based on winning a bet with a teacher.[1] Originally designed as a retail shooter game, *Fortnite* was remade into a free-to-play Battle Royale title, and the success of that version of the game quickly outpaced other competition in the genre, like *PlayerUnknown's Battlegrounds*, and displaced the player-versus-environment mode, which was renamed *Fortnite: Save the World*. Battle royale games are a twist on the conventional shooter genre, with a large number of players—100 in the case of *Fortnite*—dropped in a limited space to fight each other and eventually determine a winner. There are a variety of different modes to the game, with team or individual play, and *Fortnite* is particularly interesting as it adds *Minecraft*-style building elements to let players explore and recreate the world to best suit their needs and try to survive.

Coverage of the game focused on all kinds of things, but rarely questioned *Fortnite's* role in video games. It is accepted as appropriate and interesting in part because it conforms to traditional video game norms, like shooting and building, and also because it became so wildly popular. Monetization in the game conforms to *League of Legends*-style optional spending for cosmetic items, with the addition of seasonal, cosmetic battle passes. Players can buy battle passes each season and, based on their play that season, they can gain a variety of rewards for far less than each item would cost individually. The addition of battle passes gives players some objectives in the game and a chance to earn rewards, which is particularly useful in a genre of game when only 1 in 100 players will actually win.[2] Although battle passes were not a launch feature of *Fortnite: Battle Royale*, they fueled its growth as they garnered revenue for the game, while seeming in line with the accepted norms of video games by establishing an optional spending model. Although somewhat tongue-in-cheek, a Kotaku article claims that battle passes are "so hot right now" because

> pay-to-win games are garbage. Loot boxes are passé. Cosmetics are cute, but not a great incentive to keep playing. Game publishers have cycled through a bevy of monetization gimmicks aimed at keeping

gamers putting cash into their games, some more successful than others. Now, more and more of them seem to be coalescing around a new idea—the 'battle pass.'"[3]

This form of monetization brought developer Epic Games $223 million in March 2018 alone, with a clear route to ongoing revenue for the game, particularly as it continues to spread across platforms like PCs, consoles, and mobile devices.[4] Within months of *Fortnite's* release on iOS devices, it quickly became a top-earning game on the platform, in addition to revenues pouring in from PCs and consoles.[5] The game garnered enough money and attention that when it came time to release it for Android devices, Epic Games turned down the opportunity to use Google Play, instead requiring players to download the game from their website, which meant Google would not get its cut of any spending.[6] Coverage of *Fortnite* in the games press is always credulous, focusing on the revenue the game is earning, the press the game is attracting, or the player base the game has. *Fortnite* is hailed as a revolution, a key moment in the redefinition of how games can work and what they can be. *Fortnite* draws a broader audience than many games, but its status as a valid, legitimate game is rarely questioned.

Indicative of the coverage of *Fortnite* are details that revel in the business model of the game, as 69 percent of players buy in-game items, with the average spend at $85, according to one analysis.[7] *Fortnite* players, and the battle royale genre more generally, are hailed for their engagement, with breathless praise of the way players are more likely to pay for these games, rather than players of other free-to-play competitive games like *World of Tanks* and *League of Legends*.[8] Battle royale players also spend more time outside the game watching videos and streams and producing content of their own. Although *Fortnite* players are more likely to identify as casual than core gamers, this is held up as a reason for praise, since it indicates "appeal to a larger gamer audience."[9] Instead of being reviled for opting to go with a free-to-play business model, *Fortnite's* success is attributed to its status as a free-to-play game, with one analyst writing, "the biggest contributor to *Fortnite's* growth was its lack of entry price: anyone could drag in any of their buddies to play with only the friction of a download. Having seen this dynamic in both *League of Legends* and *Hearthstone*, it's now clear that following a paid model in core PvP [player vs. player] will at best leave you in second place."[10] *Fortnite* is hailed as something else, proof that a free-to-play business model attracts more players and can also generate truly massive amounts of money. It is the golden combination that fundamentally redefines what games can be.

To this end, *Fortnite* is also hailed as a return for games to mainstream culture. Akin to the arcade games and *Pac-Man* craze that dominated parts of the 1980s. *Fortnite* has a worldwide player base of 125 million, which is roughly equivalent to the worldwide subscriber base for Netflix.[11] Coverage of the game is simply different, with Will Luton writing, "*Fortnite*, however, feels like the first time the wider media is addressing gaming on the same terms it would music, film, TV or the press."[12] *Fortnite* is a big enough deal that it is taken seriously by both the gaming press and the mainstream press in an effort to describe the phenomenon it has become, largely because it has embraced both free-to-play as a business model and mobile gaming as a platform. *Fortnite* is referred to as such a hit that those in the video game industry find "it's hard to go a day without hearing about *Fortnite* anymore."[13] The game breaks records for viewing, setting new standards for cultural consumption of a video game, with one article about the game's impact closing with, "every day seems like some new record is being broken by this game, and I'm sure these latest ones won't be the last. Stay tuned."[14] The game is portrayed as something to catch onto, a necessary and vital part of what video games are, even as it is a free-to-play game that quickly moved from PCs and consoles to mobile devices. However, the reception of it is a picture-perfect example demonstrating the norms around video games and what is deemed acceptable.

The first key element in the reception of *Fortnite* is that it follows in the line of accepted free-to-play titles like *League of Legends*, where paying for something in the game is only tied to character customization and cosmetics, not to any game impacting elements. As a deconstruction of the game's financial model optimistically paints it,

> Much like in MOBAs [multiplayer online battle arenas], *Fortnite*'s progression and monetization only come from cosmetics. *Fortnite* is a *"free-to-win"* model: they do not sell anything that could impact the balance of the battle royale gameplay. All guns, armor, ammo is scavenged in the battle royale gameplay, but a player can choose what cosmetics they want to bring into a match.[15]

Epic Games also chose to steer away from the loot boxes that had become so contentious in the wake of *Star Wars Battlefront II*, opting for a combination of season passes that players could buy and a store with a limited number of items that change regularly (figure 8.1). The rotating store places pressure on players to buy the things they want when they see them and to check the store's offerings to see what could be added to their collection. The addition of the battle pass is a key driver of engagement with the game, as players need to play to move through their pass and claim all of its benefits. If players get too far behind, they can spend to catch back up or they can pay additional money from

Figure 8.1
The item shop in *Fortnite*.

the start to get an advantage in unlocking some cool new cosmetic before their friends. Buying a battle pass increases commitment for the season, while giving players goals to pursue as they play (figure 8.2). Even better, in an appeal to core gaming norms, players always know what they are buying if they purchase a battle pass. As one article puts it, "from a player's perspective,

Figure 8.2
The chapter 2, season 1 battle pass in *Fortnite*.

Battle Pass simply feels fair compared to the competitors' gacha systems."[16] *Fortnite* may be free-to-play and it may be on mobile, but that is framed as part of the charm of the game, as it is pushing monetization in what seems to be a player-friendly way. People can play for free, but when they choose to pay, they know exactly what they are getting. *Fortnite's* monetization strategy is discussed as a positive revolution for players, instead of greedy, grubby, or game-impacting, which mollifies any concerns about *Fortnite* being pay-to-win.

Second, the theme and genre of the game matters. *Fortnite* quickly became the biggest game in the newest and hottest genre of core video games: battle royale. At its core, the game blends two key elements of video games together: it is about killing other players and building things. The combination and quick playtime for most means that the game fits well within expectations of what a game "should" be. The earliest video games were often about battle against others, like *SpaceWar!*, or sports, like *Tennis for Two* and *Pong*. Adding in building elements, which draw from offline pursuits like blocks and Legos and video game pursuits like prior smash hit *Minecraft*, makes *Fortnite* a mix of two things that are clearly established as interesting and intriguing for the core audience for video games. *Fortnite* is about video game kinds of things, mashing them up and remixing them in a way that has resounded for millions of players.

Finally, this combination of playing within expected norms and pushing expectations in a new direction gave the game a critical mass where the attention to it snowballed. It got picked up and referenced by celebrities, from rapper Drake to sports stars. The game was well suited for YouTube videos and Twitch streams, building a robust ecosphere of talking about and consuming *Fortnite* outside of playing the game itself. As one of the indicators of how the game took over mainstream culture, prominent player Ninja was the first e-sports athlete to be on the cover of *ESPN: The Magazine*, with a story billing him as the "biggest gamer in the world."[17] *Fortnite* became something bigger, something massive, which meant that any questions about its legitimacy were effectively foreclosed.

On the other hand, *Harry Potter: Hogwarts Mystery* got no such forbearance. Released in April 2018, the game had been previewed on multiple video game sites, with explicit interest in exploring the castle of Hogwarts and the universe created by J. K. Rowling in her *Harry Potter* novels. One such preview broke down the key precepts of the game that were then known, reserving special praise for the integration of the actors from the movies reprising their roles as voice actors in the game. Running three weeks before the game's launch, the article concludes, "the return of these actors is a coup—it's not something many Harry Potter tie-ins can boast. How will the game play, though? We don't have long to find out."[18] When the game came out the reception was deafening, as the design, execution, game play, and, most importantly, the monetization were found to be deeply offensive to the traditional gaming press and the mainstream publications that chose to write about the game.

Harry Potter: Hogwarts Mystery is set shortly after the birth of Harry Potter. Players are asked to create a character that is invited to go to school at Hogwarts, from which your older brother has recently been expelled for breaking school rules. The central narrative and mystery of the game is to try and figure out why he was exploring the cursed vaults of Hogwarts. Players are introduced to some new characters, like your best friend Rowan, and some who featured in the books and movies, like the teachers and staff of Hogwarts, some of the older Weasleys, and Nymphadora

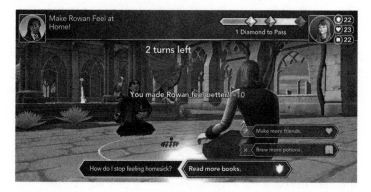

Figure 8.3
Our first character, Ellie Kwong, playing gobstones with Rowan in *Harry Potter: Hogwarts Mystery*.

Tonks. The game play is heavily derived from *Kim Kardashian: Hollywood* and Glu Mobile's line of *Stardom* games, where players are given tasks to complete and click on something until they are out of energy, then they wait for it to refill before continuing on their journey. Energy is spent quite quickly, and players are given the option to pay to refill it immediately. The game is monetized through the sale of crystals, which can be used to purchase cosmetic items, pets, and that all-important energy. The link to *Kim Kardashian: Hollywood* rarely came up in the reviews I read of the game, with only Nick Fernandez's review for Android Authority mentioning the connection, which is notable, since *Kim Kardashian: Hollywood* came out in 2014 and was estimated to still be bringing in millions of dollars a month in revenue four years later.[19] Fernandez even takes a jab at that game, referencing the players as "more than 10 million of you, somewhere."[20] Even those who see the lineage of the game are unwilling to take it seriously. However, reviews of *Hogwarts Mystery* were plentiful and consistent in tone and execution.

The general approach of a review of the game was to begin by professing a deep and abiding appreciation of the Harry Potter universe. Sometimes that story was moved into the body of the piece, and it often came back at the end, but a childhood link to Harry Potter was a frequent framework for discussing the game. In his review for IGN, David Jagneaux gives a paragraph overview of his feelings about the game, and then quickly gives the qualifications for his opinions: "As a lifelong fan of Harry Potter (I was in elementary school when the books debuted and was exactly 11 years old—the same age as Harry—when the first movie came out) all I wanted was a simple game that let me make a character and attend Hogwarts."[21] Sometimes the appreciation for Harry Potter was presented in broader terms, like how Eurogamer.net News Editor Tom Phillips has "been waiting years for a new Harry Potter video game, and the premise of *Hogwarts Mystery* is instantly interesting—a time period so far untouched by the series' lore, a chance to reconnect with well-known characters, and, yes, the simple ability to role-play being at Hogwarts, just like Harry and his pals."[22] For Kotaku, Gita Jackson makes note of her "tattoo of the sign of the Deathly Hallows on my shoulder, so I'm an easy mark for this game. When I saw a Hogwarts acceptance letter with my name on it, signed by Professor McGonagall, I kinda freaked out."[23] However, after situating their deep appreciation for the world of Harry Potter, the reviews quickly take a different tone, slamming the game for its energy system, monetization, and its simple gameplay.

Establishing one's Harry Potter bona fides is a moment where the reviewer proves to their audience that they care about this content, and that they are just looking for the kind of game they have dreamed of. Their status in Harry Potter fandom is a rhetorical shield that protects reviewers when they begin to slam the game, justifying their rage at potential left unfulfilled. The tone of the reviews is overwhelmingly harsh, almost diametrically opposed to the praise and excitement that animates discussions of *Fortnite*. On IGN, David Jagneaux describes the game as

> a trap disguised as a free-to-play RPG, seemingly designed to prey on your sense of nostalgia and childlike wonder to squeeze as much money out of you as possible. Some Wizarding World-inspired window dressing and familiar music are used as a thin veil to mask what is an otherwise offensive collection of rampant microtransactions.[24]

Gita Jackson's review for Kotaku bills the game as "fun, but you're gonna be shelling out your Galleons if you want to make the most of it. By Galleons I mean dollars."[25] The Eurogamer review by Tom Phillips describes the game as a shame, since "the manner in which it does [ask players to pay], and the frequency which you'd need to is frankly astonishing."[26] Phillip Connors bases his review on the premise that *"Harry Potter: Hogwarts Mystery* takes the trend of exploitative microtransactions much further down the rabbit hole, pushing the limits of ethical boundaries and raising the bar of how much money can be charged for nothing."[27] In the hands of reviewers like Dalton Cooper, the game becomes "a shameless cash grab that is so aggressive with its microtransactions that it's baffling, and if it weren't so predatory, it would be hilarious."[28] Making it to the mainstream press, *The Guardian* sums up Keza MacDonald's review of the game with *"Harry Potter: Hogwarts Mystery* is a dull game with a great concept, made borderline unplayable by its hyper-aggressive monetisation."[29] The primary and most consistent complaint is that it is monetized in an exceptional manner, asking more money from players than other games. However, the difference between the monetization in this game and the *Kim Kardashian: Hollywood* game is thin. The problem for *Hogwarts Mystery* is that, instead of being compared to the other games in the genre from which it came and that sit outside of the norms of traditional video games, it is implicitly compared to core video game titles.

The primary objection to the monetization in the game is the energy system. Players have energy that recharges every four minutes, but most tasks in the game will require more than one full energy bar to complete. This means that when players start a task they will be able to do some of it, but will need to come back before it ends to finish it. Effectively, this means you end up playing the game for a minute or two, put it down for an hour or so and come back for another minute or two. Objections to this mode of game design were a key focus of reviews of the game. Reviewers wrote that *"Hogwarts Mystery* does everything it can to stop you from playing it. You cannot get through even a single class without being interrupted" and *"Hogwarts Mystery* was actively trying to keep me from enjoying myself."[30] Reviewers wanted to play the game unabated, moving through the story like a book they bought, rather than as a gated, free-to-play game. Although the reviews occasionally mention the underlying logic that this kind of design means the game's content will last longer, they are frustrated by it and paint it as an aberrant kind of design that should be ridiculed and lamented for the missed opportunity.

The moment that was held out for a particular level of scorn was a sequence early in the game when your archrival in the game, Merula Snyde, tricks you into a room with Devil's Snare. Your character quickly becomes trapped, and you must use your energy to try to break free (figure 8.4). Partway through the

Figure 8.4
Our second character, Nellie Magim, trapped by Devil's Snare, with the
game asking for a purchase to get more energy in *Harry Potter: Hogwarts
Mystery*.

event, you inevitably run out of energy and you must either pay
crystals to get more energy or leave the game, with your character choking, while your energy refills. Depictions of the scene
were also filled with the kind of moralizing about the implications of games generally left to conservative video game critics.
One of those "just think about the kids" moments was authored
by Tom Phillips, who wrote:

> The first time the game engineers you *will* run out of energy is in
> its first action scene, where—creepily—your character is left in a life
> or death scenario while you wait half an hour to continue. Charita-
> bly you could say this energy system adds a certain cliffhanger-esque

nature to *Hogwarts Mystery*—but the amount of energy needed is a completely arbitrary number, and one deliberately designed to fully deplete your energy bar. The game encourages you to make a purchase and continue immediately rather than wait and leave your avatar suffering. It is especially troubling when you consider the game's audience.[31]

The combination of furor about the fact that the game is designed in a manner to make you pay or put it down and general interest in a Harry Potter game led both IGN and Kotaku to publish articles that compiled fan reactions to the game's energy system and monetization strategies.[32] It is as if huge swaths of the people picking up the game simply thought that this game should work like the games to which they were accustomed.

Concerns about energy and monetization are about how this game falls outside of the norms expected of it. Although mobile gaming review sites published strategies for not paying in the game, and the first tip was generally just to wait, outlets that focused more on traditionally monetized games sought to quantify spending in the game and what things cost.[33] Dalton Cooper began his review from the premise that games certainly need to make money, but questioned the value offered by *Hogwarts Mystery*. In the review, they describe buying crystals: they found "spending $5 on the game will yield maybe 10 minutes of uninterrupted gameplay. $10, maybe 20 minutes. In our testing of the game, we purchased $20 worth of in-game currency and were able to play for a little less than half an hour before we were completely out of energy again."[34] Unlike the Disney fans willing to wait for content, gamers sought to have the whole story on their terms and on their timeline. In follow-up articles to his review of the game, Tom Phillips of Eurogamer announced that prices were dropping for in-game currency, but only for some players. Bringing back a moralizing tone, he wrote: "And while A/B testing exists in many other smartphone games, the fact remains that *Harry Potter: Hogwarts Mystery* is an officially-licensed product backed by a massive publisher, based around a franchise associated with a certain expectation of quality, and—perhaps most of all—one aimed at kids."[35] In a separate story about the introduction of pets into the game, describing the game as one "which chokes your school-age avatar unless you wait hours for more energy or cough up money," Phillips breaks down the costs of pets, pointing out that he has not yet earned enough free currency to buy any of them.[36] Ultimately, he praises the new content, but notes that it is added "via the usual energy-gated system. It's just a shame the game's moneti-sation options like pets have to be priced so exorbitantly."[37] In violating the dominant norms and expectations of video games, *Harry Potter: Hogwarts Mystery* is transgressive, and those viola-tions are punished by shaming, regret, and moralizing by the conventional forces of the video game community in an effort to center the games they want to see.

Perhaps the clearest effort at redesign is in the way the Kotaku and IGN reviews of the game ended, asking for a game that was monetized like the other games they played, with a one-time unlock fee. Gita Jackson notes that the monetization in *Hogwarts Mystery* "is not much different from the way that many free-to-play games operate, but I still wish that I could pay a one-time fee to remove these restrictions [on energy use] instead of using my premium currency or having to wait."[38] David Jagneaux offers up a call for remaking *Hogwarts Mystery* into a game he is far more familiar with, writing,

> I can't help but feel that developer Jam City would have been better off giving us an alternative progression path to earn our way forward. At the very least you should be able to stockpile crystals and save up

lots of energy or be able to easily earn gems (the microtransaction currency) without real money. Or just sell us the whole thing for an up-front price.[39]

Although he uses two different terms for the hard currency in the game, the focus of Jagneaux's claim is to make the case that he should be able to play this game just like he plays all the other ones, framing it as helpful advice for the developer, a tip that could make them "better off." Despite the calls of Jackson and Jagneaux, *Harry Potter: Hogwarts Mystery* proved successful at generating revenue, making $55 million in its first few months of release and seeing steadily increasing downloads of the game.[40] Notably, the game made almost as much in about four months as pay-once game *Super Mario Run* made in two years, giving reason to question the wisdom of taking Jagneaux's business advice.[41]

Focusing on the outlet and target audience of games journalism offers another perspective from which to see how different it can be to talk about games in another space, to a broader group of people. While writing for *Kotaku*, Gita Jackson lambastes *Hogwarts Mystery*, largely judging it in line with her contemporaries who are staff at publications focused on appealing to gamers. Earlier in her writing career, Jackson wrote eloquently about her appreciation for *Kim Kardashian: Hollywood* for Paste Magazine, contending that the

> greatest asset for videogames as fiction, one that it holds over other forms of media, is the immediacy with which you can identify with people and experiences that are not your own. . . . With each little tap on my tablet's screen, I feel like I am closer to experiencing Mrs. Kardashian West's world, though with less pressure, and the ability to turn it off.[42]

Jackson explains the allure of the game, the way it draws her in and helps her better understand a cultural moment. She admits that she "can't stop playing it." Although the game does not conform to expectations of core gamers, the broader audience of Paste Magazine enables her to consider games differently. There are likely many reasons why Jackson does not appreciate *Hogwarts Mystery* in the same way, but the change from writing for a broad audience to one focused on core gamers is an important one. In short, the audience for both games and discussion about them really matters.

Harry Potter: Hogwarts Mystery violated the norms of video games, limiting play through an energy system and featuring a simplified mode of interaction with the game. Given that it was an intellectual property beloved by many gamers, the public reaction was stark, even if the game overall was successful. Likely propelled by the millions of *Kim Kardashian: Hollywood* players Nick Fernandez said were "somewhere," the game provoked a strong reaction because it was different in a way that the game community had a hard time accepting.[43] *Fortnite* was also different, but in a way that fed into the expected norms of games. It pushed possibilities forward in a manner that was viewed as acceptable, appreciated, and something to be excited about. In combination, these two games further illustrate key dynamics driving perceptions about what games are and should be.

Bringing It Back

The video game industry is changing as it seeks to continue to stay relevant and profitable in a changing cultural and economic environment. Free-to-play and mobile games are an increasing part of the landscape, as the kinds of people playing games expand and the need for additional revenue streams is made more urgent. The point of this project was to chart the norms around games to illustrate what is valued and what is not. Acceptance requires conforming to expectations about being able to play a game in an unlimited fashion, to show off skill, and to be able to compete on a level playing field. The themes of games matter: certain types of fighting, sports, and building feed into conventional expectations of games, while fashion and interior design fall outside of it. However, dabbling in a beloved topic or franchise can be a double-edged sword, as letting that community down will provoke an outsized reaction.

Modes of play are normalized over time as players seek out what they are familiar with or subtle twists on what they know. Sales of cosmetic items fall nicely within expected modes of play, while *Star Wars Battlefront II's* loot boxes fall well outside of it. Changes are slow to come and subject to reactionary impulses in an effort to pull the norms back to where they have been. Although the medium is rather young, there are rigid norms, pushing us toward what we can immediately remember rather than thinking through the different phases in the overarching lifespan of video games.

Games are a place where skill is displayed and labor should be done, but on terms that serve players and test them. Players are expected to persevere and get better, never buying their way ahead. Developers are expected to play into the dominant impulses of games, making what we expect and consistently remaking what we will want the next time. Moving the bar and changing expectations is a slow process, and one best tweaked by riffing off of established norms. Critiquing these games requires taking them seriously, on their terms, to start to build an understanding of norms and appropriate structures for free-to-play and mobile games. Things do not have to be as they were, but we must understand where we are to chart a new path.

The context for video games is changing as I finish writing this book. *NBA 2K19* shows one vision of the future. Lamented in Luke Plunkett's Kotaku review as a "nightmarish vision of our microtransaction-stuffed future," the game features full-on ads built into basketball games and is "*constantly* begging you to spend" premium currency.[44] Albert Burneko concludes that the integration of offline brands into the game is "evil. It's straight-up evil."[45] Just as Ultimate Team ushered in a new way to monetize games and create the philosophy of games-as-a-service, this is another case of sports games leading in a very particular way. The theme carried on with *NBA 2K20*; as Plunkett observed, things were somewhat better, but "the core of *NBA 2K20* is still rotten," and "this is a $60 video game that is asking you to buy it, take it home, then continually pay *more* money to engage in its core game modes. It's a console/PC game with the fiscal appetite of a mobile gaming scam."[46]

Nintendo brought *Mario Kart* to mobile devices complete with monthly passes and rare racers unlocked via gacha mechanics, leading Mike Fahey to argue on Kotaku that "*Mario Kart Tour* is a Nintendo game with a big extra helping of bullshit." Countering the voice of gamers, *Mario Kart Tour* saw the largest number of downloads and the second-highest amount of revenue in its first month of any Nintendo game on mobile.[47] That success caused Nintendo president Shuntaro Furukawa to announce that he expects "remarkable results" from the game, which notably was the first Mario game that conformed to typical free-to-play norms in pricing and monetization structure.[48] However, the *Mario Kart Tour* release occurred in the shadow of Apple Arcade, a $5 per month service that unlocks full games for players and was hailed by Michael Fahey and Stephen Totilo on Kotaku as "mobile gaming without all the bullshit."[49] Fahey and

Totilo contend that Apple Arcade has "none of the manipulative systems that have contaminated nearly all of mobile gaming. . . . Imagine not being screwed with while you play mobile games. What a concept!"[50] TouchArcade has turned over almost their entire site to reviewing Apple Arcade games, as the overwhelming number of offerings leaves players wondering where to start. Perhaps this is the future of mobile games, as it certainly conforms more closely to the dominant mode of pricing in console and PC games, but Fahey and Totilo observe that Apple Arcade possesses limitations. Although they contend it "seems like a good thing at the moment," Apple's curation means there are no edgy offerings, and its design applies "some not so subtle pressure to upgrade to newer devices or ones with more storage. After all, there are so many games to download and play."[51] It is notable that a new, high-end phone purchase with extra storage is likely to cost more than the overwhelming majority of whales are likely to pay on any given free-to-play game. It is further notable that Fahey and Totilo present getting a new phone and paying $5 a month as a preferable state of games to the free-to-play games found outside of Apple's Arcade.

PC games also face their own challenges, as endemic sexism has been reported in the Riot workplace and *Counter-Strike: Global Offensive (CS:GO)*was at the center of a US Federal Trade Commission investigation in 2017.[52] In the wake of the 2017 allegations about players running scams over the *CS:GO* microtransactions, developer Valve announced they were restricting sales of container keys in late 2019 because the items were predominantly used for money laundering.[53] Microtransactions change and shift how games work, and those of us in and around games need to be mindful of how our actions and design choices shape and impact who plays games, how games are played, and what games are played.

There are multiple communities at play in video games, and the ones that leave texts for me to study are especially committed to talking about and discussing them online. There are wide swaths of players who avidly play their game of choice, but who would rarely research the game online or discuss it with strangers. Mapping the boundaries in the reception of games gives an opportunity to see where our biases are, what we believe, and where we resist. The point of comparing games and analyzing the texts around them is to prompt those reading to rethink how they conceive of the norms around games and what they consider acceptable, and to question the way things have been. Anyone interested enough to read a book about video games is an outlier, and everyone who does care that much about video games should be consistently assessing what our biases are and how our preferences limit what we play, what we make, and how we think about games.

Acknowledgments

I've been fortunate enough to write several of these acknowledgments pages, and it is always one of my favorite parts of the writing process. It takes a whole lot of people to bring a book into the world, and I want to thank all of the people that helped on this project. This book started as an idea, a glimmer, and a super-short two-slide presentation. It took the contributions of a lot of people over the years to develop into what you read.

Thank you to the wide community of scholars who asked questions and challenged me to develop my ideas. Thank you to the editors and overall team at MIT Press who contributed to making this book a reality. Thanks to the anonymous reviewers. I still don't know who y'all are, but I appreciate all of your constructive and helpful guidance. Special thank yous to: Shira Chess, Mia Consalvo, Kishonna Gray, Adrienne Shaw, the awesome MIT editorial team of Doug Sery, Noah Springer, and Virginia Crossman, my copy editor Kristie Reilly, Jason Begy for indexing the book, and everyone else who made contributions to this work. Thank you to the folks I'm lucky enough to work with at Seattle University. Early work on this project was made possible through summer funding from the university and the College of Arts and Sciences. This would not have been possible without the awesome people at Mother's Place who helped take care of Piper and Ingrid, which gave me time to write. Annette, Karen, and Sylvia create a fearsome toddler room. Cathy, Carol, Mandy, and Reba rock pre-K. Alyce, Carrie, Kate, and Laura hold down preschool. And thank you Bonfigs and the specialty teachers. The crew at Dearborn Park International School and Dragon's Den helped afford time for editing. Thanks to Ms. Kwong and Zheng Lao Shi in K-1 Mandarin.

Most of all, thanks family. I wouldn't be here and wouldn't be playing games without Mom, Dad, and Lisa. The added family of Adam, Ashley, Casey, Chris, Greg, Richard, and Trudie and the found family of Addy, Amy, Beth, and Eleanor make my life better. And thanks to Erin, Piper, and Ingrid for helping me do all that I do.

Notes

Introduction

1. Schreier, "Inside Rockstar Games' Culture of Crunch"; D'Anastasio, "Inside the Culture of Sexism at Riot Games."

2. Dotson, "According to Newzoo Report, Mobile Gaming Market to Become Bigger Than Console or PC Gaming in 2016, and Only Grow from There."

3. Dotson, "Mobile Gaming's Only Going to Get Bigger, and Grow Faster Than Console Gaming, According to Report"; Handrahan, "Mobile Game Spend Will Double to $105 Billion by 2021."

4. Hodapp, "Unsurprisingly, All Future Gameloft Games Will Be Free to Play"; Kelly, "Is Premium Mobile Gaming Viable?"

5. Dotson, "Mobile Gamers Who Spend Money Almost Spend as Much as Console and PC Gamers"; Kocurek, *Coin-Operated Americans*.

6. Chess, *Ready Player Two: Women Gamers and Designed Identity*.

7. Cote, "'I Can Defend Myself': Women's Strategies for Coping with Harassment While Gaming Online"; Cote, "Writing 'Gamers': The Gendered Construction of Gamer Identity in Nintendo Power (1994–1999)."

8. Cote, "'Stupid Games' and Serious Gamers: Female Video Game Players' Ambivalent Interpretations of Casual Games' Significance."

9. Handrahan, "Mobile Game Spend Will Double to $105 Billion by 2021."

10. Chen and Burgess, "Tencent Just Overtook Facebook in Market Value." See also https://en.wikipedia.org/wiki/List_of_public_corporations_by_market_capitalization and https://www.statista.com/statistics/263264/top-companies-in-the-world-by-market-value/.

11. Futter, "Tencent Isn't Just Ubisoft's Savior—It's the World's Biggest Gaming Company." *Honor of Kings* is localized as *Arena of Valor* in the West.

12. Nieborg, "Crushing Candy: The Free-to-Play Game in Its Connective Commodity Form."

13. Brightman, "Only 3.5% of Gamers Make in-App Purchases—AppsFlyer."

14. Consalvo and Paul, *Real Games: What's Legitimate and What's Not in Contemporary Videogames*.

15. Anil DG, "What Is a Gacha?"

16. This kind of design is also found in the toy store, where brands like Hatchimals and LOL Surprise take advantages of the mystery mechanics.

17. Hodapp, "'We Own You'—Confessions of an Anonymous Free to Play Producer."

18. Chess, *Ready Player Two: Women Gamers and Designed Identity*; Salter, *Jane Jensen: Gabriel Knight, Adventure Games, Hidden Objects*.

19. Insight Team, "Women on Mobile Platforms Are the Most Valuable Gamers."

20. Robertson, "Do More Women Actually Own Game Consoles than Men?"

21. Insight Team, "Women on Mobile Platforms Are the Most Valuable Gamers."

22. Gaudiosi, "'Candy Crush' Publisher Targets Traditional Gamers with 'Legend of Solgard.'"

23. Shaw and Chess, "Reflections on the Casual Games Market in a Post-GamerGate World."

24. Nieborg, "From Premium to Freemium: The Political Economy of the App."

25. For more on this, please see Paul, *The Toxic Meritocracy of Video Games: Why Gaming Culture Is the Worst*; and Consalvo and Paul, *Real Games: What's Legitimate and What's Not in Contemporary Videogame*.

26. Phillips, "Harry Potter," April 30, 2018.

27. Lanier, "'Super Mario Run' Leaves $60 Million Revenue Mark in the Dust."

28. Fahey, "Super Mario Run's Inevitable Backlash."

29. Gilbert, "Nintendo's First iPhone Game Has a Long-Term Revenue Problem."

30. Campbell, "How Fortnite's Success Led to Months of Intense Crunch at Epic Games"; D'Anastasio, "Report."

31. Schiappa, "Second Thoughts on the Critiques of Big Rhetoric"; Burke, *Language as Symbolic Action: Essays on Life, Literature and Method*; Burke, *A Rhetoric of Motives*; Campbell and Huxman, *The Rhetorical Act: Thinking, Speaking and Writing Critically*.

32. Zarefsky, "Knowledge Claims in Rhetorical Criticism."

33. Scott, "On Viewing Rhetoric as Epistemic."

34. Humphreys, "On Being a Feminist in Games Studies."

35. James, *Beyond a Boundary*.

36. Cousins, "Snobbery and Fear Drive Criticisms of Free-to-Play Games and Ethics."

37. Cousins, "Snobbery and Fear Drive Criticisms of Free-to-Play Games and Ethics."

38. Cousins, "Snobbery and Fear Drive Criticisms of Free-to-Play Games and Ethics."

39. Cousins, "Snobbery and Fear Drive Criticisms of Free-to-Play Games and Ethics."

40. *Nontendo 4DS* is not a typo here. It's the actual name of the system Rusty's invested in within the game and the name is played for a joke throughout.

41. Kohler, "Nintendo's Take on Free-to-Play Is a Home Run."

42. GiantBoyDetective, "Rusty's Real Deal Baseball," April 4, 2014.

43. GiantBoyDetective, "Rusty's Real Deal Baseball," April 4, 2014.

44. GiantBoyDetective, "Rusty's Real Deal Baseball," April 8, 2014.

45. Kohler, "Nintendo's Take on Free-to-Play Is a Home Run."

46. Kohler, "Nintendo's Take on Free-to-Play Is a Home Run.

47. Totilo, "Where Winners Play, and Losers Pay."

48. Boyer, "The 20 Games You Shouldn't Miss in 2014."

49. Totilo, "Video Game Club 2014."

50. Totilo, "My Favorite Nintendo Is Weird Nintendo"; GiantBoyDetective, "Rusty's Real Deal Baseball," April 8, 2014.

51. Handrahan, "Super Mario Run."

52. Fahey, "Why Do Mobile Games Get a 'Free' Pass?"

53. Fahey, "Why Do Mobile Games Get a 'Free' Pass?"

54. Klepek, "College Student Found the Perfect Gamer to Win $6,000 From."

Chapter 1

1. Donovan, *Replay: The Ultimate History of Video Games*; Kent, *The Ultimate History of Video Games*.

2. Kocurek, *Coin-Operated Americans*; Chess, *Ready Player Two: Women Gamers and Designed Identity*.

3. KHAndAnime, "Where Did the Console Dungeon Crawlers Go?"

4. See https://howlongtobeat.com.

5. Huntemann, "Women in Video Games: The Case of Hardware Production and Promotion."

6. Inflation calculations made with the help of http://www.in2013dol lars.com and based on 2018 as a baseline.

7. Moriarty, "The Real Cost of Gaming."

8. Batchelor, "GTA V Is the Most Profitable Entertainment Product of All Time."

9. Handrahan, "Chinese Mobile Games Market Is Now the Most Valuable in the World." See also https://venturebeat.com/2019/05/07/niko-partners-chinas-game-market-to-hit-41-5-billion-and-767-million-players-by-2023/ and https://www.statista.com/statistics/1058001/china-mobile-game-share-in-gaming-industry/.

10. Taylor, "Games Account for 75% of App Store Spending."

11. GameRefinery, "What Separates China and the West in Mobile?"

12. GameRefinery, "What Separates China and the West in Mobile?"

13. Sue, "Culture Clash."

14. Schreier, "Why Ubisoft Is Obsessed with 'Games as a Service.'"

15. Batchelor, "Even Assassin's Creed Is a Live Service Now."

16. Ford, "'Madden NFL 25' Review—an Incredibly Disappointing Display of Football and Freemium."

17. Grubb, "Why Madden NFL Mobile Is the Last Football Game EA Will Ever Need to Release on Mobile."

18. Tylwalk, "'Madden NFL Overdrive' Guide: Get Charged Up to Win More and Play Longer for Free."

19. Nelson, "'Madden NFL Mobile' Proves Successful as EA Mobile Focuses on Games as 'Live Services.'"

Chapter 2

1. Brightman, "Only 3.5% of Gamers Make in-App Purchases—AppsFlyer."

2. Brightman, "Only 3.5% of Gamers Make in-App Purchases—AppsFlyer."

3. Rosebloom, "What You Need to Know about How Whales Spend."

4. BestUSCasinos.org, "Casino Whale Stories—Tales from Las Vegas High Rollers."

5. Hodapp, "'We Own You'—Confessions of an Anonymous Free to Play Producer."

6. Lazarides, "Gondola Wants to Rock the Boat of F2P Monetization with Realtime Player-Based IAP Adjustment."

7. McCormick, "Game of War Executive Arrested for Allegedly Stealing Trade Secrets."

8. Valleyflyin, "The Kraken Has Been Unleashed (a Conversation with Valleyflyin)—the Most Underrated Characters: MarvelStrikeForce."

9. Oxts86vv, "Foxnext Is Laughing at Us!: MarvelStrikeForce."

10. Ulanopo, "Confessions of a League Whale: A Blue Essence Rant."

11. Paul, *Wordplay and the Discourse of Video Games: Analyzing Words, Design, and Play*.

12. Consalvo, *Cheaters: Gaining Advantage in Videogames*.

13. Choudhury, "A Former Librarian Spent $89,000 in Public Money on a Mobile Game."

14. Paul, *The Toxic Meritocracy of Video Games: Why Gaming Culture Is the Worst*.

15. Valentine, "Fortnite Sold 5 Million Battle Passes on the First Day of Season 3."

16. Lazarides, "In Reponse to the Many Complaints, 'World of Tanks Blitz' Has Adjusted Profitability and Provisions."

17. Shaw, *Gaming at the Edge: Sexuality and Gender at the Margins of Gamer Culture.*

18. Davis, "Why Core Gamers Hate Free-to-Play."

19. Davis, "Why Core Gamers Hate Free-to-Play."

20. Davis, "Why Core Gamers Hate Free-to-Play."

21. Davis, "Why Core Gamers Hate Free-to-Play."

22. Davis, "Why Core Gamers Hate Free-to-Play."

23. Davis, "Why Core Gamers Hate Free-to-Play."

24. Hamilton, "In-Game Purchases Poison the Well."

25. Hamilton, "In-Game Purchases Poison the Well."

26. Totilo, "Final Fantasy Crystal Chronicles."

27. Hamilton, "In-Game Purchases Poison the Well."

28. Schreier, "A Long and Hopefully Interesting Conversation About Microtransactions."

29. Antero, "Peggle's 10th Anniversary."

30. Antero, "Peggle's 10th Anniversary."

31. McCarthy, "Final Fantasy XV's New Mobile Game Sure Is a Free-To-Play Mobile Game."

32. Fahey, "There's a New Transformers Game on the Way, and It's Just Precious."

33. Schreier, "South Park Craps All Over Free-to-Play Games."

34. For a deeper look at a previous version of *NBA2K*, please read TreaAndrea Russworm's "Computational Blackness."

35. Trusted Reviews, "Microtransactions Are an 'Unfortunate Reality' of Modern Gaming, Says NBA 2K19 Producer."

36. Valentine, "Valve."

37. Valentine, "Valve."

38. D'Anastasio, "Valve Walks Back Its Stance on Balancing Artifact Cards."

39. Valentine, "Valve."

40. Grayson, "Artifact Seems Like a Very Valve Card Game."

41. Pearson, "I Was So Fed Up of People Telling Us We Should Do Free-to-F***ing-Play."

42. Pearson, "I Was So Fed Up of People Telling Us We Should Do Free-to-F***ing-Play."

Chapter 3

1. Burford, "It's 2016 and Warframe Is Still an Excellent Free-To-Play Game."

2. Burford, "It's 2016 and Warframe Is Still an Excellent Free-To-Play Game."

3. Warr, "Dote Night."

4. Warr, "Dote Night."

5. Warr, "Dote Night."

6. Tassi, "Why I've Spent $639 On 'Hearthstone' (and Don't Regret It)."

7. Tassi, "My $1,800 'Hearthstone' Collection Is Still Incomplete."

8. Kollar, "Clash Royale's Top-Ranked Player Has Spent over $12,000 on the Game."

9. Grayson, "UFC Stars Hate How Much They're Spending On Clash of Clans."

10. Hill and Croghan, "5 Reasons I Lost $9,000 On An IPhone Game."

11. Gach, "Meet the 19-Year-Old Who Spent Over $10,000 On Micro-transactions."

12. Coavoux, Boutet, and Zabban, "What We Know About Games: A Scientometric Approach to Game Studies in the 2000s."

13. Chess and Paul, "The End of Casual: Long Live Casual."

14. Leaver and Willson, *Social, Casual, and Mobile Games: The Changing Gaming Landscape.*

15. Tassi, "Apple Promotes Strange New Game Type In IOS App Store, 'Pay Once and Play.'"

16. Dotson, "'Flop Rocket' Review—Fly Me to the Moon."

17. Hodapp, "'Sid Meier's Civilization VI' for IPad Review—Wow, Just Wow."

18. Nelson, "TouchArcade Game of the Week."

19. Nelson, "TouchArcade Game of the Week."

20. Valentine, "Frostkeep Studios Is Serious About Making 'the Game That Players Want' with Rend."

21. Fahey, "EA Trips Up on the Path from Product to Service."

22. Mannergoggle, "Play Nice Press Release."

23. Hodapp, "Strange Flavour Ditching Their 'Play Nice' IAP System, Returning to Paid Games."

24. Hodapp, "New 'SimCity BuildIt' Infographic Shows Just What a Smash Hit the Game Is."

25. Hodapp, "New 'SimCity BuildIt' Infographic Shows Just What a Smash Hit the Game Is."

26. Newman, "SimCity BuildIt Has Become the Most-Played SimCity Ever, EA Mobile Claims."

27. Harvey, "The Fame Game: Working Your Way up the Celebrity Ladder in Kim Kardashian: Hollywood."

28. Struan, "Kim Kardashian's Game Is Killing Candy Crush."

29. Robehmed, "Kim Kardashian West, Mobile Mogul: The Forbes Cover Story."

30. Hernandez, "Kim Kardashian Brags About How Much Bank Her Game Is Making."

31. Morrissey, "Oh God, I Spent $494.04 Playing the Kim Kardashian Hollywood App."

32. Morrissey, "Oh God, I Spent $494.04 Playing the Kim Kardashian Hollywood App."

33. Morrissey, "Oh God, I Spent $494.04 Playing the Kim Kardashian Hollywood App."

34. Plunkett, "Kim Kardashian's Video Game Is the Stuff of Nightmares."

35. Tassi, "Lessons Learned from a Week with 'Kim Kardashian: Hollywood.'"

36. Tassi, "Lessons Learned from a Week with 'Kim Kardashian: Hollywood.'"

37. Tassi, "Lessons Learned from a Week with 'Kim Kardashian: Hollywood.'"

38. Knoblauch, "The 10 Most Disturbing Things About 'Kim Kardashian: Hollywood'"; Valdes, "We Played 'Kim Kardashian: Hollywood' So You Don't Have To."

39. Alexander, "Gamasutra's Best of 2014: Leigh Alexander's Top 5 Games."

40. Alexander, "Gamasutra's Best of 2014: Leigh Alexander's Top 5 Games."

41. Klepek, "My Weird, Addictive Trip into Kim Kardashian: Hollywood."

42. Klepek, "My Weird, Addictive Trip into Kim Kardashian: Hollywood."

43. Hernandez, "Teen Girls Don't Care What We Think of Kim Kardashian."

44. Hernandez, "Teen Girls Don't Care What We Think of Kim Kardashian."

45. Hernandez, "Kim Kardashian: Hollywood Has the Best Rival Since Pokémon's Gary Oak."

46. Lazarides, "'Play Me Baby One More Time'—Britney Spears Is Following Kim Kardashian's F2P Footsteps"; Lazarides, "Taylor Swift Will Be the Next Pop Singer to Come to Your Mobile Device"; Jackson, "Nicki Minaj Has a New Game Where People Actually Rap for Her."

47. Chess, "Kim Kardashian: Hollywood Feminism"; Harvey, "The Fame Game: Working Your Way up the Celebrity Ladder in Kim Kardashian: Hollywood."

48. Plunkett, "'Pay to Win' Protests Hit the Streets of Black Desert Online."

49. Graft, "Dota 2 Is Free-to-Play, but Not Pay-to-Win, Says Valve."

50. Graft, "Dota 2 Is Free-to-Play, but Not Pay-to-Win, Says Valve."

51. Dotson, "How Can the Indie Developers of 'Korrigans' Do a Non-Pay-to-Win Take on 'Clash of Clans'? They Explain."

52. Petchesky, "Please Arrest Whoever Did This to Fantasy Football."

53. Herecomesthenightman, "EA Fired Plants VS Zombies Creator for Objecting to Pay2Win: Games."

54. Gach, "Players Worry Paladins' New Card System Inches Closer to Pay-To-Win."

55. Alexandra, "Star Wars Battlefront II Lets You Pay Real Money for Multiplayer Advantages."

56. Alexandra, "Star Wars Battlefront II Lets You Pay Real Money for Multiplayer Advantages."

57. Alexandra, "Star Wars Battlefront II Lets You Pay Real Money for Multiplayer Advantages."

58. Good, "I Spent $90 in Battlefront 2, and I Still Don't Have Any Control over My Characters."

59. Schreier, "EA Defense of Star Wars Battlefront II Becomes Most Downvoted Reddit Comment Ever."

60. Thier, "This Is Likely Why EA Pulled Star Wars Battlefront 2's Microtransactions."

61. Brightman, "Star Wars Battlefront II: Will EA's Concession Hurt Sales?"; Kim, "Gamers Overreacting on EA 'Star Wars' Game; Firms Should Raise Prices: Analyst."

62. Sinclair, "'You Probably Don't Want Darth Vader in Pink.'"

63. Batchelor, "EA CEO's Damage Control Speech: 'We Want to Be Better.'"

64. Sinclair, "For EA and Loot Boxes, 'Fair Is the Number One Thing.'"

Chapter 4

1. Vidyarthi, "A Brief History of FarmVille."

2. Takahashi, "Even with Half the Users, Zynga's FarmVille Made More Money than Ever before in Q1."

3. Takahashi, "Is Zynga Worth More than Electronic Arts?"

4. TranslateMedia, "The Rise and Fall of Zynga"; Constine, "Why Zynga Failed."

5. Clover, "Happy 10th Anniversary, App Store!"

6. Slivka, "Apple Opens Up 'In App Purchasing' for Free IPhone Applications."

7. Slivka, "Apple Opens Up 'In App Purchasing' for Free IPhone Applications."

8. Voorhees, "Game On."

9. Horwitz, "IOS App Store's All-Time Top Game Made $4 Billion to Top App's $1 Billion."

10. Horwitz, "Apptopia."

11. Cipriani, "3 Things Steve Jobs Had Wrong about the App Store"; Silver, "The Revolution Steve Jobs Resisted."

12. Paczkowski, "Apple SVP Eddy Cue Talks About the New Apple TV, Apps and Games."

13. Voorhees, "Game On."

14. Sauer, "How Dr. J and Larry Bird Helped Build a Video Game Empire."

15. Gaudiosi, "Madden."

16. Paul, *Wordplay and the Discourse of Video Games: Analyzing Words, Design, and Play*; Paul, "It's in the Game? Shifting the Scene with Online Play."

17. Sarkar, "With NHL 19, EA Leans into Online Play in Effort to Attract New Players."

18. Sarkar, "EA Looks Back on Five Years of the FIFA Ultimate Team Juggernaut."

19. Sarkar, "EA Looks Back on Five Years of the FIFA Ultimate Team Juggernaut."

20. For an overview of the game mode, see https://www.easports.com/uk/fifa/ultimate-team/beginners-guide-fut.

21. Sarkar, "EA Looks Back on Five Years of the FIFA Ultimate Team Juggernaut."

22. EA Sports, "Five Years of FIFA Ultimate Team."

23. Bailey, "Why I'm Finally Hooked on Madden Ultimate Team"; Sarkar, "EA Looks Back on Five Years of the FIFA Ultimate Team Juggernaut."

24. Lopes, "Brief FIFA Ultimate Team History."

25. Lopes, "Brief FIFA Ultimate Team History."

26. Schreier, "FBI Says Alleged Hackers Used FIFA to Steal Millions from EA"; Schreier, "Twenty-Five Year Old Charged with Stealing In-Game Items from EA."

27. Sarkar, "EA Looks Back on Five Years of the FIFA Ultimate Team Juggernaut."

28. Sarkar, "EA Looks Back on Five Years of the FIFA Ultimate Team Juggernaut."

29. Kurtenbach, "EA Sports Is Making a Fortune off Its Ultimate Team Modes."

30. Thier, "EA Is Making a Giant Amount of Money off Microtransactions."

31. Handrahan, "EA's Ultimate Team Now Worth $800 Million Annually."

32. Ballard, "Here's How Digital Revenue Has Benefited Electronic Arts."

33. Team, "FIFA Remains EA's Bread and Butter."

34. Takahashi, "EA Results Remind the Industry That Sports, Not Just Battlefield, Pushes Profits."

35. Davis, "EA Now Makes 40% of Its Revenue from 'Live Services.'"

36. Mc Shea, "EA Adamant Loot Boxes Aren't Gambling."

37. Taylor, "EA Sports VP Daryl Holt on Loot Boxes."

38. Glu Mobile, "MLB Tap Sports Baseball 2018."

39. Tylwalk, "MLB Tap Sports Baseball 2017 Review."

40. Hayward, "MLB Tap Sports Baseball 2017 Isn't Worth Big-League Time or Money."

41. Tylwalk, "MLB Tap Sports Baseball 2017 Review."

42. Tylwalk, "MLB Tap Sports Baseball 2018 Guide for Beginners."

43. Tylwalk, "MLB Tap Sports Baseball 2018 Guide for Beginners."

44. MSG-MLB Tap Sports Baseball, "How to Get a 5 Star Team."

45. Plunkett, "NBA 2K Is Very Sorry about Charging Players for Haircuts."

46. For revenue estimates, see https://sensortower.com/ios/us/glu-games -inc/app/mlb-tap-sports-baseball-2018/1319072708/overview.

Chapter 5

1. Coavoux, Boutet, and Zabban, "What We Know About Games: A Scientometric Approach to Game Studies in the 2000s"; Alha et al., "Free-to-Play Games: Professionals' Perspectives."

2. Alha et al., "Free-to-Play Games: Professionals' Perspectives."

3. GameCentral, "League of Legends Is Still the Biggest Video Game in the World."

4. Known as *Arena of Valor* in the West.

5. Dedmon, "League of Legends Tops Free-to-Play Revenue Charts in 2017."

6. Crossley, "Valve."

7. Heller, "Overwatch Is Coming to Humble Bundle in October."

8. LeJacq, "League of Legends Is Too Expensive."

9. LeJacq, "League of Legends Is Too Expensive."

10. Jacobs, "Redditors Explain How They Spent Thousands of Dollars League of Legends—Business Insider."

11. LoL Smurfs, "The Fastest Way to Level 30 in LoL."

12. LoL Smurfs, "Is League of Legends Free to Play? The Truth Behind LoL Being 'Free.'"

13. Musgrave, "'World of Tanks Blitz' Review—a Fine Addition to Wargaming's Cannon Canon."

14. Musgrave, "'World of Tanks Blitz' Review—a Fine Addition to Wargaming's Cannon Canon."

15. Musgrave, "'World of Tanks Blitz' Review—a Fine Addition to Wargaming's Cannon Canon."

16. Musgrave, "'World of Tanks Blitz' Review—a Fine Addition to Wargaming's Cannon Canon."

17. Musgrave, "'World of Tanks Blitz' Review—a Fine Addition to Wargaming's Cannon Canon."

18. Faraday, "Field Marshal Owen's Guide to World of Tanks Blitz | Pocket Tactics."

19. Faraday, "Field Marshal Owen's Guide to World of Tanks Blitz | Pocket Tactics."

20. Faraday, "Field Marshal Owen's Guide to World of Tanks Blitz | Pocket Tactics."

21. Faraday, "Field Marshal Owen's Guide to World of Tanks Blitz | Pocket Tactics."

22. Faraday, "Field Marshal Owen's Guide to World of Tanks Blitz | Pocket Tactics."

23. Faraday, "Field Marshal Owen's Guide to World of Tanks Blitz | Pocket Tactics."

24. Katkoff, "World of Tanks Blitz Liberates Players from Mid-Core."

25. Katkoff, "World of Tanks Blitz Liberates Players from Mid-Core."

26. Katkoff, "World of Tanks Blitz Liberates Players from Mid-Core."

27. Lazarides, "'World of Tanks Blitz' Update 2.8 Finally Makes Playing Tier IX-X Worth Your Time."

28. Lazarides, "For Some, 'World of Tanks: Blitz' 2.8 Update Might Have Pushed the Game into Pay-to-Win Territory."

29. Lazarides, "'World of Tanks Blitz' Update 2.8 Finally Makes Playing Tier IX-X Worth Your Time."

30. Lazarides, "In Reponse to the Many Complaints, 'World of Tanks Blitz' Has Adjusted Profitability and Provisions."

31. Sinclair, "'You're Stupid to Say Betting Is Bad.'"

32. Ford, "'Vainglory' Review—Portable MOBA Magic."

33. Dotson, "'Bitcoin Billionaire' Review—I'm Ashamed to Love This Game."

34. Dotson, "Carter's Top Ten Games of 2014"; Hodapp, "Eli's Top Ten Games of 2014."

35. Dotson, "'Bitcoin Billionaire' Update with Time Travel Out Now, Say Goodbye to Your Life."

36. Hodapp, "Eli's Top Ten Games of 2014."

37. Grayson, "Clicker Heroes Is Super Popular On Steam . . . for Some Reason."

38. Dotson, "'CivCrafter' Review—the Last Clicker You'll Ever Need."

39. Fahey, "Tips for Playing Bit City"; Totilo, "One Devious Microtransaction."

40. Grayson, "Clicker Game Ditches Microtransactions, Becomes Steam Best Seller"; Fragsworth, "Why Clicker Heroes 2 Is Abandoning Free-to-Play."

Chapter 6

1. Daxxari, "A New Way to Play."

2. Ham, "Rarity and Power: Balance in Collectible Object Games."

3. Good, "One of Magic."

4. Kunzelman, "Rare Magic."

5. Crecente, "Superdata"; Wilson, "PC Gaming Weekly."

6. Keganbe, "New Player Guides."

7. Curi, "Starting Stone #1: Six Steps to an Ultimate Deck."

8. Aidan, "Aidan's Free-To-Play Budget Decklists."

9. Torrid, "The New Challenge."

10. EmeraldBoar, "How Are New Players Supposed to Play?"

11. RAmarl, "How Are New Players Supposed to Play?"

12. Calixto, "Hearthstone Players Are Trapped in a Cycle of Salt."

13. Calixto, "Hearthstone Players Are Trapped in a Cycle of Salt."

14. Calixto, "Hearthstone Players Are Trapped in a Cycle of Salt."

15. Calixto, "Hearthstone Players Are Trapped in a Cycle of Salt."

16. Calixto, "Hearthstone Players Are Trapped in a Cycle of Salt."

17. This also has to do with developer pedigree, as Mia Consalvo and I discuss in *Real Games*.

18. Biden, "Hearthstone."

19. Biden, "Hearthstone."

20. Lazarides, "Collectible Card Games Are Becoming the Most Dominant Genre on Mobile, and 'Hearthstone' Is Leading the Way."

21. Lazarides, "Collectible Card Games Are Becoming the Most Dominant Genre on Mobile, and 'Hearthstone' Is Leading the Way."

22. Calixto, "Un'Goro Expansion Makes Hearthstone More Random, Probably More Expensive."

23. Calixto, "Un'Goro Expansion Makes Hearthstone More Random, Probably More Expensive."

24. Consalvo and Paul, *Real Games: What's Legitimate and What's Not in Contemporary Videogames*.

25. Nelson, "EA Releases First Trailer for 'Star Wars."

26. Ford, "'Star Wars."

27. Alfonso, "SWGOH: Beginner's Guide."

28. AlbertMyers, "EA Is Selling Star Wars Galaxy of Heroes's New Characters for 1100$."

29. Alfonso, "SWGOH: Beginner's Guide."

30. ZetaLordVader, "Dear CG, Can You Sell Us a Package That Not Cost [*sic*] a Full AAA Title?"

31. StygianUnknown, "The Three Options to Get That New Marquee Character to 7 Stars."

32. Hovahdo, "The Underpowered Guild's Guide to Clearing Heroic AAT—the 'Super Team' Strategy."

33. LukasPhoenixRebels, "The Alliance Phoenix Has Cleared the Heroic Sith Raid at 156.8M GP."

34. Mistereousone, "Dear CG Let Us Have This."

35. One of the things I learned by playing this game is that there are more than 24 time zones. For more, see https://www.timeanddate.com/time/current-number-time-zones.html.

36. Cptmarth, "The Organized Arena Shard Power Trip."

37. Stormy, "TEAM INSTINCT"; Team_iNstinct, "Team Instinct Premier #1 PVP Guild."

38. See http://teaminstinct.gg/#apply.

39. TradeMark, "Thoughts from a Former Leader of Team iNstinct."

40. TradeMark, "Thoughts from a Former Leader of Team iNstinct."

41. D'Anastasio, "Magic."

42. PepsiCo, "MTN DEW®, MTN DEW®, AMP®, GAME FUEL®, and DORITOS® Join Activision to Celebrate Call of Duty®."

Chapter 7

1. Crecente, "'Candy Crush Saga' Earned Just Under $1 Billion in Past 12 Months"; Takahashi, "Candy Crush Saga."

2. Princy, "Top-Grossing Apps of 2017."

3. The console version of the game is quite different and is a pay-upfront for a limited campaign version.

4. Kaiser, "Marvel Puzzle Quest."

5. Kaiser, "Marvel Puzzle Quest."

6. Leray, "'Marvel Puzzle Quest."

7. Gallaway, "Marvel Puzzle Quest: Dark Reign Review."

8. Gallaway, "Marvel Puzzle Quest: Dark Reign Review."

9. Barrett, "Marvel Puzzle Quest."

10. Fahey, "The Marvel Game I've Dreamt of for Six Years, Almost."

11. Fahey, "The Marvel Game I've Dreamt of for Six Years, Almost."

12. Fahey, "The Marvel Game I've Dreamt of for Six Years, Almost."

13. Fahey, "The Marvel Game I've Dreamt of for Six Years, Almost."

14. Lunden, "Activision Blizzard Closes Its $5.9B Acquisition of King, Makers of Candy Crush."

15. Karmali, "Candy Crush Founders Richer Than Grand Theft Auto Creators."

16. Fahey, "A Candy Crush Saga TV Show Is In the Works."

17. Fahey, "Candy Crush TV Show Leads to In-Game Mario Lopez."

18. Fahey, "Bejeweled Is So Over Candy Crush Saga's Bullshit."

19. Walker, "King ARE Trying to Candy-Crush the Banner Saga"; Walker, "Stealing 'Candy' from Babies"; Walker, "The Candy Crush Banner Saga Saga"; Grayson, "The Saga Continues."

20. Walker, "What to Play Instead of Candy Crush Saga."

21. Hodapp, "'Candy Crush Soda Saga' Review—Poppin' Bottles in the Ice."

22. Wales, "Candy Crush Saga Review."

23. Squires, "Candy Crush Saga Review."

24. Squires, "Candy Crush Saga Review."

25. Squires, "Candy Crush Saga Review."

26. Bell, "Candy Crush Saga—Game Review"; Morris, "Candy Crush Saga—App Review"; Morris, "Candy Crush Soda Saga—App Review."

27. Morris, "Candy Crush Saga—App Review."

28. *Marvel Avengers Academy* was released on February 4, 2016, and *Disney Magic Kingdoms* was released on March 17, 2016.

29. See https://www.marvel.com/games/marvel-avengers-academy.

30. Snyder, "'Marvel Avengers Academy' Goes Big for Second Anniversary."

31. Musgrave, "'Marvel Avengers Academy' Guide—Tips and Tricks for Assembling Your Team."

32. Martin, "Marketing and Mortality at the Avengers Academy Launch Party."

33. Martin, "Marketing and Mortality at the Avengers Academy Launch Party."

34. Martin, "Marketing and Mortality at the Avengers Academy Launch Party."

35. Karner, "What Is Marvel: Avengers Academy, and Why You Should Play It."

36. Karner, "What Is Marvel: Avengers Academy, and Why You Should Play It."

37. Karner, "Marvel's Avengers Academy—a 30-Day Follow-Up."

38. Polo, "Marvel's Avengers Academy Is More Fun Than It Has the Right to Be."

39. Polo, "Marvel's Avengers Academy Is More Fun Than It Has the Right to Be."

40. Polo, "Marvel's Avengers Academy Is More Fun Than It Has the Right to Be."

41. Polo, "Marvel's Avengers Academy Is More Fun Than It Has the Right to Be."

42. Brown, "'Marvel Avengers Academy' Has a Great Design and Story, But a Plodding Pace [Review]."

43. Brown, "'Marvel Avengers Academy' Has a Great Design and Story, But a Plodding Pace [Review]."

44. Tylwalk, "Marvel Avengers Academy Review: Teenagers, Assemble!"

45. James, "Marvel Avengers Academy Review—IPhone Reviews."

46. James, "Marvel Avengers Academy Review—IPhone Reviews."

47. Ford, "'Disney Magic Kingdoms' Adds 'Cinderella' Characters, Chest System"; Ford, "'Disney Magic Kingdoms' Updates with Pirates Characters, Quests"; Ford, "Jack Skellington Invades 'Disney Magic Kingdoms' for Halloween"; Ford, "'Disney Magic Kingdoms' Goes 'Frozen' In Holiday Update."

48. Ford, "'Disney Magic Kingdoms' Goes 'Frozen' In Holiday Update."

49. Ford, "'Disney Magic Kingdoms' Guide—Tips to Build Without Spending Real Money."

50. Ford, "'Disney Magic Kingdoms' Guide—Tips to Build Without Spending Real Money."

51. Willmott, "Disney Magic Kingdom Review—When You Wish upon a Star, You Probably Won't Wish for This."

52. Willmott, "Disney Magic Kingdom Review—When You Wish upon a Star, You Probably Won't Wish for This."

53. Andersson, "Review: Disney Magic Kingdoms Mobile Game Brings the World of Virtual Disney Theme Park Building with Extra Pixie Dust."

54. Andersson, "Review: Disney Magic Kingdoms Mobile Game Brings the World of Virtual Disney Theme Park Building with Extra Pixie Dust."

55. Andersson, "Review: Disney Magic Kingdoms Mobile Game Brings the World of Virtual Disney Theme Park Building with Extra Pixie Dust."

56. Andersson, "Review: Disney Magic Kingdoms Mobile Game Brings the World of Virtual Disney Theme Park Building with Extra Pixie Dust."

57. Headley, "8 Tips for Playing Magic Kingdoms."

58. Headley, "8 Tips for Playing Magic Kingdoms."

59. Headley, "8 Tips for Playing Magic Kingdoms."

60. Musgrave, "'Marvel Avengers Academy' Guide—Tips and Tricks for Assembling Your Team."

61. YorickSkirata, "TinyCo Has Gone Mad (and Bad): Avengersacademygame."

Conclusion

1. Schwartz, "Antoine Griezmann Did a 'Fortnite' Dance in the World Cup Final"; Fagan, "Parents Are Getting 'Fortnite' Coaches for Their Kids"; D'Anastasio, "Students Win Bet, Get Teacher to Make Final Exam About Fortnite."

2. D'Anastasio, "How Fortnite's Battle Pass Works."

3. D'Anastasio, "Battle Passes Are So Hot Right Now."

4. Sinclair, "Fortnite Earned $223 Million in March—Superdata."

5. Handrahan, "Fortnite's Five-Month IOS Revenue on Par with Clash Royale."

6. Horti and St Leger, "Fortnite Android Beta: Everything You Need to Know about the Mobile Game."

7. Batchelor, "69% of Fortnite Players Have Bought In-Game Purchases, Average Spend Is $85."

8. Taylor, "Battle Royale Players Are among the Most Engaged Gamers, Report Finds."

9. Taylor, "Battle Royale Players Are among the Most Engaged Gamers, Report Finds."

10. Luton, "Ten Surprising Things Battle Royale Can Teach Us."

11. Luton, "Ten Surprising Things Battle Royale Can Teach Us."

12. Luton, "Ten Surprising Things Battle Royale Can Teach Us."

13. Telfer and Kim, "$126 Million and Counting."

14. Tassi, "'Fortnite."

15. Telfer and Kim, "$126 Million and Counting."

16. Telfer and Kim, "$126 Million and Counting."

17. Bankhurst, "Ninja Becomes First Professional Gamer to Appear on Cover of ESPN Magazine."

18. Phillips, "Harry Potter," April 5, 2018.

19. Lanier, "'Kim Kardashian"; Fernandez, "Hogwarts Mystery Review: Harry Potter and the Prisoner of Microtransactions."

20. Fernandez, "Hogwarts Mystery Review: Harry Potter and the Prisoner of Microtransactions."

21. Jagneaux, "Harry Potter."

22. Phillips, "Harry Potter," April 30, 2018.

23. Jackson, "Mobile Game Hogwarts Mystery Is Like a Harry Potter Book That Keeps Asking for Money."

24. Jagneaux, "Harry Potter."

25. Jackson, "Mobile Game Hogwarts Mystery Is Like a Harry Potter Book That Keeps Asking for Money."

26. Phillips, "Harry Potter," April 30, 2018.

27. Connors, "Harry Potter."

28. Cooper, "Harry Potter."

29. MacDonald, "Harry Potter."

30. MacDonald, "Harry Potter"; Jagneaux, "Harry Potter."

31. Phillips, "Harry Potter," April 30, 2018.

32. Jackson, "The Internet Reacts to Hogwarts Mystery's Microtransactions"; Arif, "Harry Potter: Hogwarts Mystery Players Upset with Use of Microtransactions."

33. Tylwalk, "How to Play 'Harry Potter: Hogwarts Mystery.'"

34. Cooper, "Harry Potter."

35. Phillips, "Now Harry Potter."

36. Phillips, "Harry Potter Mobile Game Now Sells Owls for £12."

37. Phillips, "Harry Potter Mobile Game Now Sells Owls for £12."

38. Jackson, "Mobile Game Hogwarts Mystery Is Like a Harry Potter Book That Keeps Asking for Money."

39. Jagneaux, "Harry Potter."

40. Taylor, "Sensor Tower."

41. Taylor, "Super Mario Run Surpasses $60M Revenue after Two Years."

42. Jackson, "Kim Kardashian."

43. Fernandez, "Hogwarts Mystery Review: Harry Potter and the Prisoner of Microtransactions."

44. Plunkett, "NBA 2K19 Is a Nightmarish Vision of Our Microtransaction-Stuffed Future."

45. Burneko, "NBA 2K19's Brand Humping Is Craven, Shameless, and Straight-Up Evil."

46. Plunkett, "Surprise, NBA 2K20 Is Still Full of Bullshit Microtransactions."

47. Valentine, "Mario Kart Tour's First-Month Downloads Zoom Past 123M."

48. Handrahan, "Nintendo Expects 'Remarkable Results' from Mario Kart Tour."

49. Fahey and Totilo, "Apple Arcade Is Mobile Gaming Without All the Bullshit."

50. Fahey and Totilo, "Apple Arcade Is Mobile Gaming Without All the Bullshit."

51. Fahey and Totilo, "Apple Arcade Is Mobile Gaming Without All the Bullshit."

52. D'Anastasio, "Inside the Culture of Sexism at Riot Games"; Dent, "YouTubers Avoid Fine over Valve 'CS.'"

53. Gault, "'Nearly All' Counter-Strike Microtransactions Are Being Used for Money Laundering"; Hern, "Counter-Strike Trading Found to Be 'Nearly All' Money Laundering."

Bibliography

Aidan. "Aidan's Free-to-Play Budget Decklists." Team Metaminds, November 7, 2015. http://teammetaminds.com/blog/aidans-deck-lists.

AlbertMyers. "EA Is Selling Star Wars Galaxy of Heroes's New Characters for 1100$." Reddit, 2017. https://www.reddit.com/r/Games/comments/5s0k6t/ea_is_selling_star_wars_galaxy_of_heroess_new.

Alexander, Leigh. "Gamasutra's Best of 2014: Leigh Alexander's Top 5 Games." Gamasutra, December 19, 2014. http://www.gamasutra.com/view/news/232790/Gamasutras_Best_of_2014_Leigh_Alexanders_Top_5_Games.php.

Alexandra, Heather. "Star Wars Battlefront II Lets You Pay Real Money for Multiplayer Advantages." Kotaku, November 10, 2017. https://kotaku.com/star-wars-battlefront-ii-lets-you-pay-real-money-for-mu-1820333246.

Alfonso, Juan D. "SWGOH: Beginner's Guide." LevelSkip, July 7, 2018. https://levelskip.com/mobile/SWGOH-Beginners-Guide.

Alha, Kati, Elina Koskinen, Janne Paavilainen, and Juho Hamari. "Free-to-Play Games: Professionals' Perspectives." DIGRA Nordic '14: Proceedings of the 2014 International DIGRA Nordic Conference. 2014.

Andersson, Corinne. "Review: Disney Magic Kingdoms Mobile Game Brings the World of Virtual Disney Theme Park Building with Extra Pixie Dust." Inside the Magic, March 16, 2016. https://insidethemagic

.net/2016/03/review-disney-magic-kingdoms-mobile-game-brings-the
-world-of-virtual-disney-theme-park-building-with-extra-pixie-dust.

Anil, DG. "What Is a Gacha?" Both Guns Blazing, August 7, 2013. https://
bothgunsblazingblog.wordpress.com/2013/08/07/gacha.

antero, henrique. "Peggle's 10th Anniversary." henrique antero, February 26, 2017. https://medium.com/@hernique/peggles-10th-anniversary
-439941ae5773.

Arif, Shabana. "Harry Potter: Hogwarts Mystery Players Upset with
Use of Microtransactions." IGN, April 30, 2018. https://www.ign.com/
articles/2018/04/30/harry-potter-hogwarts-mystery-players-upset-with
-use-of-microtransactions.

Bailey, Kat. "Why I'm Finally Hooked on Madden Ultimate Team," USG,
September 2, 2015. http://www.usgamer.net/articles/ive-finally-gotten
-hooked-on-madden-ultimate-team.

Ballard, John. "Here's How Digital Revenue Has Benefited Electronic
Arts." The Motley Fool, September 9, 2017. https://www.fool.com/inves
ting/2017/09/09/heres-how-digital-revenue-has-benefited-electronic
.aspx.

Bankhurst, Adam. "Ninja Becomes First Professional Gamer to Appear
on Cover of ESPN Magazine." IGN, September 17, 2018. https://www
.ign.com/articles/2018/09/18/ninja-becomes-first-professional-gamer
-to-appear-on-cover-of-espn-magazine.

Barrett, Ben. "Marvel Puzzle Quest: No, Really, It's Good." Rock, Paper,
Shotgun, October 12, 2014. https://www.rockpapershotgun.com/2014/
10/12/marvel-puzzle-quest.

Batchelor, James. "69% of Fortnite Players Have Bought In-Game Purchases, Average Spend Is $85." GamesIndustry.biz, June 27, 2018.
https://www.gamesindustry.biz/articles/2018-06-27-69-percent-of-fort
nite-players-have-bought-in-game-purchases-average-spend-is-usd85.

Batchelor, James. "EA CEO's Damage Control Speech: 'We Want to Be
Better.'" GamesIndustry.biz, June 9, 2018. https://www.gamesindustry
.biz/articles/2018-06-09-ea-ceo-damage-control-speech-we-want-to-be

-better?utm_source=newsletter&utm_medium=email&utm_campaign =e3.

Batchelor, James. "Even Assassin's Creed Is a Live Service Now." Games-Industry.biz, June 13, 2018. https://www.gamesindustry.biz/articles/ 2018-06-13-even-assassins-creed-is-a-live-service-now.

Batchelor, James. "GTA V Is the Most Profitable Entertainment Product of All Time." GamesIndustry.biz, April 9, 2018. https://www.games industry.biz/articles/2018-04-09-gta-v-is-the-most-profitable-entertain ment-product-of-all-time.

Bell, Erin. "Candy Crush Saga—Game Review." Common Sense Media, September 30, 2013. https://www.commonsensemedia.org/game-reviews/ candy-crush-saga.

BestUSCasinos.org. "Casino Whale Stories—Tales from Las Vegas High Rollers." BestUSCasinos.org, 2018. https://www.bestuscasinos.org/high -rollers-whales.

Biden, Ed. "Hearthstone: A Game Changer for Mobile F2P?" Gamasutra, June 8, 2015. http://gamasutra.com/blogs/EdBiden/20150608/245378/ Hearthstone_A_Game_Changer_for_Mobile_F2P.php.

Boyer, Brandon. "The 20 Games You Shouldn't Miss in 2014." Boing Boing, December 22, 2014. https://boingboing.net/2014/12/22/the-20 -games-you-shouldnt-mi.html.

Brightman, James. "Only 3.5% of Gamers Make in-App Purchases—AppsFlyer." GamesIndustry.biz, June 30, 2016. https://www.games industry.biz/articles/2016-06-30-only-3-5-percent-of-gamers-make-in -app-purchases-appsflyer.

Brightman, James. "Star Wars Battlefront II: Will EA's Concession Hurt Sales?" GamesIndustry.biz, November 17, 2017. https://www.games industry.biz/articles/2017-11-17-star-wars-battlefront-ii-will-eas-con cession-hurt-sales.

Brown, Luke. "'Marvel Avengers Academy' Has a Great Design and Story, But a Plodding Pace [Review]." Comics Alliance, February 9, 2016. http://comicsalliance.com/marvel-avengers-academy-mobile-review.

Burford, G. B. "It's 2016 and Warframe Is Still an Excellent Free-to-Play Game." Kotaku, March 31, 2016. https://kotaku.com/its-2016-and -warframe-is-still-an-excellent-free-to-pla-1768070371.

Burke, Kenneth. *A Rhetoric of Motives*. Berkeley, CA: University of California Press, 1969.

Burke, Kenneth. *Language as Symbolic Action: Essays on Life, Literature and Method*. Berkeley, CA: University of California Press, 1966.

Burneko, Albert. "NBA 2K19's Brand Humping Is Craven, Shameless, and Straight-Up Evil." The Concourse, October 1, 2018. https://thecon course.deadspin.com/nba-2k19s-brand-humping-is-craven-shameless -and-strai-1829440522.

Calixto, Joshua. "Hearthstone Players Are Trapped in a Cycle of Salt." Kotaku, May 23, 2017. https://kotaku.com/hearthstone-players-are -trapped-in-a-cycle-of-salt-1795447060.

Calixto, Joshua. "Un'Goro Expansion Makes Hearthstone More Random, Probably More Expensive." Kotaku, April 11, 2017. https://kota ku.com/ungoro-expansion-makes-hearthstone-more-random-probabl -1794231571.

Campbell, Colin. "How Fortnite's Success Led to Months of Intense Crunch at Epic Games." Polygon, April 23, 2019. https://www.polygon .com/2019/4/23/18507750/fortnite-work-crunch-epic-games.

Campbell, Karlyn Kohrs, and Susan Schultz Huxman. *The Rhetorical Act: Thinking, Speaking and Writing Critically*. Belmont, CA: Wadsworth Cengage Learning, 2009.

Chen, Lulu Yilun, and Matthew Burgess. "Tencent Just Overtook Facebook in Market Value: Chart." *Bloomberg.com*, November 21, 2017. https:// www.bloomberg.com/news/articles/2017-11-21/tencent-overtakes-face book-and-joins-global-top-five-chart.

Chess, Shira. "Kim Kardashian: Hollywood Feminism." In *How to Play Video Games*, edited by Matthew Thomas Payne and Nina B. Huntemann, 93–100. New York: NYU Press, 2019.

Chess, Shira. *Ready Player Two: Women Gamers and Designed Identity.* Minneapolis: University of Minnesota Press, 2017.

Chess, Shira, and Christopher A. Paul. "The End of Casual: Long Live Casual." *Games and Culture* 14, no. 2 (March 1, 2019): 107–118.

Choudhury, Saheli Roy. "A Former Librarian Spent $89,000 in Public Money on a Mobile Game." CNBC, August 15, 2018. https://www.cnbc .com/2018/08/16/a-former-librarian-spent-89000-in-public-money-on -a-mobile-game.html.

Cipriani, Jason. "3 Things Steve Jobs Had Wrong about the App Store." ZDNet, July 27, 2018. https://www.zdnet.com/article/3-things-steve-jobs -had-wrong-about-the-app-store.

Clover, Juli. "Happy 10th Anniversary, App Store!" Mac Rumors, July 10, 2018. https://www.macrumors.com/2018/07/10/happy-10th-anniversary -app-store.

Coavoux, Samuel, Manuel Boutet, and Vinciane Zabban. "What We Know About Games: A Scientometric Approach to Game Studies in the 2000s." *Games and Culture* 12, no. 6 (2017): 563–584.

Connors, Phillip. "Harry Potter: Hogwarts Mystery Review—Why It's So HORRIBLE!" *GamingScan*, June 27, 2018. https://www.gamingscan.com/ harry-potter-hogwarts-mystery-review.

Consalvo, Mia. *Cheaters: Gaining Advantage in Videogames.* Cambridge, MA: The MIT Press, 2007.

Consalvo, Mia, and Christopher A. Paul. *Real Games: What's Legitimate and What's Not in Contemporary Videogames.* Cambridge, MA: MIT Press, 2019.

Constine, Josh. "Why Zynga Failed." TechCrunch, October 5, 2012. http:// social.techcrunch.com/2012/10/05/more-competitors-smarter-gamers -expensive-ads-less-virality-mobile.

Cooper, Dalton. "Harry Potter: Hogwarts Mystery Review." Game Rant, May 14, 2018. https://gamerant.com/harry-potter-hogwarts-mystery -review.

Cote, Amanda C. "'I Can Defend Myself': Women's Strategies for Coping with Harassment While Gaming Online." *Games and Culture* 12, no. 2 (2017): 136–155.

Cote, Amanda C. "'Stupid Games' and Serious Gamers: Female Video Game Players' Ambivalent Interpretations of Casual Games' Significance." In *Game, Play and the Emerging Ludo-Mix*. DIGRA Nordic '19: Proceedings of the 2019 International DIGRA Nordic Conference. Kyoto, Japan: 2019.

Cote, Amanda C. "Writing 'Gamers': The Gendered Construction of Gamer Identity in Nintendo Power (1994–1999)." *Games and Culture* 13, no. 5 (2018): 479–503.

Cousins, Ben. "Snobbery and Fear Drive Criticisms of Free-to-Play Games and Ethics." Polygon, April 9, 2014. https://www.polygon.com/2014/4/9/5597062/snobbery-and-fear-drive-ethical-criticisms-of-free-to-play-games.

Cptmarth. "The Organized Arena Shard Power Trip." Reddit, August 2018. https://www.reddit.com/r/SWGalaxyOfHeroes/comments/93f6q8/the_organized_arena_shard_power_trip.

Crecente, Brian. "'Candy Crush Saga' Earned Just Under $1 Billion in Past 12 Months." *Variety*, August 16, 2018. https://variety.com/2018/gaming/news/candy-crush-saga-1-billion-1202908004.

Crecente, Brian. "Superdata: Hearthstone Pulls in $20 Million a Month as It Disrupts the Card Game Industry." Polygon, August 11, 2015. https://www.polygon.com/2015/8/11/9130779/superdata-hearthstone-pulls-in-20-million-a-month-as-it-disrupts-the.

Crossley, Rob. "Valve: Team Fortress 2 Is Free Forever | Game Development." Develop, June 24, 2011. https://web.archive.org/web/20110627082805/http://www.develop-online.net/news/38103/Team-Fortress-2-becomes-free-forever.

Curi. "Starting Stone #1: Six Steps to an Ultimate Deck." Liquid Hearth, November 4, 2013. https://www.liquidhearth.com/forum/general-strategy/458083-starting-stone-1-six-steps-to-an-ultimate-deck.

D'Anastasio, Cecilia. "Battle Passes Are So Hot Right Now." Kotaku, June 21, 2018. https://kotaku.com/battle-passes-are-so-hot-right-now-182702 6722.

D'Anastasio, Cecilia. "How Fortnite's Battle Pass Works." Kotaku, May 3, 2018. https://kotaku.com/how-fortnite-s-battle-pass-works-1825750598.

D'Anastasio, Cecilia. "Inside the Culture of Sexism at Riot Games." Kotaku, August 7, 2018. https://kotaku.com/inside-the-culture-of-sexism -at-riot-games-1828165483.

D'Anastasio, Cecilia. "Magic: The Gathering Arena: The Kotaku Review." Kotaku, September 26, 2019. https://kotaku.com/magic-the-gathering -arena-the-kotaku-review-1834790330.

D'Anastasio, Cecilia. "Report: Fortnite Developers Describe Severe Ongoing Crunch." Kotaku, April 23, 2019. https://kotaku.com/report-fortnite -developers-are-severely-overworked-1834243520.

D'Anastasio, Cecilia. "Students Win Bet, Get Teacher to Make Final Exam About Fortnite." Kotaku, February 26, 2018. https://kotaku.com/ students-win-bet-get-teacher-to-make-final-exam-about-1823334480.

D'Anastasio, Cecilia. "Valve Walks Back Its Stance on Balancing Artifact Cards." Kotaku, December 21, 2018. http://www.kotaku.co.uk/ 2018/12/21/valve-walks-back-its-stance-on-balancing-artifact-cards.

Davis, Chris. "EA Now Makes 40% of Its Revenue from 'Live Services.'" Chris Davis, May 8, 2018. https://cdavisgames.com/2018/05/08/ea-now -makes-forty-percent-of-its-revenue-from-live-services.

Davis, Justin. "Why Core Gamers Hate Free-to-Play." IGN, July 29, 2013. http://www.ign.com/articles/2013/07/29/why-core-gamers-hate-free -to-play.

Daxxari. "A New Way to Play." Hearthstone Official Game Site, February 2, 2016. https://playhearthstone.com/en-us/blog/19995505.

Dedmon, Tanner. "League of Legends Tops Free-to-Play Revenue Charts in 2017." WWG, January 30, 2018. https://comicbook.com/ gaming/2018/01/30/league-of-legends-top-free-to-play-revenue-chart -in-2017.

Dent, Steve. "YouTubers Avoid Fine over Valve 'CS:GO' Gambling Scam." Engadget, September 8, 2017. https://www.engadget.com/2017/09/08/youtube-csgo-lotto-fcc-no-fine.

Donovan, Tristan. *Replay: The Ultimate History of Video Games*. East Sussex, UK: Yellow Ant, 2010.

Dotson, Carter. "According to Newzoo Report, Mobile Gaming Market to Become Bigger than Console or PC Gaming in 2016, and Only Grow from There." TouchArcade, April 22, 2016. https://toucharcade.com/2016/04/22/according-to-newzoo-report-mobile-gaming-market-to-become-bigger-than-console-or-pc-gaming-in-2016-and-only-grow-from-there.

Dotson, Carter. "'Bitcoin Billionaire' Review—I'm Ashamed to Love This Game." TouchArcade, November 7, 2014. https://toucharcade.com/2014/11/07/bitcoin-billionaire-review.

Dotson, Carter. "'Bitcoin Billionaire' Update with Time Travel Out Now, Say Goodbye to Your Life." TouchArcade, August 6, 2015. https://toucharcade.com/2015/08/06/bitcoin-billionaire-update-2.

Dotson, Carter. "Carter's Top Ten Games of 2014." TouchArcade, December 25, 2014. https://toucharcade.com/2014/12/26/carters-top-ten-games-of-2014.

Dotson, Carter. "'CivCrafter' Review—the Last Clicker You'll Ever Need." TouchArcade, April 8, 2015. https://toucharcade.com/2015/04/08/civcrafter-review.

Dotson, Carter. "'Flop Rocket' Review—Fly Me to the Moon." TouchArcade, March 13, 2015. https://toucharcade.com/2015/03/13/flop-rocket-review.

Dotson, Carter. "How Can the Indie Developers of 'Korrigans' Do a Non-Pay-to-Win Take on 'Clash of Clans'? They Explain." TouchArcade, June 15, 2015. https://toucharcade.com/2015/06/15/how-can-the-indie-developers-of-korrigans-do-a-non-pay-to-win-take-on-clash-of-clans-they-explain.

Dotson, Carter. "Mobile Gamers Who Spend Money Almost Spend as Much as Console and PC Gamers." TouchArcade, April 4, 2016. https://

toucharcade.com/2016/04/04/mobile-gamers-who-spend-money-almost
-spend-as-much-as-console-and-pc-gamers.

Dotson, Carter. "Mobile Gaming's Only Going to Get Bigger, and Grow Faster than Console Gaming, According to Report." TouchArcade, May 4, 2015. https://toucharcade.com/2015/05/04/mobile-gamings-only-going -to-get-bigger-and-grow-faster-than-console-gaming-according-to -report.

EA Sports. "Five Years of FIFA Ultimate Team." EA SPORTS, March 19, 2015. https://www.easports.com/uk/fifa/news/2014/five-years-of-fifa-ultimate -team.

EmeraldBoar. "How Are New Players Supposed to Play?" Hearthstone Forums, August 28, 2018. https://us.battle.net/forums/en/hearthstone/ topic/20767639207.

Fagan, Kaylee. "Parents Are Getting 'Fortnite' Coaches for Their Kids." Business Insider, August 1, 2018. https://www.businessinsider.com/fortnite -coaches-2018-7.

Fahey, Michael, and Stephen Totilo. "Apple Arcade Is Mobile Gaming Without All the Bullshit." Kotaku, September 19, 2019. https:// kotaku.com/apple-arcade-is-mobile-gaming-without-all-the-bullshit -1838258655.

Fahey, Mike. "A Candy Crush Saga TV Show Is in the Works." Kotaku, October 18, 2016. https://kotaku.com/a-candy-crush-saga-tv-show-is-in -the-works-1787928194.

Fahey, Mike. "Bejeweled Is So Over Candy Crush Saga's Bullshit." Kotaku, May 15, 2016. https://kotaku.com/bejeweled-is-so-over-candy-crush -sagas-bullshit-1776745361.

Fahey, Mike. "Candy Crush TV Show Leads to In-Game Mario Lopez." Kotaku, July 6, 2017. https://kotaku.com/candy-crush-tv-show-leads-to -in-game-mario-lopez-1796672578.

Fahey, Mike. "The Marvel Game I've Dreamt of for Six Years, Almost." Kotaku, October 3, 2013. https://kotaku.com/the-marvel-game-ive-dreamt -of-for-six-years-almost-1440832229.

Fahey, Mike. "There's a New Transformers Game on the Way, and It's Just Precious." Kotaku, December 10, 2014. https://kotaku.com/theres-a-new-transformers-game-on-the-way-and-its-just-1669294074.

Fahey, Mike. "Tips for Playing Bit City." Kotaku, March 20, 2017. https://kotaku.com/tips-for-playing-bit-city-1793455056.

Fahey, Rob. "EA Trips up on the Path from Product to Service." Games Industry.biz, December 1, 2017. https://www.gamesindustry.biz/articles/2017-12-01-ea-trips-up-on-the-path-from-product-to-service.

Fahey, Rob. "Super Mario Run's Inevitable Backlash." GamesIndustry.biz, December 22, 2016. https://www.gamesindustry.biz/articles/2016-12-22-super-mario-runs-inevitable-backlash.

Fahey, Rob. "Why Do Mobile Games Get a 'Free' Pass?" GamesIndustry.biz, May 4, 2018. https://www.gamesindustry.biz/articles/2018-05-04-why-do-mobile-games-get-a-free-pass.

Faraday, Owen. "Field Marshal Owen's Guide to World of Tanks Blitz." Pocket Tactics, June 28, 2014. https://www.pockettactics.com/articles/field-marshal-owens-guide-world-tanks-blitz.

Fernandez, Nick. "Hogwarts Mystery Review: Harry Potter and the Prisoner of Microtransactions." Android Authority, April 27, 2018. https://www.androidauthority.com/harry-potter-hogwarts-mystery-review-859269.

Ford, Eric. "'Disney Magic Kingdoms' Adds 'Cinderella' Characters, Chest System." TouchArcade, August 3, 2016. https://toucharcade.com/2016/08/03/disney-magic-kingdoms-adds-cinderella-characters-chest-system.

Ford, Eric. "'Disney Magic Kingdoms' Goes 'Frozen' in Holiday Update." TouchArcade, December 8, 2016. https://toucharcade.com/2016/12/08/disney-magic-kingdoms-frozen-update.

Ford, Eric. "'Disney Magic Kingdoms' Guide—Tips to Build Without Spending Real Money." TouchArcade, April 8, 2016. https://toucharcade.com/2016/04/08/disney-magic-kingdoms-guide-tips-to-build.

Ford, Eric. "'Disney Magic Kingdoms' Updates with Pirates Characters, Quests." TouchArcade, September 14, 2016. https://toucharcade.com/

2016/09/14/disney-magic-kingdoms-updates-with-pirates-characters
-quests.

Ford, Eric. "Jack Skellington Invades 'Disney Magic Kingdoms' for Halloween." TouchArcade, October 13, 2016. https://toucharcade.com/2016/
10/13/jack-skellington-invades-disney-magic-kingdoms-for-halloween.

Ford, Eric. "'Madden NFL 25' Review—an Incredibly Disappointing Display of Football and Freemium." TouchArcade, August 27, 2013. https://
toucharcade.com/2013/08/27/madden-25-review.

Ford, Eric. "'Star Wars: Galaxy of Heroes'—Tips to Awaken the Force Without Spending Real Money." TouchArcade, December 8, 2015. https://
toucharcade.com/2015/12/08/star-wars-galaxy-of-heroes-tips-guide.

Ford, Eric. "'Vainglory' Review—Portable MOBA Magic." TouchArcade,
November 20, 2014. https://toucharcade.com/2014/11/20/vainglory
-review.

Fragsworth. "Why Clicker Heroes 2 Is Abandoning Free-to-Play." Clicker
Heroes 2, November 20, 2017. http://www.clickerheroes2.com/payto
win.php.

Futter, Michael. "Tencent Isn't Just Ubisoft's Savior—It's the World's
Biggest Gaming Company." Polygon, March 29, 2018. https://www
.polygon.com/2018/3/29/17172326/tencent-ubisoft-explained.

Gach, Ethan. "Meet the 19-Year-Old Who Spent Over $10,000 on Micro-
transactions." Kotaku, November 29, 2017. https://kotaku.com/meet-the
-19-year-old-who-spent-over-10-000-on-microtra-1820854953.

Gach, Ethan. "Players Worry Paladins' New Card System Inches Closer
to Pay-to-Win." Kotaku, November 30, 2017. https://kotaku.com/play
ers-worry-paladins-new-card-system-inches-closer-to-1820894074.

Gallaway, Brad. "Marvel Puzzle Quest: Dark Reign Review." Game-
Critics.com, January 28, 2014. https://gamecritics.com/brad-gallaway/
marvel-puzzle-quest-dark-reign-review.

GameCentral. "League of Legends Is Still the Biggest Video Game in the
World." *Metro News*, August 4, 2017. https://metro.co.uk/2017/08/04/
league-of-legends-is-still-the-biggest-video-game-in-the-world-6828565.

GameRefinery. "What Separates China and the West in Mobile?" Games Industry.biz, May 2, 2018. https://www.gamesindustry.biz/articles/2018 -05-02-what-separates-china-and-the-west-in-mobile.

Gaudiosi, John. "'Candy Crush' Publisher Targets Traditional Gamers with 'Legend of Solgard.'" The Star Online, August 27, 2018. https://www .thestar.com.my/tech/tech-news/2018/08/27/candy-crush-publisher -targets-traditional-gamers-with-legend-of-solgard.

Gaudiosi, John. "Madden: The $4 Billion Video Game Franchise." CNNMoney, September 5, 2013. https://money.cnn.com/2013/09/05/ technology/innovation/madden-25/index.html.

Gault, Matthew. "'Nearly All' Counter-Strike Microtransactions Are Being Used for Money Laundering." Vice, October 29, 2019. https:// www.vice.com/en_ca/article/8xw7nx/nearly-all-counter-strike-micro transactions-are-being-used-for-money-laundering.

GiantBoyDetective. "Rusty's Real Deal Baseball: The Right Way to Do In-Game Purchases." Talk Amongst Yourselves, April 4, 2014. https://tay.kinja.com/rustys-real-deal-baseball-the-right-way-to-do-in -game-1558215409.

GiantBoyDetective. "Rusty's Real Deal Baseball: The TAY Review." Talk Amongst Yourselves, April 8, 2014. https://tay.kinja.com/rustys-real -deal-baseball-the-tay-review-1559409222.

Gilbert, Ben. "Nintendo's First iPhone Game Has a Long-Term Revenue Problem." Business Insider, January 3, 2017. https://www.business insider.com/nintendo-super-mario-run-revenue-2017-1.

Glu Mobile. "MLB Tap Sports Baseball 2018." Glu, 2018. https://www .glu.com/games/mlb-tap-sports-baseball-2018.

Good, Owen S. "I Spent $90 in Battlefront 2, and I Still Don't Have Any Control over My Characters." Polygon, November 16, 2017. https:// www.polygon.com/2017/11/16/16658476/star-wars-battlefront-2-loot -crate-costs-analysis.

Good, Owen S. "One of Magic: The Gathering's Rarest Cards Was Bought for $87,000." Polygon, July 28, 2018. https://www.polygon

.com/2018/7/28/17625830/magic-the-gathering-black-lotus-auction
-sold.

Graft, Kris. "Gamasutra—Dota 2 Is Free-to-Play, but Not Pay-to-Win, Says Valve." Gamasutra, June 1, 2012. http://gamasutra.com/view/news/ 171570/Dota_2_is_freetoplay_but_not_paytowin_says_Valve.php.

Grayson, Nathan. "Artifact Seems Like a Very Valve Card Game." Steamed, September 4, 2018. https://steamed.kotaku.com/artifact-seems -like-a-very-valve-card-game-1828815941.

Grayson, Nathan. "Clicker Game Ditches Microtransactions, Becomes Steam Best Seller." Kotaku, July 18, 2018. https://steamed.kotaku.com/ clicker-game-ditches-microtransactions-becomes-steam-b-1827703881.

Grayson, Nathan. "Clicker Heroes Is Super Popular on Steam . . . for Some Reason." Kotaku, May 18, 2015. https://steamed.kotaku.com/ clicker-heroes-is-super-popular-on-steam-for-some-re-1705380774.

Grayson, Nathan. "The Saga Continues: King Abandons 'Candy' TM in US." Rock, Paper, Shotgun, February 26, 2014. https://www.rockpaper shotgun.com/2014/02/26/king-abandons-candy-trademark-in-us.

Grayson, Nathan. "UFC Stars Hate How Much They're Spending on Clash of Clans." Kotaku, May 22, 2015. https://kotaku.com/ufc-stars -hate-how-much-theyre-spending-on-clash-of-cla-1706396864.

Grubb, Jeff. "Why Madden NFL Mobile Is the Last Football Game EA Will Ever Need to Release on Mobile." Venture Beat, January 15, 2015. https://venturebeat.com/2015/01/15/why-madden-nfl-mobile-is-the -last-football-game-ea-will-ever-need-to-release-on-mobile.

Ham, Ethan. "Rarity and Power: Balance in Collectible Object Games." Game Studies 10, no. 1 (2010). http://gamestudies.org/1001/articles/ham.

Hamilton, Kirk. "In-Game Purchases Poison the Well." Kotaku, November 29, 2017. https://kotaku.com/in-game-purchases-poison-the-well-1820 844066.

Handrahan, Matthew. "Chinese Mobile Games Market Is Now the Most Valuable in the World." GamesIndustry.biz, May 3, 2016. https://www

.gamesindustry.biz/articles/2016-05-03-chinese-mobile-market-is-now -the-most-valuable-in-the-world.

Handrahan, Matthew. "EA's Ultimate Team Now Worth $800 Million Annually." GamesIndustry.biz, March 1, 2017. https://www.games industry.biz/articles/2017-03-01-eas-ultimate-team-now-worth-USD800 -million-annually.

Handrahan, Matthew. "Fortnite's Five-Month iOS Revenue on Par with Clash Royale." GamesIndustry.biz, August 22, 2018. https://www.games industry.biz/articles/2018-08-22-fortnites-five-month-ios-revenue-on -par-with-clash-royale.

Handrahan, Matthew. "Mobile Game Spend Will Double to $105 Billion by 2021." GamesIndustry.biz, March 30, 2017. https://www.games industry.biz/articles/2017-03-30-mobile-game-spend-will-double-to -usd105-billion-by-2021.

Handrahan, Matthew. "Nintendo Expects 'Remarkable Results' from Mario Kart Tour." GamesIndustry.biz, November 11, 2019. https://www .gamesindustry.biz/articles/2019-11-11-nintendo-expects-remarkable -results-from-mario-kart-tour.

Handrahan, Matthew. "Super Mario Run: Critical Consensus." Games Industry.biz, December 21, 2016. https://www.gamesindustry.biz/ articles/2016-12-21-super-mario-run-critical-consensus.

Harvey, Alison. "The Fame Game: Working Your Way Up the Celebrity Ladder in Kim Kardashian: Hollywood." *Games and Culture* 13, no. 7 (November 1, 2018): 652–670.

Hayward, Andrew. "MLB Tap Sports Baseball 2017 Isn't Worth Big-League Time or Money." Macworld, May 1, 2017. https://www.mac world.com/article/3190665/ios/mlb-tap-sports-baseball-2017-isnt -worth-big-league-time-or-money.html.

Headley, Jaysen. "8 Tips for Playing Magic Kingdoms." Jaysen Headly Writes, May 19, 2016. https://jaysenheadleywrites.com/2016/05/19/8 -tips-for-playing-magic-kingdoms.

Heller, Emily. "Overwatch Is Coming to Humble Bundle in October." Polygon, September 7, 2018. https://www.polygon.com/deals/2018/9/7/17829338/overwatch-sale-humble-bundle-october-blizzard-charity.

Herecomesthenightman. "EA Fired Plants VS Zombies Creator for Objecting to Pay2Win: Games." Reddit, January 2018. https://www.reddit.com/r/Games/comments/7ea983/ea_fired_plants_vs_zombies_creator_for_objecting/?st=jkx30jgu&sh=9b2c414e.

Hern, Alex. "Counter-Strike Trading Found to Be 'Nearly All' Money Laundering." The Guardian, October 30, 2019. https://www.theguardian.com/games/2019/oct/30/counter-strike-trading-found-to-be-nearly-all-money-laundering.

Hernandez, Patricia. "Kim Kardashian Brags About How Much Bank Her Game Is Making." Kotaku, March 8, 2016. https://kotaku.com/kim-kardashian-brags-about-how-much-bank-her-game-is-ma-1763459919.

Hernandez, Patricia. "Kim Kardashian: Hollywood Has the Best Rival Since Pokémon's Gary Oak." Kotaku, July 28, 2014. https://kotaku.com/kim-kardashian-hollywood-has-the-best-rival-since-poke-1612138200.

Hernandez, Patricia. "Teen Girls Don't Care What We Think of Kim Kardashian." Kotaku, August 15, 2014. https://kotaku.com/teen-girls-dont-care-what-we-think-of-kim-kardashian-1611225640.

Hill, Mark, and Jason Croghan. "5 Reasons I Lost $9,000 on an iPhone Game." Cracked.com, July 29, 2015. http://www.cracked.com/personal-experiences-1762-5-reasons-i-lost-249000-iphone-game.html.

Hodapp, Eli. "'Candy Crush Soda Saga' Review—Poppin' Bottles in the Ice." TouchArcade, November 12, 2014. https://toucharcade.com/2014/11/12/candy-crush-soda-saga-review.

Hodapp, Eli. "Eli's Top Ten Games of 2014." TouchArcade, December 26, 2014. https://toucharcade.com/2014/12/26/elis-top-ten-games-of-2014.

Hodapp, Eli. "New 'SimCity BuildIt' Infographic Shows Just What a Smash Hit the Game Is." TouchArcade, January 15, 2015. https://touch

arcade.com/2015/01/15/new-simcity-buildit-infographic-shows-just
-what-a-smash-hit-the-game-is.

Hodapp, Eli. "'Sid Meier's Civilization VI' for IPad Review—Wow, Just
Wow." TouchArcade, December 21, 2017. https://toucharcade.com/
2017/12/21/sid-meiers-civilization-vi-for-ipad-review.

Hodapp, Eli. "Strange Flavour Ditching Their 'Play Nice' IAP System,
Returning to Paid Games." TouchArcade, July 28, 2015. https://touch
arcade.com/2015/07/28/strange-flavour-ditching-their-play-nice-iap
-system-returning-to-paid-games.

Hodapp, Eli. "Unsurprisingly, All Future Gameloft Games Will Be Free
to Play." TouchArcade, April 4, 2016. https://toucharcade.com/2016/04
/04/unsurprisingly-all-future-gameloft-games-will-be-free-to-play.

Hodapp, Eli. "'We Own You'—Confessions of an Anonymous Free to
Play Producer." TouchArcade, September 16, 2015. https://toucharcade
.com/2015/09/16/we-own-you-confessions-of-a-free-to-play-producer.

Horti, Samuel, and Henry St Leger. "Fortnite Android Beta: Everything
You Need to Know about the Mobile Game." Tech Radar, September 13,
2018. https://www.techradar.com/news/fortnite-on-android.

Horwitz, Jeremy. "Apptopia: iOS Games Peak Quickly, and Top 50 Take
76% of Revenues." VentureBeat, June 21, 2018. https://venturebeat
.com/2018/06/21/apptopia-ios-games-peak-quickly-and-top-50-take-76
-of-revenues.

Horwitz, Jeremy. "iOS App Store's All-Time Top Game Made $4 Billion
to Top App's $1 Billion." VentureBeat, July 2, 2018. https://venturebeat
.com/2018/07/02/top-ios-apps-of-all-time.

Hovahdo. "The Underpowered Guild's Guide to Clearing Heroic AAT—
the 'Super Team' Strategy." Star Wars Galaxy of Heroes Forums, December 1, 2016. https://forums.galaxy-of-heroes.starwars.ea.com/discussion/
79590/the-underpowered-guilds-guide-to-clearing-heroic-aat-the-super
-team-strategy.

Humphreys, Sal. "On Being a Feminist in Games Studies." Games and
Culture 14, no. 7-8 (2017): 825–842.

Huntemann, Nina B. "Women in Video Games: The Case of Hardware Production and Promotion." In *Gaming Globally: Production, Play, and Place*, edited by Nina B. Huntemann and Ben Aslinger, 41–57. New York: Palgrave Macmillan, 2013.

Insight Team. "Women on Mobile Platforms Are the Most Valuable Gamers." Deltadna.com, December 14, 2017. https://deltadna.com/blog/women-mobile-platforms-valuable-gamers.

Jackson, Gita. "Kim Kardashian: Hollywood and the Price of Fame." *Paste*, July 22, 2014. https://www.pastemagazine.com/articles/2014/07/kim-kardashian-hollywood-and-the-price-of-fame.html.

Jackson, Gita. "Mobile Game Hogwarts Mystery Is Like a Harry Potter Book That Keeps Asking for Money." Kotaku, April 26, 2018. https://kotaku.com/mobile-game-hogwarts-mystery-is-like-a-harry-potter-boo-1825576677.

Jackson, Gita. "Nicki Minaj Has a New Game Where People Actually Rap for Her." Kotaku, December 7, 2016. https://kotaku.com/nicki-minaj-has-a-new-game-where-people-actually-rap-fo-1789794906.

Jackson, Gita. "The Internet Reacts to Hogwarts Mystery's Microtransactions." Kotaku, April 27, 2018. https://kotaku.com/the-internet-reacts-to-hogwarts-mystery-s-microtransact-1825598054.

Jacobs, Harrison. "Redditors Explain How They Spent Thousands of Dollars on League of Legends." Business Insider, March 20, 2015. https://www.businessinsider.com/redditors-explain-how-they-spent-thousands-of-dollars-league-of-legends-2015-3.

Jagneaux, David. "Harry Potter: Hogwarts Mystery Review." IGN, May 3, 2018. https://www.ign.com/articles/2018/05/03/harry-potter-hogwarts-mystery-review.

James, Chris. "Marvel Avengers Academy Review—IPhone Reviews." Pocket Gamer, February 8, 2016. http://www.pocketgamer.co.uk/r/iPhone/Marvel+Avengers+Academy/review.asp?c=68988.

James, C. L. R. *Beyond a Boundary*. Durham, NC: Duke University Press, 1993.

Kaiser, Rowan. "Marvel Puzzle Quest: Dark Reign Review." IGN, October 11, 2013. http://www.ign.com/articles/2013/10/11/marvel-puzzle-quest-dark-reign-review.

Karmali, Luke. "Candy Crush Founders Richer than Grand Theft Auto Creators." IGN, May 19, 2014. https://www.ign.com/articles/2014/05/19/candy-crush-founders-richer-than-grand-theft-auto-creators.

Karner, Jen. "Marvel's Avengers Academy—a 30-Day Follow-Up." Android Central, April 7, 2016. https://www.androidcentral.com/avengers-academy-30-day-followup.

Karner, Jen. "What Is Marvel: Avengers Academy, and Why You Should Play It." Android Central, February 14, 2016. https://www.androidcentral.com/what-marvel-avengers-academy-and-why-should-i-play-it.

Katkoff, Michail. "World of Tanks Blitz Liberates Players from Mid-Core—Deconstructor of Fun." Deconstructor of Fun, June 21, 2015. https://www.deconstructoroffun.com/blog//2015/06/world-of-tanks-blitz-liberates-players.html?rq=world%20of%20tanks.

Keganbe. "New Player Guides." Hearthstone Forums, March 12, 2014. https://us.battle.net/forums/en/hearthstone/topic/12034043452.

Kelly, Tadhg. "Is Premium Mobile Gaming Viable?" TechCrunch, February 8, 2015. http://social.techcrunch.com/2015/02/08/is-premium-mobile-gaming-viable.

Kent, Steven L. *The Ultimate History of Video Games.* New York: Three Rivers Press, 2001.

KHAndAnime. "Where Did the Console Dungeon Crawlers Go?—Games Discussion." GameSpot, January 2010. https://www.gamespot.com/forums/games-discussion-1000000/where-did-the-console-dungeon-crawlers-go-27139491.

Kim, Tae. "Gamers Overreacting on EA 'Star Wars' Game; Firms Should Raise Prices: Analyst." CNBC, November 20, 2017. https://www.cnbc.com/2017/11/20/gamers-overreacting-on-ea-star-wars-game-firms-should-raise-prices.html.

Klepek, Patrick. "College Student Found the Perfect Gamer to Win $6,000 From." Kotaku, January 9, 2015. https://kotaku.com/college-student -found-the-perfect-gamer-to-win-6000-fr-1678359567.

Klepek, Patrick. "My Weird, Addictive Trip into Kim Kardashian: Hollywood." Giant Bomb, August 6, 2014. https://www.giantbomb.com/ articles/my-weird-addictive-trip-into-kim-kardashian-hollyw/1100-4980.

Knoblauch, Max. "The 10 Most Disturbing Things About 'Kim Kardashian: Hollywood.'" Mashable, July 23, 2014. https://mashable .com/2014/07/23/weird-kardashian-hollwood/#FfRTyWSWXPqP.

Kocurek, Carly A. *Coin-Operated Americans: Rebooting Boyhood at the Video Game Arcade.* Minneapolis: University of Minnesota Press, 2015.

Kohler, Chris. "Nintendo's Take on Free-to-Play Is a Home Run." *Wired*, April 10, 2014. https://www.wired.com/2014/04/rusty-real-deal-baseball.

Kollar, Philip. "Clash Royale's Top-Ranked Player Has Spent over $12,000 on the Game." Polygon, March 31, 2016. https://www.poly gon.com/2016/3/31/11340798/clash-royales-top-ranked-player-has -spent-over-12000-on-the-game.

Kunzelman, Cameron. "Rare Magic: The Gathering Card Sells for $87,000." Kotaku, July 28, 2018. https://kotaku.com/rare-magic-the -gathering-card-sells-for-87-000-1827945703.

Kurtenbach, Dieter. "EA Sports Is Making a Fortune off Its Ultimate Team Modes." FOX Sports, March 2, 2016. http://www.foxsports.com/ soccer/story/ea-sports-ultimate-team-mode-revenue-per-year-fut-fifa -ultimate-team-650-billion-030216.

Lanier, Liz. "'Kim Kardashian: Hollywood' Brings in $8 Million for Glu Mobile." *Variety*, August 6, 2018. https://variety.com/2018/gaming/news/ kim-kardashian-hollywood-brings-in-8-million-1202896344.

Lanier, Liz. "'Super Mario Run' Leaves $60 Million Revenue Mark in the Dust." *Variety*, July 2, 2018. https://variety.com/2018/gaming/news/ super-mario-run-hits-60-million-revenue-mark-1202863810.

Lazarides, Tasos. "Collectible Card Games Are Becoming the Most Dominant Genre on Mobile, and 'Hearthstone' Is Leading the Way." TouchArcade, August 11, 2015. https://toucharcade.com/2015/08/11/collectible-card-games-are-becoming-the-most-dominant-genre-on-mobile-and-hearthstone-is-leading-the-way.

Lazarides, Tasos. "For Some, 'World of Tanks: Blitz' 2.8 Update Might Have Pushed the Game into Pay-to-Win Territory." TouchArcade, April 8, 2016. https://toucharcade.com/2016/04/08/for-some-world-of-tanks-blitz-2-8-update-might-have-pushed-the-game-into-pay-to-win-territory.

Lazarides, Tasos. "Gondola Wants to Rock the Boat of F2P Monetization with Realtime Player-Based IAP Adjustment." TouchArcade, April 6, 2015. https://toucharcade.com/2015/04/06/gondola-wants-to-rock-the-boat-of-f2p-monetization-with-realtime-player-based-iap-adjustment.

Lazarides, Tasos. "In Response to the Many Complaints, 'World of Tanks Blitz' Has Adjusted Profitability and Provisions." TouchArcade, April 21, 2016. https://toucharcade.com/2016/04/21/after-the-many-complaints-world-of-tanks-blitz-has-adjusted-profitability-and-provisions.

Lazarides, Tasos. "'Play Me Baby One More Time'—Britney Spears Is Following Kim Kardashian's F2P Footsteps." TouchArcade, April 30, 2015. https://toucharcade.com/2015/04/30/play-me-baby-one-more-time-britney-spears-is-following-kim-kardashians-f2p-footsteps.

Lazarides, Tasos. "Taylor Swift Will Be the Next Pop Singer to Come to Your Mobile Device." TouchArcade, February 4, 2016. https://toucharcade.com/2016/02/04/taylor-swift-mobile-game.

Lazarides, Tasos. "'World of Tanks Blitz' Update 2.8 Finally Makes Playing Tier IX-X Worth Your Time." TouchArcade, April 6, 2016. https://toucharcade.com/2016/04/06/world-of-tanks-blitz-update-2-8-finally-makes-playing-tier-ix-x-worth-your-time.

Leaver, Tama, and Michele Willson, eds. *Social, Casual, and Mobile Games: The Changing Gaming Landscape*. New York: Bloomsbury, 2017.

LeJacq, Yannick. "League of Legends Is Too Expensive." Kotaku, May 12, 2015. https://kotaku.com/league-of-legends-is-too-expensive-1704015868.

Leray, Joseph. "'Marvel Puzzle Quest: Dark Reign' Review—Match-3 RPG in the Marvel Universe." TouchArcade, October 12, 2013. https://touch arcade.com/2013/10/12/marvel-puzzle-quest-dark-reign-review.

LoL Smurfs. "Is League of Legends Free to Play? The Truth Behind LoL Being 'Free.'" LoL-Smurfs, May 23, 2018. https://www.lol-smurfs.com/blog/is-league-of-legends-free.

LoL Smurfs. "The Fastest Way to Level 30 in LoL." LoL-Smurfs, January 30, 2015. https://www.lol-smurfs.com/blog/fastest-way-level-30.

Lopes, Rodrigo. "Brief FIFA Ultimate Team History." FIFA AU Team, 2015. https://www.fifauteam.com/brief-fifa-ultimate-team-history.

LukasPhoenixRebels. "The Alliance Phoenix Has Cleared the Heroic Sith Raid at 156.8M GP." Reddit, March 2018. https://www.reddit.com/r/SW GalaxyOfHeroes/comments/829r3z/the_alliance_phoenix_has_cleared _the_heroic_sith.

Lunden, Ingrid. "Activision Blizzard Closes Its $5.9B Acquisition of King, Makers of Candy Crush." TechCrunch, 2015. http://social.tech crunch.com/2016/02/23/activision-blizzard-closes-its-5-9b-acquisition -of-king-makers-of-candy-crush.

Luton, Will. "Ten Surprising Things Battle Royale Can Teach Us." GamesIndustry.biz, August 30, 2018. https://www.gamesindustry.biz/articles/2018-08-30-ten-surprising-things-battle-royale-can-teach-us.

MacDonald, Keza. "Harry Potter: Hogwarts Mystery Review: A Shameless Shake-Down." *The Guardian*, May 4, 2018. https://www.theguardian.com/games/2018/may/04/harry-potter-hogwarts-mystery-review.

Mannergoggle. "Play Nice Press Release." Strange Flavour, August 31, 2013. http://www.strangeflavour.com/news/play-nice-press-release.

Martin, Garrett. "Marketing and Mortality at the Avengers Academy Launch Party." *Paste*, February 10, 2016. https://www.pastemagazine.com/articles/2016/02/marketing-and-mortality-at-the-avengers-academy -la.html.

Mc Shea, Tom. "EA Adamant Loot Boxes Aren't Gambling." GamesIndustry.biz, May 9, 2018. https://www.gamesindustry.biz/articles/2018-05-09-ea-adamant-loot-boxes-arent-gambling.

McCarthy, Caty. "Final Fantasy XV's New Mobile Game Sure Is a Free-to-Play Mobile Game." USG, June 29, 2017. https://www.usgamer.net/articles/final-fantasy-xvs-new-mobile-game-sure-is-a-free-to-play-mobile-game.

McCormick, Rich. "Game of War Executive Arrested for Allegedly Stealing Trade Secrets." The Verge, August 26, 2015. https://www.theverge.com/2015/8/26/9209593/game-of-war-fire-age-executive-arrested-stealing-secrets.

Mistereousone. "Dear CG Let Us Have This." Reddit, March 2018. https://www.reddit.com/r/SWGalaxyOfHeroes/comments/82ah7k/dear_cg_let_us_have_this.

Moriarty, Colin. "The Real Cost of Gaming: Inflation, Time, and Purchasing Power." IGN, October 15, 2013. http://www.ign.com/articles/2013/10/15/the-real-cost-of-gaming-inflation-time-and-purchasing-power.

Morris, Chris. "Candy Crush Saga—App Review." Common Sense Media, January 24, 2013. https://www.commonsensemedia.org/app-reviews/candy-crush-saga.

Morris, Chris. "Candy Crush Soda Saga—App Review." Common Sense Media, November 14, 2014. https://www.commonsensemedia.org/app-reviews/candy-crush-soda-saga.

Morrissey, Tracie Egan. "Oh God, I Spent $494.04 Playing the Kim Kardashian Hollywood App." Jezebel, July 1, 2014. https://jezebel.com/oh-god-i-spent-494-04-playing-the-kim-kardashian-holl-1597154346.

MSG-MLB Tap Sports Baseball. "How to Get a 5 Star Team | Tips and Tricks." 2018. https://www.youtube.com/watch?v=KSNWFky09k0.

Musgrave, Shaun. "'Marvel Avengers Academy' Guide—Tips and Tricks for Assembling Your Team." TouchArcade, February 26, 2016. https://

toucharcade.com/2016/02/26/marvel-avengers-academy-guide-tips
-and-tricks-for-assembling-your-team.

Musgrave, Shaun. "'World of Tanks Blitz' Review—a Fine Addition to
Wargaming's Cannon Canon." TouchArcade, July 8, 2014. https://touch
arcade.com/2014/07/08/world-of-tanks-blitz.

Nelson, Jared. "EA Releases First Trailer for 'Star Wars: Galaxy of Heroes,'
a Hero Collecting Game with Turn-Based Battling." TouchArcade,
August 31, 2015. https://toucharcade.com/2015/08/31/star-wars-galaxy
-of-heroes-trailer.

Nelson, Jared. "'Madden NFL Mobile' Proves Successful as EA Mobile
Focuses on Games as 'Live Services.'" TouchArcade, January 15, 2015.
https://toucharcade.com/2015/01/15/madden-nfl-mobile-success.

Nelson, Jared. "TouchArcade Game of the Week: 'Guardians of the Galaxy: The Universal Weapon.'" TouchArcade, July 18, 2014. https://touch
arcade.com/2014/07/18/game-of-the-week-guardians-of-the-galaxy.

Newman, Heather. "SimCity BuildIt Has Become the Most-Played Sim-
City Ever, EA Mobile Claims." VentureBeat, June 6, 2015. https://ven
turebeat.com/2015/06/06/simcity-buildit-has-become-the-most-played
-simcity-ever.

Nieborg, David. "From Premium to Freemium: The Political Economy
of the App." In *Social, Casual and Mobile Games: The Changing Gaming
Landscape*, edited by Tama Leaver and Michele Willson, 225–240. New
York: Bloomsbury, 2017.

Nieborg, David B. "Crushing Candy: The Free-to-Play Game in Its Connective Commodity Form." *Social Media and Society* 1, no. 2 (2015).
https://journals.sagepub.com/doi/10.1177/2056305115621932.

Oxts86vv. "Foxnext Is Laughing at Us!: MarvelStrikeForce." Reddit, July
2018. https://www.reddit.com/r/MarvelStrikeForce/comments/8ui9kc/
foxnext_is_laughing_at_us/?st=jloac8bc&sh=f2ab22ac.

Paczkowski, John. "Apple SVP Eddy Cue Talks About the New Apple
TV, Apps and Games." BuzzFeed News, December 9, 2015. https://www

.buzzfeednews.com/article/johnpaczkowski/eddy-cue-on-apple-tv-app
-store-best-of-2015.

Paul, Christopher A. "It's in the Game? Shifting the Scene with Online Play." In *Sports Videogames*, edited by Mia Consalvo, Konstantin Mitgutsch, and Abe Stein, 138–155. New York: Routledge, 2013.

Paul, Christopher A. *The Toxic Meritocracy of Video Games: Why Gaming Culture Is the Worst*. Minneapolis: University of Minnesota Press, 2018.

Paul, Christopher A. *Wordplay and the Discourse of Video Games: Analyzing Words, Design, and Play*. New York: Routledge, 2012.

Pearson, Dan. "I Was So Fed Up of People Telling Us We Should Do Free-to-F***ing-Play." GamesIndustry.biz, June 26, 2014. https://www.gamesindustry.biz/articles/2014-06-25-so-fed-up-of-people-telling-us-we-should-do-free-to-f-ing-play.

PepsiCo. "MTN DEW®, MTN DEW®, AMP®, GAME FUEL®, and DORITOS® Join Activision to Celebrate Call of Duty®: Modern Warfare®," September 10, 2019. https://www.prnewswire.com/news-releases/mtn-dew-mtn-dew-amp-game-fuel-and-doritos-join-activision-to-celebrate-call-of-duty-modern-warfare-300915165.html.

Petchesky, Barry. "Please Arrest Whoever Did This to Fantasy Football." Deadspin, October 21, 2016. https://deadspin.com/please-arrest-whoever-did-this-to-fantasy-football-1788065809.

Phillips, Tom. "Harry Potter: Hogwarts Mystery Forces You to Pay—or Wait—to Save a Kid from Being Strangled." *Eurogamer*, April 30, 2018. https://www.eurogamer.net/articles/2018-04-27-harry-potter-hogwart-mystery-is-ruined-by-its-in-game-payments.

Phillips, Tom. "Harry Potter: Hogwarts Mystery Will Feature Some Familiar Voices." *Eurogamer*, April 5, 2018. https://www.eurogamer.net/articles/2018-04-05-harry-potter-hogwarts-mystery-will-feature-some-familiar-voices.

Phillips, Tom. "Harry Potter Mobile Game Now Sells Owls for £12." *Eurogamer*, June 27, 2018. https://www.eurogamer.net/articles/2018-06-27-now-harry-potter-mobile-game-now-sells-owls-for-12.

Phillips, Tom. "Now Harry Potter: Hogwarts Mystery Has Slashed the Price of Its Microtransactions." *Eurogamer*, May 1, 2018. https://www .eurogamer.net/articles/2018-05-01-now-harry-potter-hogwarts-mys tery-is-heavily-discounting-energy-microtransactions.

Plunkett, Luke. "Kim Kardashian's Video Game Is the Stuff of Night- mares." Kotaku, June 17, 2014. https://kotaku.com/kim-kardashians -video-game-is-the-stuff-of-nightmares-1592324887.

Plunkett, Luke. "NBA 2K Is Very Sorry about Charging Players for Hair- cuts." Kotaku, September 9, 2018. https://kotaku.com/nba-2k-is-very -sorry-about-charging-players-for-haircut-1828924933.

Plunkett, Luke. "NBA 2K19 Is a Nightmarish Vision of Our Micro- transaction-Stuffed Future." Kotaku, September 11, 2018. https://kotaku .com/nba-2k19-is-a-nightmarish-vision-of-our-microtransactio-1828 954456.

Plunkett, Luke. "'Pay to Win' Protests Hit the Streets of Black Desert Online." Kotaku, August 7, 2016. https://kotaku.com/pay-to-win-protests -hit-the-streets-of-black-desert-o-1784949509.

Plunkett, Luke. "Surprise, NBA 2K20 Is Still Full of Bullshit Microtrans- actions." Kotaku, September 10, 2019. https://kotaku.com/surprise-nba -2k20-is-still-full-of-bullshit-microtrans-1838000636.

Polo, Susana. "Marvel's Avengers Academy Is More Fun than It Has the Right to Be." Polygon, February 16, 2016. https://www.polygon .com/2016/2/16/11006882/avengers-academy-game.

Princy. "Top Grossing Apps of 2017." Zco Corporation, January 23, 2018. https://www.zco.com/blog/top-grossing-apps-of-2017.

RAmarl. "How Are New Players Supposed to Play?" Hearthstone Forums, August 29, 2018. https://us.battle.net/forums/en/hearthstone/ topic/20767639207.

Robehmed, Natalie. "Kim Kardashian West, Mobile Mogul: The Forbes Cover Story." *Forbes*, July 11, 2016. https://www.forbes.com/sites/natalie robehmed/2016/07/11/kim-kardashian-mobile-mogul-the-forbes-cover -story/#3feff58b7e4f.

Robertson, Adi. "Do More Women Actually Own Game Consoles than Men? It's Hard to Say." The Verge, November 4, 2015. https://www.theverge.com/2015/11/4/9670524/pew-survey-women-men-console-ownership-by-gender-2015.

Rosebloom, Isaac. "What You Need to Know about How Whales Spend." Deltadna.com, April 13, 2016. https://deltadna.com/blog/how-whales-spend.

Russworm, TreaAndrea M. "Computational Blackness: The Procedural Logics of Race, Game, and Cinema, or How Spike Lee's *Livin' Da Dream* Productively 'Broke' a Popular Video Game." *Black Camera* 10, no. 1 (2018): 193–212. https://www.muse.jhu.edu/article/707694.

Salter, Anastasia. *Jane Jensen: Gabriel Knight, Adventure Games, Hidden Objects*. London: Bloomsbury Academic, 2017.

Sarkar, Samit. "EA Looks Back on Five Years of the FIFA Ultimate Team Juggernaut." Polygon, March 19, 2014. https://www.polygon.com/2014/3/19/5525710/fifa-ultimate-team-fifth-anniversary-ea-sports-interview.

Sarkar, Samit. "With NHL 19, EA Leans into Online Play in Effort to Attract New Players." Polygon, June 20, 2018. https://www.polygon.com/2018/6/20/17446816/nhl-19-release-date-preview-ea-sports-ps4-xbox-one.

Sauer, Patrick. "How Dr. J and Larry Bird Helped Build a Video Game Empire." *Sports*, May 25, 2017. https://sports.vice.com/en_us/article/wje9kq/how-dr-j-and-larry-bird-helped-build-a-video-game-empire.

Schiappa, Edward. "Second Thoughts on the Critiques of Big Rhetoric." *Philosophy and Rhetoric* 34, no. 3 (2001): 260–274.

Schreier, Jason. "A Long and Hopefully Interesting Conversation About Microtransactions." Kotaku, October 14, 2018. https://kotaku.com/a-long-and-hopefully-interesting-conversation-about-mic-1829687571.

Schreier, Jason. "EA Defense of Star Wars Battlefront II Becomes Most Downvoted Reddit Comment Ever." Kotaku, November 13, 2017.

https://kotaku.com/ea-defense-of-star-wars-battlefront-ii-becomes-most-dow-1820396527.

Schreier, Jason. "FBI Says Alleged Hackers Used FIFA to Steal Millions from EA." Kotaku, November 14, 2016. https://kotaku.com/man-goes-on-trial-for-allegedly-stealing-millions-from-1788948231.

Schreier, Jason. "Inside Rockstar Games' Culture of Crunch." Kotaku, October 23, 2018. https://kotaku.com/inside-rockstar-games-culture-of-crunch-1829936466.

Schreier, Jason. "South Park Craps All Over Free-to-Play Games." Kotaku, November 6, 2014. https://kotaku.com/south-park-craps-all-over-free-to-play-games-1655328455.

Schreier, Jason. "Twenty-Five-Year-Old Charged with Stealing In-Game Items from EA." Kotaku, August 10, 2018. https://kotaku.com/twenty-five-year-old-charged-with-stealing-in-game-item-1828259867.

Schreier, Jason. "Why Ubisoft Is Obsessed with 'Games as a Service.'" Kotaku, February 12, 2018. https://kotaku.com/why-ubisoft-is-obsessed-with-games-as-a-service-1822938255.

Schwartz, Nick. "Antoine Griezmann Did a 'Fortnite' Dance in the World Cup Final." *USA Today*, July 15, 2018. https://ftw.usaday.com/2018/07/what-dance-did-frances-antoine-griezmann-do-after-scoring-at-the-world-cup.

Scott, Robert L. "On Viewing Rhetoric as Epistemic." *Central States Speech Journal* 18 (1967): 9–17.

Shaw, Adrienne. *Gaming at the Edge: Sexuality and Gender at the Margins of Gamer Culture.* Minneapolis: University of Minnesota Press, 2014.

Shaw, Adrienne, and Shira Chess. "Reflections on the Casual Games Market in a Post-GamerGate World." In *Social, Casual and Mobile Games: The Changing Gaming Landscape*, edited by Tama Leaver and Michele Willson, 277–289. New York: Bloomsbury, 2017.

Silver, Stephen. "The Revolution Steve Jobs Resisted: Apple's App Store Marks 10 Years of Third-Party Innovation." AppleInsider, July 10, 2018.

https://appleinsider.com/articles/18/07/10/the-revolution-steve-jobs
-resisted-apples-app-store-marks-10-years-of-third-party-innovation.

Sinclair, Brendan. "For EA and Loot Boxes, 'Fair Is the Number One Thing.'" GamesIndustry.biz, June 21, 2018. https://www.gamesindustry .biz/articles/2018-06-21-for-ea-and-loot-boxes-fair-is-the-number-one -thing.

Sinclair, Brendan. "Fortnite Earned $223 Million in March—Superdata." GamesIndustry.biz, April 26, 2018. https://www.gamesindustry.biz/ articles/2018-04-26-fornite-earned-usd223-million-in-march-superdata.

Sinclair, Brendan. "'You Probably Don't Want Darth Vader in Pink.'" GamesIndustry.biz, November 28, 2017. https://www.gamesindustry .biz/articles/2017-11-28-you-probably-dont-want-darth-vader-in-pink.

Sinclair, Brendan. "'You're Stupid to Say Betting Is Bad'—Wargaming." GamesIndustry.biz, April 7, 2017. https://www.gamesindustry.biz/ articles/2017-04-07-youre-stupid-to-say-betting-is-bad-wargaming.

Slivka, Eric. "Apple Opens Up 'In-App Purchasing' for Free iPhone Applications." Mac Rumors, October 15, 2009. https://www.macrumors .com/2009/10/15/apple-opens-up-in-app-purchasing-for-free-iphone -applications.

Snyder, Justin. "'Marvel Avengers Academy' Goes Big for Second Anniversary." Marvel.com, February 5, 2018. https://www.marvel.com/arti cles/games/marvel-avengers-academy-goes-big-for-second-anniversary.

Squires, Jim. "Candy Crush Saga Review." Gamezebo, April 14, 2012. http://www.gamezebo.com/2012/04/14/candy-crush-saga-review.

Stormy. "TEAM INSTINCT." Star Wars Galaxy of Heroes Forums, September 3, 2016. https://forums.galaxy-of-heroes.starwars.ea.com/discus sion/65809/%EF%B8%8Fteam-instinct-%EF%B8%8F.

Struan, John. "Kim Kardashian's Game Is Killing Candy Crush." Kotaku, August 13, 2014. https://kotaku.com/kim-kardashians-game-is-killing -candy-crush-1621017294.

StygianUnknown. "The Three Options to Get That New Marquee Character to 7 Stars." Reddit, June 2018. https://www.reddit.com/r/SWGalaxy

OfHeroes/comments/8nnrlu/the_three_options_to_get_that_new_mar
quee.

Sue, Jeff. "Culture Clash: Why Arena of Valor Is Struggling in America." GamesIndustry.biz, August 10, 2018. https://www.gamesindustry
.biz/articles/2018-08-10-culture-clash-why-arena-of-valor-is-struggling-in
-america.

Takahashi, Dean. "Candy Crush Saga: 2.73 Billion Downloads in Five
Years and Still Counting." VentureBeat, November 17, 2017. https://
venturebeat.com/2017/11/17/candy-crush-saga-2-73-billion-down
loads-in-five-years-and-still-counting.

Takahashi, Dean. "EA Results Remind the Industry That Sports, Not
Just Battlefield, Pushes Profits." VentureBeat, October 31, 2017. https://
venturebeat.com/2017/10/31/ea-results-remind-the-industry-that
-sports-not-just-battlefield-pushes-profits.

Takahashi, Dean. "Even with Half the Users, Zynga's FarmVille Made
More Money than Ever before in Q1." VentureBeat, July 5, 2011.
https://venturebeat.com/2011/07/05/even-with-half-the-users-zyngas
-farmville-made-more-money-than-ever-before-in-q1.

Takahashi, Dean. "Is Zynga Worth More than Electronic Arts?" Venture-
Beat, October 26, 2010. https://venturebeat.com/2010/10/26/is-zynga
-worth-more-than-electronic-arts.

Tassi, Paul. "Apple Promotes Strange New Game Type in iOS App Store,
'Pay Once and Play.'" Forbes, February 13, 2015. https://www.forbes
.com/sites/insertcoin/2015/02/13/apple-promotes-strange-new-game
-type-in-ios-app-store-pay-once-and-play-2.

Tassi, Paul. "'Fortnite: Battle Royale' Is Breaking Records on YouTube,
Not Just Twitch." Forbes, March 27, 2018. https://www.forbes.com/sites/
insertcoin/2018/03/27/fortnite-battle-royale-is-breaking-records-on
-youtube-not-just-twitch.

Tassi, Paul. "Lessons Learned from a Week with 'Kim Kardashian: Hollywood.'" Forbes, July 23, 2014. https://www.forbes.com/sites/insert
coin/2014/07/23/lessons-learned-from-a-week-with-kim-kardashian
-hollywood/#209099d673e6.

Tassi, Paul. "My $1,800 'Hearthstone' Collection Is Still Incomplete." *Forbes*, November 18, 2017. https://www.forbes.com/sites/insertcoin/2017/11/18/my-1800-hearthstone-collection-is-still-incomplete.

Tassi, Paul. "Why I've Spent $639 on 'Hearthstone' (and Don't Regret It)," December 22, 2014. http://www.forbes.com/sites/insertcoin/2014/12/22/why-ive-spent-639-on-hearthstone-and-dont-regret-it.

Taylor, Haydn. "Battle Royale Players Are among the Most Engaged Gamers, Report Finds." GamesIndustry.biz, May 24, 2018. https://www.gamesindustry.biz/articles/2018-05-24-battle-royale-players-are-more-engaged-and-spend-more-money-than-their-peers-in-other-games.

Taylor, Haydn. "EA Sports VP Daryl Holt on Loot Boxes: 'Our Model Is Sustainable.'" GamesIndustry.biz, June 29, 2018. https://www.gamesindustry.biz/articles/2018-06-29-ea-sports-vp-daryl-holt-on-loot-boxes-our-model-is-sustainable.

Taylor, Haydn. "Games Account for 75% of App Store Spending." GamesIndustry.biz, June 1, 2018. https://www.gamesindustry.biz/articles/2018-06-01-games-account-for-75-percent-of-app-store-spending.

Taylor, Haydn. "Sensor Tower: Harry Potter: Hogwarts Mystery Revenue Surpasses $55M." GamesIndustry.biz, August 9, 2018. https://www.gamesindustry.biz/articles/2018-08-09-sensor-tower-harry-potter-hogwarts-mystery-revenue-surpasses-usd50m.

Taylor, Haydn. "Super Mario Run Surpasses $60M Revenue after Two Years." GamesIndustry.biz, July 3, 2018. https://www.gamesindustry.biz/articles/2018-07-03-super-mario-run-surpasses-usd60m-revenue-after-two-years.

Team, Trefis. "FIFA Remains EA's Bread and Butter." *Forbes*, October 10, 2017. https://www.forbes.com/sites/greatspeculations/2017/10/10/fifa-remains-eas-bread-and-butter.

Team_iNstinct. "Team Instinct Premier #1 PVP Guild." Star Wars Galaxy of Heroes Forums, April 19, 2016. https://forums.galaxy-of-heroes.starwars.ea.com/discussion/30214/team-instinct-premier-1-pvp-guild.

Telfer, Adam, and Joseph Kim. "$126 Million and Counting: Fortnite, How Do They Do It?" Deconstructor of Fun, April 23, 2018. https://

www.deconstructoroffun.com/blog/2018/4/21/aegai526kyjvsn69x
m6uc2x02we48x.

Thier, Dave. "EA Is Making a Giant Amount of Money off Microtransactions." *Forbes*, March 3, 2016. https://www.forbes.com/sites/
davidthier/2016/03/03/ea-is-making-a-giant-amount-of-money-off
-microtransactions.

Thier, Dave. "This Is Likely Why EA Pulled Star Wars Battlefront 2's
Microtransactions." *Forbes*, November 17, 2017. https://www.forbes
.com/sites/davidthier/2017/11/17/this-is-likely-why-ea-took-action
-with-star-wars-battlefront-2s-microtransactions/#6f0fb3b3bdd5.

Torrid. "The New Challenge: Reaching Legend Rank + 12 Arena Wins
Without Paying for Cards!" Hearthstone Forums, September 8, 2018.
https://us.battle.net/forums/en/hearthstone/topic/20768756854.

Totilo, Stephen. "Final Fantasy Crystal Chronicles: My Life as a Darklord
Micro-Review: A Horrifying Thought." Kotaku, August 5, 2009. https://
kotaku.com/5330810/final-fantasy-crystal-chronicles-my-life-as-a-dark
lord-micro-review-a-horrifying-thought.

Totilo, Stephen. "My Favorite Nintendo Is Weird Nintendo." Kotaku,
January 26, 2018. https://kotaku.com/my-favorite-nintendo-is-weird
-nintendo-1822460818.

Totilo, Stephen. "One Devious Microtransaction." Kotaku, March 17,
2017. https://kotaku.com/one-devious-microtransaction-1793392082.

Totilo, Stephen. "Video Game Club 2014." *Slate*, December 29, 2014.
http://www.slate.com/articles/arts/gaming/features/2014/video_game
_club_2014/best_video_games_2014_rusty_s_real_deal_baseball_and
_shadow_of_mordor.html.

Totilo, Stephen. "Where Winners Play, and Losers Pay." *The New York
Times*, May 23, 2014. https://www.nytimes.com/2014/05/24/arts/video
-games/rustys-real-deal-baseball-video-game-tests-haggling-skills.html.

TradeMark. "Thoughts from a Former Leader of Team iNstinct." Reddit,
March 2018. https://www.reddit.com/r/SWGalaxyOfHeroes/comments/
7zvlpb/thoughts_from_a_former_leader_of_team_instinct.

TranslateMedia. "The Rise and Fall of Zynga: A Cautionary Tale for Mobile Game Developers." TranslateMedia, June 7, 2017. https://www.translatemedia.com/us/blog-usa/rise-fall-zynga-cautionary-tale-game-developers.

Trusted Reviews. "Microtransactions Are an 'Unfortunate Reality' of Modern Gaming, Says NBA 2K19 Producer." Trusted Reviews, September 4, 2018. https://www.trustedreviews.com/news/microtransactions-unfortunate-reality-modern-gaming-says-nba-2k19-producer-3550636.

Tylwalk, Nick. "How to Play 'Harry Potter: Hogwarts Mystery' as Long as Possible for Free." TouchArcade, April 26, 2018. https://toucharcade.com/2018/04/26/harry-potter-hogwarts-mystery-cheats-and-tips.

Tylwalk, Nick. "'Madden NFL Overdrive' Guide: Get Charged Up to Win More and Play Longer for Free." TouchArcade, August 14, 2018. https://toucharcade.com/2018/08/14/madden-nfl-overdrive-guide-get-charged-up-to-win-more-and-play-longer-for-free.

Tylwalk, Nick. "Marvel Avengers Academy Review: Teenagers, Assemble!" Gamezebo, February 8, 2016. https://www.gamezebo.com/2016/02/08/marvel-avengers-academy-review-teenagers-assemble.

Tylwalk, Nick. "MLB Tap Sports Baseball 2017 Review: More Legit than Ever." Gamezebo, April 3, 2017. https://www.gamezebo.com/2017/04/03/mlb-tap-sports-baseball-2017-review-legit-ever.

Tylwalk, Nick. "MLB Tap Sports Baseball 2018 Guide for Beginners." Gamezebo, April 15, 2018. https://www.gamezebo.com/2018/04/15/mlb-tap-sports-baseball-2018-guide-beginners.

Ulanopo. "Confessions of a League Whale: A Blue Essence Rant." December 2017. League of Legends Boards. Accessed September 4, 2018. https://boards.na.leagueoflegends.com/en/c/gameplay-balance/ihGleXF4-confessions-of-a-league-whale-a-blue-essence-rant.

Valdes, Armand. "We Played 'Kim Kardashian: Hollywood' So You Don't Have To." Mashable, July 21, 2014. https://mashable.com/2014/07/21/kardashian-hollywood-game/#Sr1wZeFelsqP.

Valentine, Rebekah. "Fortnite Sold 5 Million Battle Passes on the First Day of Season 3." GamesIndustry.biz, May 25, 2018. https://www.games industry.biz/articles/2018-05-25-fortnite-sold-5-million-battle-passes -on-the-first-day-of-season-3.

Valentine, Rebekah. "Frostkeep Studios Is Serious about Making 'the Game That Players Want' with Rend." GamesIndustry.biz, August 2, 2018. https://www.gamesindustry.biz/articles/2018-08-02-with-rend-frost keep-studios-hopes-to-make-the-game-that-players-want.

Valentine, Rebekah. "Mario Kart Tour's First-Month Downloads Zoom Past 123M." GamesIndustry.biz, October 29, 2019. https://www.games industry.biz/articles/2019-10-29-mario-kart-tours-first-month-down loads-zoom-past-123m.

Valentine, Rebekah. "Valve: Creating Artifact Is Not a 'Zero-Sum Game.'" GamesIndustry.biz, September 3, 2018. https://www.gamesindustry.biz/ articles/2018-09-03-valve-creating-artifact-is-not-a-zero-sum-game.

Valleyflyin. "The Kraken Has Been Unleashed (a Conversation with Valleyflyin)—the Most Underrated Characters: MarvelStrikeForce." Reddit, July 2018. https://www.reddit.com/r/MarvelStrikeForce/comments/ 8t6h5c/the_kraken_has_been_uleashed_a_conversation_with/?st=jlo a6ce0&sh=a82109c3.

Vidyarthi, Neil. "A Brief History of FarmVille," January 25, 2010. https:// www.adweek.com/digital/farmville-history.

Voorhees, John. "Game On: A Decade of iOS Gaming." *MacStories*, July 13, 2018. https://www.macstories.net/stories/game-on-a-decade-of-ios -gaming.

Wales, Matt. "Candy Crush Saga Review." Pocket Gamer, 2013. http:// www.pocketgamer.co.uk/r/iPhone/Candy+Crush+Saga/review.asp?c =46983.

Walker, John. "King ARE Trying to Candy-Crush the Banner Saga," January 22, 2014. http://www.rockpapershotgun.com/2014/01/22/king-are -trying-to-candy-crush-the-banner-saga.

Walker, John. "Stealing 'Candy' from Babies: King Embrace the Aristocracy." Rock, Paper, Shotgun, January 21, 2014. https://www.rockpaper shotgun.com/2014/01/21/stealing-candy-from-babies-king-embrace -the-aristocracy.

Walker, John. "The Candy Crush Banner Saga Saga: Stoic Speaks Up." Rock, Paper, Shotgun, January 22, 2014. https://www.rockpapershot gun.com/2014/01/22/the-candy-crush-banner-saga-saga-stoic-speak-up.

Walker, John. "What to Play Instead of Candy Crush Saga." Rock, Paper, Shotgun, February 18, 2014. https://www.rockpapershotgun.com/2014/ 02/18/what-to-play-instead-of-candy-crush-saga.

Warr, Philippa. "Dote Night: How Did I Spend £215 on a 'Free' Game!?" Rock, Paper, Shotgun, August 20, 2014. https://www.rockpapershotgun .com/2014/08/20/dote-night.

Willmott, Ray. "Disney Magic Kingdom Review—When You Wish upon a Star, You Probably Won't Wish for This." Pocket Gamer, March 18, 2016. http://www.pocketgamer.co.uk/r/iPhone/Disney+Magic+Kingdom/ review.asp?c=69456.

Wilson, Jason. "PC Gaming Weekly: Watch out, Hearthstone—Here Comes Artifact." VentureBeat, August 10, 2017. https://venturebeat .com/2017/08/10/pc-gaming-weekly-watch-out-heartstone-here-comes -artifact.

YorickSkirata. "TinyCo Has Gone Mad (and Bad): Avengersacademy game." Reddit, September 21, 2018. https://www.reddit.com/r/avengers academygame/comments/9hos60/tinyco_has_gone_mad_and_bad/?st =jmcmlwee&sh=a023f9d6.

Zarefsky, David. "Knowledge Claims in Rhetorical Criticism." Journal of Communication 58, no. 4 (2008): 629–640.

ZetaLordVader. "Dear CG, Can You Sell Us a Package That Not Cost [sic] a Full AAA Title?" Reddit, March 2018. https://www.reddit.com/r/ SWGalaxyOfHeroes/comments/84m1rs/dear_cg_can_you_sell_us_a _package_that_not_cost_a.

Index

Note: page numbers in italics indicate figures.